WORDS

SPELLING, PRONUNCIATION, DEFINITION, and APPLICATION

Compiled by

RUPERT P. SoRELLE

AND

CHARLES W. KITT

THIRD EDITION

*Revised by the Editorial Staff
of the Gregg Publishing Company*

THE GREGG PUBLISHING COMPANY

NEW YORK   CHICAGO   BOSTON   SAN FRANCISCO
TORONTO   LONDON   SYDNEY

Copyright, 1903, By JOHN R. GREGG

Copyright, 1911, 1929, 1941, by
THE GREGG PUBLISHING COMPANY

H–68–KP–15

Printed in the United States of America

PREFACE TO THIRD EDITION

Words, which was first published in 1903 and revised in 1911 and again in 1929, has owed its continued popularity to several features that distinguish it from the usual "business speller."

With the thought of making the material still more helpful to the student and more teachable by the instructor, the organization of the content has been changed as follows:

1. In illustrating the rules for spelling the derivatives of words, both the root word and its derivative are given in each case. (See lessons in Part I.)

2. Spelling and pronunciation "demons" have been distributed through the text instead of being presented together in separate sections.

3. The lists in Part VI, "Words Used in Special Businesses and Industries," consist of some fifty of the most commonly used terms in each industry. Each term is pronounced and has been defined by an authority.

4. Brief review tests are included for Parts I to IV inclusive.

5. Suggestions on the use of the dictionary point the way to further purposeful study by the earnest student.

One of the features of preceding editions as well as of this edition that is always mentioned by students as being particularly helpful consists of illustrative sentences showing the use of the words being studied. It is possible to know how to spell and pronounce a word, and even understand its definition, and still not grasp its full implication in actual use. A sentence incorporating the word in its natural setting removes the uncertainty at once. This sentence feature makes *Words* a vocabulary builder rather than a mere spelling book. Shorthand and typewriting teachers have found the sentences in *Words* especially valuable also as dictation material.

Webster's New International Dictionary, Second Edition, has been used as authority for the spelling, syllabication, and pronunciation of the words. Wherever two spellings or two pronunciations of a word are allowable, only the preferred form is given.

The descriptions of word origins likewise are based on Webster's Dictionary and on *Picturesque Word Origins*, which is also published by

G. & C. Merriam Company, to whom grateful acknowledgment is made for editorial co-operation.

The definitions have been kept as brief as possible, as the student should be encouraged to form the habit of consulting a dictionary for more detailed study of words.

In the revising of the technical terms in Part VI, the publishers have had the valuable co-operation of experts in each field included in these lessons. To each of the following persons and organizations appreciation is expressed for their editorial assistance and guidance in the selection of the most commonly used technical terms and their definition and use.

American Bankers Association; Arnon W. Welch, attorney; The Thrift, Brooklyn (Mr. Philip S. Clarke); Edward Ellsworth Hipsher, Associate Editor, *The Etude*; G. & C. Merriam Company; Fred H. Montgomery, Montgomery & Montgomery, Insurance; Wm. W. Higgins, Editor, *Rural New-Yorker*; R. L. Taylor, Assistant Editor, *Chemical & Metallurgical Engineering*; W. C. Pank, Editor, *Furniture Record*; A. E. Knowlton, Associate Editor, *Electrical World*; G. Ricciardi, Associate Editor, *The Iron Age*; Erik Oberg, Editor, *Machinery*; Arthur D. Ferris; Terry Ramsaye, Editor, *Motion Picture Herald*; James G. Peede, Managing Editor, *Hide and Leather*; B. Dudley, Associate Editor, *Electronics*; Arthur D. Ferris, *Hardware Age*; Morris Buck, Engineering Editor, *Transit Journal*; S. Paul Johnston, Editor, *Aviation*; E. E. R. Tratman, Civil Engineer; Douglas G. Woolf, Editor, *Textile World*; Evan Johnson, Editor, *Office Appliances*; Edward Sagarin, Assistant Editor, *Drug Topics*; H. E. Blank, Jr., Assistant Editor, *Automotive Industries*; J. Rodman Keagy, Associate Editor, *Jewelers' Circular-Keystone*; William D. McNeil, President, American National Retail Jewelers Assoc.; B. L. Johnson, Editor, *American Builder*; Elizabeth Scharff, Fashion Counsel.

Acknowledgment is also made to Mr. Clyde I. Blanchard, general editor of the Gregg Publishing Company, for planning the revision of this as well as the preceding edition; to Miss E. Lillian Hutchinson, of our editorial staff, for compiling the material; and to Mrs. John Robert Gregg and Miss Harriet P. Banker, for their critical reading of the manuscript.

THE GREGG PUBLISHING COMPANY

CONTENTS

	Page
The Use of the Dictionary	vii
Key to Pronunciation	x

Part I. Rules for Spelling ... 1

Lesson		
1	When Silent Final E Is Omitted	2–3
2	When Silent Final E Is Retained	4–5
3	When a Final Consonant Is Doubled	6–7
4	When a Final Consonant Is Not Doubled	8–9
5	When Final Y Is Changed to I	10–11
6	Ei and Ie Words	12–13
7	Regular Plurals; Plurals of Nouns Ending in Y	14–15
8	Plurals of Nouns Ending in O; in F, Fe, and Ff	16–17
9	Irregular Plurals	18–19
10	Possessives	20–21
11	Compound Words	22–23
12	Words Often Misspelled	24
13	Words Often Mispronounced	25
	Brief Test on Part I	26

Part II. Word Beginnings and Endings (Prefixes and Suffixes) ... 27

14	Common Word Beginnings	28–29
15	Common Word Endings	30–31
16	Ant and Ent Suffixes	32–33
17	Ance and Ence Suffixes	34–35
18	Able and Ible Suffixes	36–37
19	Ise, Ize, Yze; Tion, Sion Suffixes	38–39
20	Er (Eer, Ier), Or Suffixes	40–41
21	Words Often Misspelled	42
22	Words Often Mispronounced	43
	Brief Test on Part II	44

Part III. Word Usage ... 45

23–26	Words That Sound Exactly Alike (Homonyms)	46–53
27–32	Words That Sound or Look Somewhat Alike	54–65
33–36	Words That Mean the Same Thing (Synonyms)	66–73
37–39	Words That Mean the Opposite Thing (Antonyms)	74–76
40	Prepositions	77
41	Words Often Misspelled	78
42	Words Often Mispronounced	79
	Brief Test on Part III	80

Lesson		Page
Part IV. New Words; Words of Foreign Origin; Geographic Names		81
43	New Words and Old Words with New Meanings	82
44–46	Commonly Used Words and Phrases of Foreign Origin	83–85
47	Legal and Business Terms of Latin Origin	86
48	States and Territories of the United States	87–88
49	Other North and South American Countries	89
50	Fifty Large Cities of the United States	90
51	Fifty Large Cities of the World	91
52	Words Often Misspelled	92
53	Words Often Mispronounced	93
	Brief Test on Part IV	94
Part V. Words Used in Business		95
54–60	General Business Terms	96–109
61–62	Accounting Terms	110–113
63–64	Advertising, Publishing, and Printing Terms	114–117
65–68	Banking and Investment Terms	118–125
69–70	Insurance Terms	126–129
71–74	Legal Terms	130–137
75–76	Office Supplies and Equipment Terms	138–141
77	Real Estate Terms	142–143
78–79	Transportation and Shipping Terms	144–147
80	Commercial Abbreviations	148
Part VI. Words Used in Special Businesses and Industries		149
81	Agricultural Terms	150–151
82	Architectural and Building Terms	152–154
83	Automobile Terms	155–157
84	Aviation Terms	158–161
85	Chemical Terms	161–164
86	Civil Engineering Terms	164–167
87	Educational Terms	168–170
88–89	Electrical and Radio Terms	171–177
90	Fashion and Textile Terms	177–179
91	Fuel and Oil Terms	180–183
92	Furniture and Interior-Decoration Terms	183–185
93	Government Terms	186–188
94	Grocery Terms	189–191
95	Hardware and Cutlery Terms	191–194
96	Jewelry and Silverware Terms	194–195
97	Leather Goods Terms	195–197
98	Machinery Terms	197–199
99–101	Medical and Drug Terms	200–208
102	Mining and Metallurgical Terms	208–209
103	Motion Picture and Photographic Terms	209–211
104	Musical Terms	211–212
	Index	213–214
	The Division of Words	Back fly leaf

THE USE OF THE DICTIONARY

The modern dictionary is the most comprehensive reference book ever published. Like any machine or tool, however, the technique of using it correctly must be mastered if the greatest benefits are to be obtained.

First, Know Your Alphabet. A knowledge of the correct sequence of the letters of the alphabet is essential. If you lack this knowledge, you will be handicapped:

1. In using the thumb index for opening the dictionary at the initial letter of the word you seek.
2. In finding the guide words at the top of the page containing the word you seek.
3. In quickly locating the word on the page.

Remember: words are arranged, first, according to the alphabetic order of their initial letters; then according to the alphabetic order of their second, third, and remaining letters.

Verifying Spelling. When you check the spelling of a word, be sure:

1. That you read the letters in their correct order; for example, it is *drudgery*—not *drugdery*.
2. That you do not insert letters that are not there; for example, it is *caress*—not *carress*.
3. That you do not leave out letters; for example, it is *aghast*, not *agast*.
4. That you have not found some other word pronounced exactly like the word you seek; for example, the noun *mucus* instead of the adjective *mucous*.
5. That you have not found some other word spelled somewhat like the word you seek; for example, *ordnance* instead of *ordinance*.
6. That, when more than one spelling of the word sought is allowed, you choose the preferred spelling. Each dictionary has its own method of indicating whether the varying forms are of equal or nearly equal standing, or whether one is distinctly preferable.
7. That, in looking up compound words, you notice whether the word is one solid word (as *baseball*), two separate words (as

dining room), or hyphenated (as *half-mast*). Be sure you understand how the dictionary you are using indicates hyphens; that is, do not confuse a real hyphen with a hyphen indicating syllable division. Also, do not overlook the extra space between two-word compounds.

Checking Syllabication. Stenographers, typists, and proofreaders, especially, should consult the dictionary constantly for the correct syllabication of words in order to determine where a word may be correctly divided at the end of a written or printed line. (See also back fly leaf.) Various dictionaries have various styles of indicating syllabication—by spacing, by hyphens, by dots. An accent always indicates the end of a syllable.

Looking up Pronunciations. In looking up the pronunciation of a word, notice:

1. How the word is separated into syllables. This has a great bearing on the pronunciation. For example, if *hy-poc-ri-sy* were divided *hypo-crisy*, how different the pronunciation would be! Also, the syllabication alone may determine the meaning of a word; for example, *prod-uce* (noun) and *pro-duce* (verb).

2. Where the accents fall. The accent alone may determine the meaning of the word—for example, *con'test* and *con test'* and *ob'ject* and *ob ject'*—and whether there are two accents, called a *primary* and a *secondary* accent, the primary, of course, being the stronger, as in *ex-hil'a-ra'tion*. Dictionaries differ in the method of distinguishing between these accents. Notice that every word of more than one syllable contains an accent.

3. How the vowels and some of the consonants are sounded. Dictionaries indicate these sounds by respelling the words, usually in parentheses, immediately following the word, in a speech-sound (phonetic) alphabet in which the vowels are marked with small marks called *diacritical marks*. The key to the meaning of these marks is printed at the foot of every open pair of pages. (See also page x.) Example: *anniversary* (ăn'ĭ vûr'sà rĭ).

4. Whether the word may be pronounced in more than one way. If such is the case, the preferred form is placed first; for example, *grease* (*verb*) (grēs; grēz).

Finding Meanings of Words. When you look up the meaning of a word, you should:

1. Understand how the dictionary you are using presents definitions. Some dictionaries give the meanings in the historical order in

which the word developed; some give the most common meaning first; others give separate entries when the word has entirely different meanings.

2. Read, in addition to the definition, any illustrative sentence or quotation incorporating the word.

3. Look up the meaning of any word contained in the definition that you do not understand.

4. Notice any indications of special meanings. These indications are usually printed in italics and indicate the department of knowledge in which the meaning occurs, as *Law*, *Com.* (Commerce), *Med.* (Medicine), *Shipbuilding;* or matters of usage, as *Colloq.* (Colloquial), *Dial.* (Dialectal).

5. Look up any cross references to other words.

Other Uses of the Dictionary. The dictionary contains a great deal of other valuable information; for example:

1. Grammatical information. The part of speech (noun, verb, whether transitive or intransitive, adjective, etc.), irregular plurals, principal parts of verbs, irregular comparatives and superlatives of adjectives and adverbs, and cases of pronouns.
2. Synonyms and antonyms.
3. Capitalization of proper nouns and adjectives.
4. The origin of all words listed (etymology).
5. Commonly used foreign words and phrases.
6. Prefixes and suffixes.
7. Illustrations.

In addition, many supplementary tables are given, sometimes in the body of the dictionary and sometimes in an appendix. These include:

1. Abbreviations.
2. Names of places (gazetteer).
3. Names of famous persons (biographical dictionary).
4. Tables of weights and measures.
5. Common Christian names of men and women.
6. Vocabulary of rhymes.
7. Atlas.
8. Chronological tables.
9. Preparation of copy for the printer.

KEY TO PRONUNCIATION

A

ā as in āle
ȧ as in chȧotic
â as in câre

ă as in ădd
ä as in ärm
ȧ as in ȧsk

E

ē as in ēve
ẹ as in hẹre
ĕ as in ĕvent

ĕ as in ĕnd
ē as in makēr

I

ī as in īce

ĭ as in ĭll

O

ō as in ōld
ŏ as in ŏbey
ô as in ôrb
ŏ as in ŏdd

ŏ as in sŏft
oo as in foōd
oŏ as in foŏt

U

ū as in cūbe
ŭ as in ŭnite

û as in ûrn
ŭ as in ŭp

Other Sounds

ou as in out
tụ̄ as in natụ̄re
th as in thin
N (French nasal *n*) as in penchant (päN shäN)

oi as in oil
ç as in çent
th as in then

For other markings not given in this key, see Webster's New International Dictionary, Second Edition, published by G. & C. Merriam Company.

The names of the diacritical marks are: (⁺) suspended bar; (^) circumflex; (¨) dieresis; (˙) dot; (~) tilde; (¯) macron; (˘) breve.

PART I

Rules for Spelling

Part I of this book covers the principal rules of spelling. If you master these rules, your efforts will be repaid a hundredfold. Employers rank ability to spell correctly as perhaps the most important qualification of a stenographer.

In studying each word in each lesson, (1) notice how the word illustrates the application of the particular spelling rule being presented; (2) try to define the word yourself, and then see whether your definition agrees with the brief definition given in the lesson; (3) read the sentence on the facing page, in which the word is used in a natural setting.

To help you master the "spelling demons," 400 such words, in groups of 100 words, are given at the end of Parts I, II, III, and IV. These words should be given particular study and frequent review. The habit of entering individual demons in a small notebook, where they can be easily reviewed and gradually mastered, will be found an effective means of conquering them.

Words often mispronounced likewise appear, in groups of fifty words, at the end of Parts I, II, III, and IV. The notebook habit will be useful also in acquiring correct pronunciations.

Here are two final study hints: (1) From the first lesson, form the dictionary habit. (See pages vii–ix for suggestions for "The Use of the Dictionary.") (2) Form the habit of syllabifying each word studied. Correct syllabification is the basis of correct word division. (See the back fly leaf.)

LESSON 1

When Silent Final E Is Omitted

Words ending with a silent *e* usually drop the *e* before a termination beginning with a vowel.

1.	enclose, enclosure [1]	Something included; that which is surrounded or closed in.
2.	obscure, obscurity	Dimness; indistinctness.
3.	measure, measurable	Capable of being estimated or computed.
4.	force, forcible	Vigorous; powerful.
5.	guide, guidance	Direction; supervision.
6.	ensue, ensuing	Following as a consequence; coming afterward.
7.	discipline, disciplinary	Pertaining to strict discipline; corrective.
8.	use, usage	Treatment; long-continued custom or practice.
9.	imitate, imitator	One who copies, or strives to copy, another.
10.	appraise, appraisal	Estimate; valuation.
11.	desire, desirous	Experiencing a wish or craving for; eager.
12.	advise, advisory	Having power to suggest or counsel.
13.	congratulate, congratulatory	Expressive of pleasure over another's good fortune.
14.	abuse, abusive	Inclined to indulge in cruel or ill treatment.
15.	base, basic	Fundamental.

Exceptions [2]

16.	shoe, shoeing	Furnishing with shoes.
17.	canoe, canoeing	Paddling in a canoe.
18.	notice, noticeable	Capable of being regarded or observed.
19.	manage, manageable	Obedient; subject to guidance.
20.	advantage, advantageous	Beneficial; profitable.
21.	outrage, outrageous	Violent; atrocious; shocking.
22.	dye, dyeing	Tinting by immersing in a coloring fluid.
23.	singe, singeing	Burning slightly at the edge or on the surface; scorching.
24.	mile, mileage	Aggregate distance in miles; an allowance for traveling expenses at a certain rate per mile.

---

[1] Only the derivative is defined.
[2] Exceptions sometimes occur because the application of a spelling rule would result in mispronouncing the word or mistaking it for another word.

WORDS USED IN SENTENCES

1. Caution the mail clerks not to overlook the *enclosures* for these letters.
2. The origin of the term "baronial" to indicate a style of envelope is lost in *obscurity*.
3. No *measurable* advantage has been gained from all this added work.
4. Such *forcible* remarks are entirely uncalled for.
5. Much is heard today about vocational *guidance*.
6. The *ensuing* report will elaborate on many of the statements just made.
7. The student was sent to the principal's office for *disciplinary* reasons.
8. The expression "quite a few," meaning a considerable number, is not good *usage*.
9. Be yourself—do not be an *imitator*.
10. Before insuring his collection of jade, he wishes to have an *appraisal* made.
11. The boy's parents are *desirous* of giving him a liberal education.
12. He is to serve the board in an *advisory* capacity.
13. The actor received many *congratulatory* telegrams on the opening night of his new play.
14. Even though the offender did a great deal of damage, there was no excuse for such *abusive* language.
15. The *basic* reason for all this preparation is the necessity for absolute accuracy of results.
16. Horse*shoeing* is all but an extinct trade in New York City today.
17. Those who do not swim should not indulge in *canoeing*.
18. Erasures should be made carefully so that they will not be *noticeable*.
19. The problem boy is becoming much more *manageable*.
20. An exit to the side street will be most *advantageous* in loading shipments.
21. The money lenders made *outrageous* demands on those who were obliged to borrow from them.
22. She is *dyeing* the slippers so that they will match her gown.
23. You were fortunate, indeed, to escape with a mere *singeing* of that long-haired fabric—it might have scorched in that heat.
24. What *mileage* have you had from your old car?

LESSON 2

When Silent Final E Is Retained

Words ending with a silent *e* usually retain the *e* before a termination beginning with a consonant.

1. encourage, encouragement — The act of heartening; an incentive.
2. arrange, arrangement — Preparation; adjustment; system.
3. disgrace, disgraceful — Causing shame; dishonorable; unbecoming.
4. care, carefully — Attentively; cautiously.
5. noise, noiseless — Silent; quiet.
6. tire, tireless — Unwearying.
7. venture, venturesome — Inclined to run a risk; daring.
8. complete, completely — Entirely; fully.
9. apprentice, apprenticeship — Time served by a novice.
10. entire, entirety — Completeness; the whole.
11. safe, safety — Freedom from danger or loss.
12. like, likeness — Resemblance; similarity.
13. home, homeward — In the direction of home.
14. false, falsehood — An untrue assertion; misrepresentation.

Exceptions

15. acknowledge, acknowledgment — An admission of something that has been concealed or of the receipt of something that has been sent or given.
16. judge, judgment — The mental act of discriminating.
17. argue, argument — A reason or the reasons offered in proof; controversy.
18. wise, wisdom — Ability to judge soundly; discretion; sagacity.
19. true, truly — In agreement with fact; honestly, sincerely.
20. awe, awful — Terrible; appalling.
21. whole, wholly — In a complete manner; entirely.
22. nine, ninth — After eighth.

WORDS USED IN SENTENCES

1. Mr. Stone needs a little *encouragement* to complete that task.

2. The *arrangement* meets with the approval of all.

3. The whole affair is *disgraceful*.

4. Check the inventory *carefully*.

5. Our office is equipped throughout with *noiseless* typewriters.

6. He has been *tireless* in his efforts to produce more business.

7. The enterprise is *venturesome*, but it is well worth the risk.

8. The factory is *completely* equipped with the latest safety devices.

9. The junior statistician may now be said to have served his *apprenticeship*, as he is ready for a major assignment.

10. Copy the will in its *entirety*.

11. *Safety* of principal is a major consideration in making this investment.

12. The portrait of the president is an excellent *likeness*.

13. The picnickers were *homeward* bound after the day's outing when the accident occurred.

14. His statement proved to be a deliberate *falsehood*.

15. He sent a telegram in *acknowledgment* of the receipt of the shipment.

16. Use your *judgment* in deciding whether to travel by air or by train.

17. The *argument* between the two men resulted in hard feelings.

18. The *wisdom* of these protective measures is unquestioned.

19. It is obvious that the clerk has stated the facts *truly*.

20. The news of the *awful* wreck was received by radio.

21. He was *wholly* at ease in reading his report.

22. His *ninth* experiment proved his theory.

LESSON 3

When a Final Consonant Is Doubled

Words of one syllable and words of more than one syllable accented on the last syllable, ending in a single consonant preceded by a single vowel, double the final consonant before a termination beginning with a vowel.

1.	plan, planning	Devising; contriving; scheming.
2.	acquit, acquitted	Freed from an accusation.
3.	ship, shipped	Sent through any regular channel of transportation.
4.	compel, compelling	Causing one to yield or submit.
5.	bag, baggage	Trunks and suitcases used in travel.
6.	remit, remittance	Transmittal of money, bills; the thing transmitted.
7.	control, controllable	Capable of being restrained or directed.
8.	occur, occurrence	A happening; an incident.
9.	slim, slimmest	Most slender; slightest.
10.	incur, incurred	Became liable to; brought down on oneself.
11.	regret, regrettable	Admitting of, deserving, or demanding remorse.
12.	clan, clannish	Disposed to cling together; bound by class prejudices; narrow.
13.	hot, hotter	Having more heat; more fiery.
14.	wit, witty	Humorous; droll; clever.
15.	abet, abettor	One who instigates or incites.
16.	transfer, transferred	Removed; passed; conveyed.
17.	rebel, rebellion	Revolt.
18.	equip, equipped	Fitted out for any service or undertaking.
19.	repel, repellent	Driving back; forbidding; unfriendly.

Exceptions

20.	transfer, transferable	Capable of being carried from one person or place to another; negotiable.
21.	defer, deference	Respectful yielding; regard.
22.	infer, inference	A logical conclusion from given data.
23.	chagrin, chagrined	Dismayed; humiliated.
24.	gas, gaseous	Having the nature or form of a gas.

WORDS USED IN SENTENCES

1. Mr. Hull is *planning* an extended trip through the Far West.
2. The general feeling is that the prisoner will be *acquitted*.
3. The goods ordered by telegram have been *shipped* by air express.
4. Adverse conditions are *compelling* us to close our branch office.
5. Please have my *baggage* checked through to my destination.
6. May we have your *remittance* covering your long-overdue account?
7. Surely the situation is *controllable*.
8. The delay in this shipment was a very unfortunate *occurrence*.
9. The doctor gives only the *slimmest* hope of the patient's recovery.
10. Mr. Thorpe *incurred* a great many debts in establishing his own business.
11. Such an unfortunate outcome, of course, is *regrettable*.
12. Any *clannish* tendencies in an office should be discouraged.
13. The handle on the cheaper flatiron gets much *hotter* than that on the better-quality iron.
14. *Witty* remarks during business conferences are usually out of place.
15. He admitted that he had been an *abettor* in the robbery.
16. I wish to have the balance of my savings account *transferred* to my checking account.
17. Such armed resistance to constituted authority is *rebellion*.
18. The architect's office is fully *equipped* with all instruments used in that profession.
19. The special finish on this fabric makes it water-*repellent*.
20. This ticket is not *transferable*.
21. Out of *deference* to his father's wishes, my friend decided not to expand the business.
22. The *inference* is that someone outside the company is giving unauthorized advice.
23. He was greatly *chagrined* when confronted with the accusations.
24. The chemical in the beaker was giving off a *gaseous* vapor.

LESSON 4

When a Final Consonant Is Not Doubled

1. The final consonant of a word is *not* doubled before a termination beginning with a vowel:
   a. When the word is accented on any syllable except the last.

1.	benefit, benefited	Improved; profited.
2.	profit, profited	Gained; brought good.
3.	differ, differing	Disagreeing; disputing.

   b. When the word ends in more than one consonant.

4.	perform, performance	Carrying out an act; a deed.
5.	confirm, confirming	Corroborating; verifying.
6.	act, actor	A doer; a player.

   c. When the word ends in a single consonant preceded by more than one vowel.

7.	appear, appeared	Became visible; seemed.
8.	need, needy	Destitute; very poor.
9.	brief, briefest	Shortest; most condensed.

2. Verbs ending in *unaccented el*, and a few other words, may be spelled with either a single or a double final consonant when adding a termination beginning with a vowel. Webster prefers the single consonant.

10.	counsel, counselor	One who advises; a lawyer.
11.	travel, traveler	One who goes on journeys.
12.	enamel, enameled	Coated with a shiny, opaque substance.
13.	equal, equality [1]	Character or condition of being the same in extent, number, or magnitude.
14.	jewel, jeweler	One who makes or deals in jewels or gems.
15.	marvel, marvelous	Extraordinary; incredible.
16.	kidnap, kidnaped	Stolen or carried away, said of a human being.
17.	worship, worshiper	One who adores or shows honor to.

Exception

18.	cancel, cancellation	The act of annulling or revoking.

3. Words ending in a double consonant usually retain both consonants when adding terminations.

19.	skill, skillful	Adept; deft; proficient.
20.	odd, oddly	Strangely; unevenly; uncommonly.
21.	enroll, enrolling	Placing on record in a list or register.
22.	install, installment	The act of establishing in a position or office; a portion of a debt to be paid.

Exception

23.	full, fully	Entirely; completely.

[1] Spelled with one *l* only.

WORDS USED IN SENTENCES

1. The long sea voyage *benefited* his health.
2. He *profited* greatly from his early experiments in a similar kind of work.
3. Because of *differing* opinions, the meeting was adjourned.
4. We can judge his ability only by his past *performance*.
5. A letter *confirming* our telephone conversation of this morning has been mailed to you.
6. The *actor* received many curtain calls.
7. That *appeared* to be the sole reason for the adverse decision.
8. There is great suffering among the *needy* during extremely cold weather.
9. We received only the *briefest* acknowledgment of the gift.
10. I am endeavoring to obtain a position as camp *counselor* for the summer.
11. *Traveler's* checks are the safest means of carrying money while traveling.
12. Be careful not to drop this *enameled* vanity case.
13. *Equality* of opportunity is the privilege of all Americans.
14. The *jeweler* advertised a new line of costume jewelry.
15. He has made a *marvelous* recovery from a serious illness.
16. No news of the *kidnaped* child has been received.
17. The chapel was thronged with *worshipers*.
18. The *cancellation* mark on the stamp cannot be deciphered.
19. A *skillful* mechanic could have repaired the break in a few minutes.
20. An *oddly* wrought pattern added to the beauty of the jeweled pendant.
21. We are *enrolling* in the Music Appreciation course.
22. The third *installment* on the Federal income tax is due on September 15.
23. I feel I am *fully* prepared for the position.

LESSON 5

When Final Y Is Changed to I

1. Words ending in *y* preceded by a consonant usually change the *y* to *i* before any termination except one beginning with *i*.

1.	likely, likelihood	Probability; prospect.
2.	beauty, beautiful	Handsome; comely; fair.
3.	lonely, loneliness	Seclusion; solitude.
4.	ordinary, ordinarily	Usually; customarily.
5.	heavy, heaviest	Most weighty; most ponderous.
6.	try, trying	Testing; endeavoring; annoying.
7.	accompany, accompanying	Attending; going along with.
8.	modify, modifies	Limits; restricts; varies.

Exceptions

9.	shy, shyness	Timidity; bashfulness.
10.	spry, spryly	Nimbly; briskly; actively.
11.	lady, ladylike	Courteous; well bred.
12.	secretary, secretaryship	The term of office, or office, of a secretary.
13.	baby, babyish	Infantile.

2. Words ending in *y* preceded by a vowel usually retain the *y* before all terminations.

14.	obey, obeyed	Complied with the orders of.
15.	delay, delaying	Staying; detaining; retarding.
16.	betray, betrayal	The giving over into the hands of an enemy by treachery.
17.	annoy, annoyance	Irritation; vexation.

Exceptions

18.	say, said	Uttered; told; already referred to.
19.	slay, slain	Killed by violence.
20.	lay, laid	Placed; caused to lie.
21.	day, daily	Every day.

WORDS USED IN SENTENCES

1. There is little *likelihood* that the loan will go through.
2. Notice the intricate and colorful patterns in this *beautiful* mosaic.
3. The *loneliness* of life in a big city is often acute.
4. *Ordinarily*, we do not recommend washing this fabric.
5. The *heaviest* carton in the shipment weighs over 50 pounds.
6. The customer, after *trying* several cars, selected a roadster.
7. Please notice the changes in the *accompanying* schedule of prices.
8. The change in train schedules *modifies* our plans somewhat.
9. You should endeavor to overcome your *shyness*.
10. The salesclerk stepped forward *spryly* to serve the customer.
11. The little girls were commended for their *ladylike* manners.
12. The *secretaryship* in the mayor's office is open.
13. It is unfortunate that Miss Long has such a *babyish* voice.
14. He has *obeyed* instructions to the letter.
15. *Delaying* the matter will not affect the final outcome.
16. His imprudent remarks amounted to a *betrayal* of company secrets.
17. The salesclerk concealed his *annoyance* while serving the unreasonable customer.
18. He *said* that he had had five years of practical laboratory experience.
19. I fear he was *slain* by a maniac.
20. The chairman *laid* his plan before the members of the committee on finance.
21. Each agent in the field is required to submit a *daily* report to the head office.

LESSON 6

Ei and Ie Words

> Put *i* before *e*
> Except after *c*
> Or when sounded like *a*
> As in *neighbor* and *weigh*.

I before *E*

1. **chief**   Principal; foremost; the person at the head of a group.
2. **field**   A piece of land cleared for cultivation, pasture, etc.
3. **fierce**   Savage; wild; vehement.
4. **niece**   The daughter of one's brother or sister.
5. **pier**   A support for the end of a bridge span; a structure built on piles at the water's edge.
6. **relieve**   To aid; ease; allay.
7. **shield**   A piece of armor; a protection; to defend.
8. **variety**   Diversity; state of being different.

After *C*

9. **conceit**   Self-esteem; vanity.
10. **deceive**   To betray; cheat; mislead.

Sounded like *A*

11. **weight**   Heaviness; gravity; import; significance.
12. **heir**   One who receives property of a deceased person.
13. **reign**   Royal power; sovereignty; to hold sway.

Exceptions

14. **ancient**   Very old.
15. **forfeit**   A fine or penalty; to lose something by neglect.
16. **height**   Altitude; highest position.
17. **inveigle**   To entice; allure.
18. **leisure**   Spare time at one's disposal.
19. **neither**   Not either.
20. **weird**   Uncanny; strange; eerie.

WORDS USED IN SENTENCES

1. The *chief* reason for her dismissal was her failure to follow her *chief's* instructions.

2. The farmer is proud of his 10-acre *field* of potatoes.

3. The press launched a *fierce* attack on the policies of the administration.

4. The treasurer's *niece* is now ready for a position.

5. I will meet you at the *pier* with final instructions for you.

6. The new rules will *relieve* traffic congestion during rush hours.

7. An erasing *shield* is helpful in making neat erasures.

8. The *variety* of canned goods on the market today is astonishing.

9. His overbearing manner toward his fellow employees is only one indication of his *conceit*.

10. Misleading advertising may *deceive* the public.

11. His opinions have great *weight* with her.

12. The sole *heir* to the property is a minor son.

13. Queen Victoria's *reign* covered a period of sixty-four years.

14. They discovered an *ancient* statute that would cover the case.

15. Because of tardiness, you must *forfeit* your claim to the prize.

16. This new honor has come at the *height* of his career.

17. I regret that I allowed the salesclerk to *inveigle* me into buying so expensive an article as this chair.

18. We have an interesting program of *leisure*-time activities.

19. *Neither* the manufacturer nor our jobber can supply the goods in time to fill this order.

20. Motion-picture technique is capable of producing *weird* effects.

LESSON 7

Regular Plurals; Plurals of Nouns Ending in Y

A. The plurals of English nouns are regularly formed by adding *s* to the singular.

    1. apartment, apartments   2. college, colleges

B. When the singular form (of both common and proper nouns) ends with *s* or an *s* sound—*ss*, *x*, *ch*, and *sh*—the plural is formed by adding *es* to the singular.

    3. chorus, choruses   6. dispatch, dispatches
    4. dress, dresses   7. sash, sashes
    5. annex, annexes   8. Mr. Evans, the Evanses

Note: Words ending in silent *s* do not change their form in the plural.

    9. one corps, ten corps   10. one chassis, five chassis

C. When a noun ends in *y* preceded by a consonant, the plural is formed by changing *y* to *i* and adding *es* to the singular.

    11. authority, authorities   14. cruelty, cruelties
    12. boundary, boundaries   15. enemy, enemies
    13. century, centuries   16. vacancy, vacancies

Note: To proper nouns ending in *y*, however, simply add *s;* as *the Marys.*

D. When a noun ends in *y* preceded by a vowel, the plural is formed by adding *s* to the singular.

    17. attorney, attorneys   20. valley, valleys
    18. holiday, holidays   21. Wednesday, Wednesdays
    19. key, keys

Word Origin

Cancel. The literal meaning of the Latin *cancellare*, from which *cancel* is derived, is "to make lines across, like latticework."

The same root word, through the French form, developed into **chancel**, as that part of the church was originally enclosed with lattices or crossbars. The doorkeeper who sat at a latticed bar was known as a **chancellor**, whose position became increasingly important throughout history, finally becoming, in England, the official secretary of the king and the keeper of the royal seal.

WORDS USED IN SENTENCES

1. This real estate broker has several desirable *apartments* to rent.

2. The deans of all the leading *colleges* were asked to answer the questionnaire.

3. The glee club practiced the *choruses* of both selections.

4. Women's *dresses* are on the third floor of the store.

5. Both *annexes* to the hospital were crowded.

6. The latest *dispatches* from Europe are of a reassuring nature.

7. *Sashes* are not becoming to large women.

8. The *Evanses* have invited a large number of friends to a reception.

9. The drum *corps* of both companies need additional drummers.

10. In his difficult travels, the explorer wore out two *chassis*.

11. *Authorities* differ on some rules of capitalization.

12. The south and west *boundaries* of the forest preserve end at the state road.

13. Many important scientific inventions were perfected in the nineteenth and twentieth *centuries*.

14. The *cruelties* of war cannot be described.

15. The germs of disease are *enemies* to mankind.

16. We have no *vacancies* in our stenographic department.

17. The court reprimanded the *attorneys* for their dilatory tactics.

18. It is imperative that we receive these goods in time for the *holidays*.

19. We make *keys* to fit any lock.

20. All the *valleys* are flooded by the spring thaw.

21. Dr. Grant has evening office hours on *Wednesdays* only.

LESSON 8

Plurals of Nouns Ending in O; in F, FE, and FF

A. The plurals of nouns ending in *o* usually are formed by adding *s* to the singular.

1. Merino, Merinos
2. piano, pianos
3. ratio, ratios
4. tobacco, tobaccos

B. Certain nouns ending in *o* preceded by a consonant add *es* in forming the plural.

5. innuendo, innuendoes
6. tomato, tomatoes
7. veto, vetoes

Note: Some nouns ending in *o* have two plural forms. (The preferred forms appear first.)

8. cargo, cargoes or cargos
9. fresco, frescoes or frescos
10. memento, mementos or mementoes
11. proviso, provisos or provisoes

C. The plurals of most nouns ending in *f*, *fe*, and *ff* are formed by adding *s* to the singular.

12. handkerchief, handkerchiefs
13. strife, strifes
14. rebuff, rebuffs
15. roof, roofs

D. A few commonly used nouns ending in *f* or *fe* form their plural by changing the *f* or *fe* to *ve* and adding *s*.

16. half, halves
17. leaf, leaves
18. life, lives
19. knife, knives
20. self, selves
21. shelf, shelves
22. thief, thieves
23. wharf, wharves or wharfs
24. wife, wives

Word Origin

Check. When one speaks of *checking* a person's accounts, one is using the language of the game of chess, in which *check* is a term for a repulse. The word was derived through the Arabic from the Persian *shah*, meaning a king. The king is the only chess piece that can be checked.

WORDS USED IN SENTENCES

1. Our new fall stock includes some fine *Merinos*.
2. Each of the used *pianos* on sale bears the signature of the opera star who formerly owned it.
3. In at least five department stores, the *ratios* of sales to advertising cost have increased markedly.
4. This cigarette is made of the best Virginia and Turkish *tobaccos*.
5. By various *innuendoes*, our competitors have gradually undermined the public's faith in our product.
6. Only sun-ripened *tomatoes* are used in our catchup.
7. This bill has already received two *vetoes*.
8. This season our ships have carried several *cargoes* of scrap iron to southern ports.
9. The artist was given a contract to paint all the *frescoes* for the Art Building at the Fair.
10. I will keep this program and invitation as *mementos* of this occasion.
11. The contract contained several *provisos*.
12. All our *handkerchiefs* are packed in gift boxes.
13. It is most unfortunate that strikes and *strifes* are so prevalent in the world today.
14. Despite many *rebuffs*, the persistent insurance salesman finally succeeded in writing that policy.
15. All these cottages have *roofs* of fireproof shingles.
16. First, divide the bananas into *halves*.
17. Due to carelessness, several *leaves* in the new dictionary have been torn.
18. The *lives* of successful men are often more thrilling than those of characters in fiction.
19. In this pattern, the table *knives* are in the new viand style.
20. Be sure the blanks are filled in by the applicants them*selves*.
21. The blueprints call for built-in book*shelves* on either side of the fireplace.
22. This job was obviously the work of professional *thieves*.
23. Trucks lined the *wharves* as far as we could see.
24. This broadcast is intended especially for house*wives*.

LESSON 9

Irregular Plurals

A. The plurals of some nouns are formed by a change of vowels.

    1. woman, women   3. tooth, teeth
    2. foot, feet   4. mouse, mice

B. The plurals of a few words end in *en*.

    5. child, children

C. Some nouns of foreign origin retain their foreign plurals.

    6. analysis, analyses   9. stimulus, stimuli
    7. parenthesis, parentheses   10. alumna, alumnae
    8. datum, data   11. phenomenon, phenomena

D. Some nouns of foreign origin have two plurals, the foreign and the English form.

    12. criterion, criteria or criterions   14. medium, mediums or media
    13. formula, formulas or formulae

E. Some nouns have the same form in both singular and plural.

    15. cattle   16. wheat   17. species   18. Portuguese

F. Some nouns, though ending in *s*, are rarely, if ever, used in the singular form.

    19. annals   20. athletics   21. goods   22. spectacles

G. The plurals of letters, signs, numbers, and words mentioned without regard to their meaning are formed by the addition of an apostrophe and *s*.

    23. A, A's   10, 10's   +, +'s   if, if's

H. Plurals of compound nouns are usually formed by adding the plural sign to the chief element of the compound.

    24. brothers-in-law   notaries public   lieutenant colonels

WORDS USED IN SENTENCES

1. The Country Club is now open to *women*.
2. The hall is nearly 20 *feet* long.
3. Only through daily care can you expect to keep your *teeth* in good condition.
4. We are obliged to engage an exterminating concern to rid our store of *mice*.
5. Typewriting is now being taught to very young *children*.
6. The *analyses* submitted by various experts all point to the same conclusion.
7. When *parentheses* form a part of the preceding sentence, the period is placed outside (as, for instance, here).
8. The *data* reveal a marked trend toward technical training.
9. The nerves react to the *stimuli* of heat, cold, and dampness.
10. The *alumnae* of seven women's colleges sent out a joint appeal for funds.
11. The advancements in the aviation industry are among the *phenomena* of the age.
12. By what *criteria* do you decide whether a book should be for library purchase?
13. The chemical *formulas* in tomorrow's assignment are most important.
14. What advertising *media* do you propose to use in launching the sale of your new product?
15. The dairyman sold fifteen head of *cattle*.
16. *Wheat* gives the largest yields in fertile black soils.
17. Several *species* of salmon are found in this river.
18. The *Portuguese* were famous explorers.
19. The *annals* of the state historical society are to be illustrated with interesting pictures.
20. He received a medal for excelling in *athletics*.
21. All our *goods* are made in our own factories.
22. His shell-rimmed *spectacles* make him look like an owl.
23. His parents were delighted that his report card contained three *A*'s and two *B+*'s. Now there are no *if*'s about his promotion.
24. Both *brothers-in-law* were *lieutenant colonels*. Compile a list of the *notaries public* in this county.

LESSON 10

Possessives

A. To form the possessive of *singular* nouns *not* ending in *s*, add an apostrophe followed by an *s*.

 1. customer, customer's
 2. month, month's
 3. world, world's
 4. Frank, Frank's

B. If a *singular* noun ends in *s* or an *s*-sound, add an apostrophe and an *s* if a new syllable is formed in the pronunciation of the possessive.

 5. boss, boss's
 6. miss, miss's
 7. fox, fox's
 8. Jones, Jones's
 9. Thomas, Thomas's
10. witness, witness's

If, however, the final syllable of the original word is preceded by an *s* sound, add only an apostrophe.

11. hostess, hostess'
12. princess, princess'
13. Frances, Frances'

Note: Some authorities differ on this rule.

C. The possessive of *regular plurals* is formed by adding only the apostrophe after the *s*.

14. lawyers, lawyers'
15. sheriffs, sheriffs'
16. celebrities, celebrities'
17. negroes, negroes'

Caution: In forming the possessive of a noun ending in *s*, the apostrophe must not be placed *before* that *s*.

Wrong: Burn's, misse's   *Right:* Burns's, misses'

D. The possessive of *irregular plurals* is formed by adding the apostrophe followed by *s*.

18. freshmen, freshmen's
19. Englishwomen, Englishwomen's

E. Possessive personal pronouns do not require an apostrophe.

20. they, theirs
21. he, his
22. we, ours
23. you, yours
24. it, its
25. she, hers
26. who, whose

Caution: The possessive pronouns *its*, *theirs*, and *whose* must not be confused with the contractions *it's*, meaning "it is"; *there's*, meaning "there is"; and *who's*, meaning "who is" or "who has."

F. The sign of the possessive is added at the end of a compound noun.

27. somebody else's
28. bookkeeper-secretary's

WORDS USED IN SENTENCES

1. The *customer's* complaint was justifiable.
2. At the end of the first *month's* business, the new company showed a tidy profit.
3. In his enthusiasm, he cried that he would go to the *world's* end for the sake of the cause.
4. *Frank's* duties are many.
5. The office boy was told to sharpen the *boss's* pencils every morning.
6. This dress is a *miss's* size.
7. The silver *fox's* fur is highly prized.
8. Mr. *Jones's* entire family is musical.
9. Mrs. *Thomas's* social secretary addressed the invitations for the reception.
10. The *witness's* replies were scarcely audible.
11. The *hostess'* gracious manner put the guests at ease.
12. Because of adverse conditions, the *princess'* fortune has shrunk considerably.
13. *Frances'* grades last term were excellent.
14. The *lawyers'* fees in the case amounted to more than the damages awarded.
15. *Sheriffs'* terms of office vary in length.
16. *Celebrities'* autographs are in great demand.
17. The contribution by the *Negroes'* auxiliary enabled our district to make its quota.
18. All *freshmen's* electives for next year are to be submitted to the office by May.
19. *Englishwomen's* complexions are famous for their clearness.
20. That dilapidated car of *theirs* is an eyesore. *There's* no reason why they should not buy a new one.
21. *His* best friend would not have recognized him.
22. Their windshield is not made of shatterproof glass; *ours* is.
23. The next step is *yours*.
24. *It's* too late to ask the mailing department for *its* report now.
25. The recommendation is *hers*.
26. It is difficult to tell *whose* fault this is. *Who's* been reading my "*Who's* Who"?
27. It is most unfair to blame him for *somebody else's* mistake.
28. The *bookkeeper-secretary's* schedule indicates that the annual report is due next week.

LESSON 11

Compound Words

Some compound words are written as one solid word; others are two separate words; still others are hyphenated. Authorities do not agree on the rules, and practice changes from time to time. An up-to-date dictionary is the only sure guide. The following rules represent the best present-day practice.

PREFIXES AND SUFFIXES

When the first element of a compound word is a prefix or the last element is a suffix, the compound is usually written solid. For illustrations, see Lessons 14 and 15.

Exceptions

1. When the last letter of a prefix is the same as the first letter of the word to which it is being added, a hyphen is inserted.

co-operate	**semi-independent**	**re-enter**	**pre-existing**

When, in adding a suffix, the same letter occurs three times, the hyphen is inserted.

bell-like **shell-less**

2. When the second element is a capitalized word, a hyphen is inserted after the prefix.

pro-British **trans-Pacific** **anti-American** **semi-Diesel** **extra-League**

3. The prefix *self* is always followed by a hyphen.

self-esteem **self-confidence**

4. The hyphen is necessary in some verbs beginning with the prefix *re* to distinguish them from identically spelled words of different meanings.

re-count	**recount**	**re-cover**	**recover**
re-form	**reform**	**re-mark**	**remark**

COMPOUND NOUNS

Compound nouns are more often written solid or as two words than hyphenated.

Solid

armchair	breakup	hardwood	papermaking
background	businessman	homestead	postmark
bondholder	cabinetworker	lawsuit	quitclaim

Two Words

air pump	common sense	half dollar	piece goods
all right	cross reference	money order	real estate
bank note	day labor	per cent	week end

Hyphenated

actor-manager	give-and-take	kilowatt-hour	son-in-law
car-mile	go-between	man-of-war	take-off
cure-all	horsepower-hour	mother-of-pearl	trade-mark

1. Compound numerals from *twenty-one* to *ninety-nine* are hyphenated.

    fifty-two   one hundred forty-seven

2. Fractions are hyphenated, the hyphen being placed between the numerator and the denominator unless one element or both already contain a hyphen.

  one-eighth   forty-six hundredths   twenty-one thirty-seconds

3. Combinations with *vice*, *ex*, and *elect* are hyphenated.

    ex-president   vice-chairman   senator-elect

COMPOUND ADJECTIVES

1. When two or more words are used *before* a noun as if they were but one adjective, the expression is hyphenated.

able-bodied man	light-blue letterhead	time-honored custom
change-of-address card	middle-aged man	top-heavy load
clear-cut distinction	never-to-be-	twelve-year-old child
double-quick time	forgotten event	uncalled-for remark
first-class condition	100-watt bulb	up-to-date method

Exceptions

a. Compound adjectives containing an adverb ending in *ly*.

  finely drawn distinction   rapidly falling barometer

Caution: Some commonly used *adjectives*, however, end in *ly*.

    a friendly-appearing person   a worldly-looking woman

b. Two-word proper nouns used as adjectives.

New York style   Park Avenue shop   South American product

2. When a compound adjective *follows* a noun, it is usually not hyphenated.

the plan above described   a man well groomed   a method that is up to date

COMPOUND VERBS

When a verb is built up from two or more words, it should be hyphenated.

  to dry-clean   to hard-finish   to blue-pencil   to double-check

Note: For the plurals and possessive of compound nouns, see Lessons 9 and 10.

LESSON 12

Words Often Misspelled

abeyance	annual	buoyant	concern
abridgment	anticipate	career	conference
absence	antique	carriage	confident
absolutely	anxious	caucus	congested
abutting	apparently	characteristic	congratulations
accommodation	appeal	charity	congressional
achieve	appetite	Chattanooga	conquer
achievement	appreciate	Chesapeake	conscience
acquaintance	appropriate	choice	consequence
acquiesce	architecture	chute	consist
acquisition	arrival	cipher	conspicuous
activities	assassin	circular	contempt
actual	assess	citizen	continuity
additional	assistance	cleanse	contribution
adjournment	assured	clearance	controversy
adjustment	average	cogent	cordially
administer	awkward	colonel	criminal
administrative	banquet	color	cubic
affectionately	bargain	colossal	customary
affirmative	basement	commemorate	damage
aggregate	beginning	commissioners	dangerous
agitation	believing	committee	dealer
agreement	Berkeley	competitive	debt
allege	building	complacence	decide
animal	bulletin	concede	decision

Word Origin

Salary. The exact meaning of the Latin word from which *salary* is derived is "salt money." The Roman soldiers received *salarium*, an allowance for salt, as part of their pay. This original meaning still survives in the common saying of being "worth one's salt."

LESSON 13

Words Often Mispronounced

accidentally	ăk′sĭ děn′tăl lĭ	Bayreuth	bī′roit′
acclimate	ă klī′mĭt	Beyrouth (Beirut)	bā′ro͞ot
accompaniment	ă kŭm′pȧ nĭ měnt	biography	bī ŏg′rȧ fĭ
acoustics	ȧ ko͞os′tĭks	blatant	blā′tănt
admirable	ăd′mĭ rȧ b'l	Bologna	bō lō′nyä
adult	ȧ dŭlt′	Bordeaux	bôr′dō′
affluent	ăf′flû ĕnt	bouquet	bo͞o kā′
Albuquerque	ăl′bû kûr′kĕ	Butte	būt
alienate	āl′yĕn āt	Cannes	kȧn
ally	ă lī′	caramel	kăr′ȧ měl
almond	ä′mŭnd	Caribbean	kăr′ĭ bē′ăn
alternative	ôl tûr′nȧ tĭv	chauffeur	shō fûr′
apparatus	ăp′ȧ rā′tŭs	coadjutor	kō ăj′o͞o tēr
applicable	ăp′lĭ kȧ b'l	combat (v.)	kŏm′băt
apricot	ā′prĭ kŏt	comparable	kŏm′pȧ rȧ b'l
arctic	ärk′tĭk	condolence	kŏn dō′lĕns
artistically	är tĭs′tĭ kăl lĭ	consummate (v.)	kŏn′sŭ māt
aspirant	ăs pīr′ănt	culinary	kū′lĭ nĕr′ĭ
associate (v.)	ȧ sō′shĭ āt	curator	kû rā′tēr
athlete	ăth′lēt	data	dā′tȧ
attacked	ă tăkt′	deaf	děf
authoritatively	ô thŏr′ĭ tā′tĭv lĭ	decade	děk′ād
auxiliary	ôg zĭl′yȧ rĭ	decorous	děk′ō rŭs
avenue	ăv′ĕ nū	demonstrate	děm′ŭn strāt
aviator	ā′vĭ ā′tēr	demonstrative	dĕ mŏn′strȧ tĭv

Word Origin

Cash comes from the Italian *cassa*, meaning "money box," which, in turn, was derived from the Latin *capsa*, "a box." When one speaks of a "cash box," the word *cash* is really being used twice in the same sense.

BRIEF TEST ON PART I

1. State the rule that governs the spelling of each of the following words:

advertisement	curbing	ratifying	shopping
analyzing	forbidden	replied	solicited
arguing	genuineness	satisfactorily	dutiful

2. Spell the plurals of:

alley	foreman	sheaf
church	invoice	statement
city	potato	studio
crisis	4	tweezers

3. Spell the possessives of:

boys	laymen	tourist
it	Max	students

4. Indicate whether the following words are preferably written solid, with a hyphen, or as separate words.

streetcar	motorcycle	timesaver	bankbook	reexamine
tomorrow	preColonial	letterwriting	nevertheless	pricelist
antifriction	goodby	redraw	semiconscious	profitsharing
southwest	preempt	tinplate	highschool	intercity
transcontinental	selfcontrol	worldwide	schoolhouse	precool

5. Indicate the correct pronunciation of the following words.

aerial	appreciative	centenary
treasure	robust	earnest

6. Write sentences containing the following words:

absurd	certain	sacrifice
ascertain	precarious	scrupulous

7. Write a short paragraph concerning the origin of *slogan;* of *plaster of Paris.*

8. State the rule regarding the hyphenation of compound numerals.

9. Are words containing the prefix *self* written solid or with a hyphen?

10. How can you decide whether or not to double the final consonant when adding a termination?

PART II

Word Beginnings and Endings (Prefixes and Suffixes)

The lessons of Part II contribute to an understanding of how words are built. Through the laws of association, you will thus be able to master certain common spelling difficulties.

Especially in Lessons 14 and 15, analyze the words that illustrate the various prefixes and suffixes and see whether you can detect the influence of that element on the meaning of the word.

Students who enjoy carrying on research projects will be greatly interested in referring to the dictionary for the complete enumeration and explanation of the meanings of the various prefixes and suffixes. For example, look up the suffix *-ery*.

The suggestions on page 1 for the study of words often misspelled and words often mispronounced should be faithfully followed throughout this and subsequent parts of the text.

LESSON 14

Common Word Beginnings

Prefix	Meaning	Illustration
a	at, in, on	ahead, across, abroad, asleep
a (an) (Gk.)	without, not	atheist, anarchy, aneroid
ab (abs)	from	abnormal, abhor, abolish, absent, abstain
ad (a, ac, af, ag, al, an, ap, ar, as, at)	to	admit, advocate, aspect, accustom, acquire, affix, aggregate, allocate, annotate, appoint, arrive, ascend, attempt
after	subsequent to	afterthought, afternoon, aftermath
ante	before	antedate, antecedent, anteroom, antediluvian
anti (ant)	against, opposite	anticlimax, antipathy, antibody, antitrust, antarctic
be	to make, by	benumb, besiege, before, beside
bi (bis)	two, twice	bimonthly, bicentenary, bimetallism, bicycle
by	secondary	bygone, byword, bystander, byplay
circum	around	circumstance, circumference, circumspect, circumscribed, circumnavigate
con (co, col, com, cor)	with, together	confer, collapse, compress, composite, consult, correspond, co-worker, coalesce
contra (counter)	against	contravene, contradict, counteract, counterbalance, countersign
de	down	depose, demerit, depend, debase, detract
dis	away, apart reversal	disastrous, dispossess, dispense, discharge
en (em)	in	enrich, enlarge, embody, employ, embrace
ex (e, ec, ef)	out of, from	extract, excerpt, extemporaneous, eject, eclectic, efface
extra	beyond	extrajudicial, extraneous, extraterritorial
for	away, prohibition, neglect, thoroughly	forgive, forget, forgo, forbid, forbear, forsake, forlorn
fore	in front, previous	forearm, foreclosure, foreknowledge, foregoing
hyper	over, above, excessive	hypercritical, hyperconscious, hyperacidity
hypo	under, a low degree	hypocrite, hypodermic, hypochondriac, hypoblast
in (il, im, ir)	in, on, not	inapplicable, intolerant, inconvenient, illegal, import, irresponsible, irreconcilable

Prefix	Meaning	Illustration
inter (intra, intro, enter)	between, among	intercollegiate, intercede, intramural, introduce, introspective, entertain
mis	wrong, wrongly	misapply, misrule, misrepresent
mono	one, alone	monograph, monogram, monosyllable
non	not	nonobservance, nonsubscriber, nonessential, nonexistent
off	away, removed	offcast, offshore, offshoot, offhand
out	beyond	outweigh, outbreak, outbalance
over	above, to an excessive degree	overthrow, overrule, overconfident, overproduction
per	through, throughout	pervade, peruse, perennial, perforate
poly	many, much, often	polysyllabic, polyglot, polygon
post	after	postpone, postscript, postlude, posterity
pre	before	prevail, prefix, preamble, pre-eminence, premeditate
pro	for, forth	promotion, pronoun, propel, progress, propensity
pseudo	false, spurious	pseudopermanent, pseudonym, pseudoconservative
re	back, again	re-establish, reorganize, reunion, re-elect
retro	backward	retroactive, retrospect, retrogradation
semi	half, partly	semiannual, semicolon, semicircular
step	combining form denoting a relative by remarriage	stepmother, stepfather, stepbrother
sub (suc, suf, sug, sum, sup, sus)	under	subway, subdue, succumb, suffice, suggest, summon, supplant, suspect
super (Fr. sur)	above, over	supersede, survey, superabundant, surpass
there	in, at a point in relation to place	thereupon, thereby, thereto
thorough	through, throughout	thoroughbred, thoroughfare, thoroughgoing
trans (tra)	across, beyond	transact, transship, translate, traverse
tri	having three parts	tricolor, triangle, tripod
ultra	beyond	ultrafashionable, ultracritical, ultraviolet
un	not, reverse of	unskilled, unbusinesslike, uncertainty, uncivil
under	beneath	undercurrent, underrate, underhanded
up	up, upward	uphold, upraise, uproot, upturn, upkeep
where	at or in which place	whereabouts, wherefore, whereupon
with	from, against	withdraw, withstand, without

LESSON 15

Common Word Endings

Suffix	Meaning	Illustration
able (ible, ble)	See Lesson 18	
acious	abounding in, tending to	pugnacious, fallacious, mendacious
acy	state or quality of being	obstinacy, accuracy, candidacy
age	state of being, act of, that which, a collection of	savage, homage, voyage, stoppage, heritage, vintage
al	pertaining to, having the characteristic of, act of	electoral, general, critical, departmental, horizontal, approval
an (ian)	pertaining to, one who	comedian, historian, American, human, custodian
ance (ancy)	See Lesson 17	
ant (ent)	See Lesson 16	
ary	belonging to, one who, place for	judiciary, secondary, solitary, hereditary, dietary, actuary, apiary
ate	having, one who	confederate, moderate, corporate, delegate
dom	state of being, domain of	random, freedom, kingdom
ee	one who receives	employee, assignee, nominee, refugee
en	made of, to make	wooden, molten, brighten, darken
ence (ency)	See Lesson 17	
er (eer, ier)	See Lesson 20	
ery (ry)	place where, state of being, collection, art of	distillery, cookery, entry, jewelry, savagery, infantry, pedantry, gentry, finery, millinery
escence (escent)	beginning to be, slightly	iridescence, incandescent, coalescent
ess	feminine	patroness, heiress, waitress
est	most	largest, smallest, fastest
ful	full of	careful, resourceful, thoughtful, useful, successful, thankful, powerful
fy	to make	disqualify, identify, syllabify
hood	state or quality of being	hardihood, livelihood, neighborhood
ic (ical, ac)	pertaining to, made of, one who	automatic, athletic, volcanic, dramatic, democratic, mechanical, maniac

Suffix	Meaning	Illustration
ician	a specialist	electrician, musician, technician
ics	science of	mathematics, tactics, politics, dynamics, statistics
id	quality of	valid, lucid, frigid
ile (il)	capable of, relating to	virile, servile, docile, civil
ine	pertaining to, like	feminine, sanguine, adamantine
ing	the act of	pending, accounting, applying
ion	See Lesson 19	
ise (ize)	See Lesson 19	
ish	resembling	bookish, womanish, English, bluish, boyish
ism	state of being, doctrine	cynicism, communism, despotism, socialism, criticism
ist	one who	journalist, copyist, organist, humorist
ite	a native of, an adherent of, being	suburbanite, favorite
ity (ty)	state or quality of being	duplicity, velocity, calamity, fidelity, vivacity, twenty, thirty
ive	having the quality or power of	conclusive, corrective, extensive, operative, conducive
less	without	speechless, countless, nerveless
ly	in the manner in which	approximately, tightly, indifferently, friendly
ment	state of being, act of, that which	excitement, appointment, assessment, impeachment
mony	state of being, that which	harmony, ceremony, acrimony, matrimony
ness	state or quality of being	business, flatness, costliness
or	See Lesson 20	
ory	relating to, place for	accessory, auditory, peremptory, dormitory
ose (ous)	full of, having	verbose, glucose, ponderous, unanimous, bilious, infectious, pernicious
ple	fold, increase	multiple, couple, triple
ship	state of, office of, art of	receivership, penmanship, leadership
some	like	tiresome, loathesome, lonesome
ster	one who does	teamster, spinster
tude	state of being	quietude, latitude, gratitude
ule	diminutive	ridicule, globule, molecule
ulent	full of	corpulent, fraudulent, virulent
ure	state or act of	pleasure, exposure, culture, tenure, signature
ward (wards)	in the direction of	backward, upward, afterwards

LESSON 16

Ant and Ent Suffixes

The terminations *ant* and *ent* have two uses: (1) to form adjectives having the force of a present participle, and (2) to form nouns denoting one who or that which.

1. applicant — One who makes a request.
2. assistant — One who helps; helping.
3. attendant — Accompanying; also, one who or that which accompanies.
4. elegant — Very choice; pleasing to good taste.
5. exorbitant — Excessive.
6. ignorant — Lacking in knowledge.
7. incessant — Unceasing.
8. pleasant — Agreeable; pleasing.
9. relevant — Bearing upon the case; pertinent.
10. reluctant — Unwilling; disinclined.
11. servant — One who serves or attends.
12. stimulant — That which stimulates or excites.
13. competent — Fit; answering all requirements.
14. correspondent — One who communicates with another by letter.
15. delinquent — Failing in duty; also, one who violates the law or who is not fully responsible for his conduct.
16. dependent — Relying on something else for support; also, one who thus relies.
17. different — Not the same; dissimilar.
18. diligent — Careful; industrious.
19. equivalent — Equal to; also, a thing of the same value, weight, power.
20. excellent — Superior; of great worth.
21. incident — That which happens; an event.
22. permanent — Durable; constant.
23. persistent — Tenacious; enduring.
24. president — One who presides.

WORDS USED IN SENTENCES

1. This *applicant's* references are most satisfactory.
2. The *assistant* superintendent is responsible for having all doors and windows closed at night.
3. *Attendant* circumstances make the scheme impossible. Please reserve a room for the invalid and her *attendant*.
4. Mr. Roland's home is furnished in *elegant* simplicity.
5. The charge for repairing the watch is *exorbitant*.
6. There is no excuse for his remaining *ignorant* of the facts in this case.
7. I am utterly bored by her *incessant* chatter.
8. Our relationship with them has always been *pleasant*.
9. Here is all the correspondence *relevant* to the Hyde case.
10. We are *reluctant* to take such drastic measures.
11. Public office holders are *servants* of the people.
12. The good news has affected him like a *stimulant*.
13. She is *competent* to do the work of a laboratory technician.
14. The autobiography of the famous war *correspondent* contains a vivid account of his experiences.
15. Please prepare a list of all *delinquent* customers.
16. The success of the plan is *dependent* on the co-operation of every member of the organization.
17. It is our plan to install an entirely *different* model soon.
18. The boy proved to be *diligent* in the performance of his duties.
19. The shorter hours are the *equivalent* of an increase in salary.
20. His *excellent* sales approach won favorable comment.
21. Here is another *incident* of failure to follow instructions.
22. He obtained a *permanent* position with the local transit company.
23. *Persistent* rumors are afloat that the corporation is in financial difficulties.
24. The *president* of the club was unable to preside at the last business meeting.

LESSON 17

Ance and Ence Suffixes

The terminations *ance* and *ence*, and *ancy* and *ency*, form nouns meaning act or state of, or quality of.

1. **accordance** — Harmony; conformity.
2. **appearance** — External aspect; mien.
3. **assurance** — The act of making certain; self-reliance.
4. **compliance** — The act of yielding, as to a demand or proposal; obedience; assent.
5. **continuance** — A holding on or remaining in a particular state.
6. **entrance** — Entry; access.
7. **hindrance** — An obstruction; delay.
8. **importance** — Consequence; weight; significance.
9. **observance** — The act of taking notice; attentiveness.
10. **predominance** — Ascendancy; prevalence.
11. **reluctance** — Unwillingness.
12. **buoyancy** — The property of floating on the surface of a liquid; vivacity; cheerfulness.
13. **hesitancy** — Vacillation; indecision.
14. **confidence** — Faith; credence; certitude.
15. **convenience** — Freedom from discomfort; fitness.
16. **dependence** — Reliance; trust.
17. **experience** — Knowledge derived from one's own action.
18. **influence** — Weight; power to sway.
19. **innocence** — Purity of thought and feeling; guilelessness.
20. **preference** — Prior choice; the power or opportunity of choosing.
21. **recurrence** — Returning or reappearing regularly or frequently.
22. **reticence** — Reserve in speech.
23. **inefficiency** — Lack of power or skill to accomplish something.
24. **presidency** — The office or the term of office of a chief executive.

WORDS USED IN SENTENCES

1. In *accordance* with our agreement, we will send a remittance on the fifteenth.
2. His disheveled *appearance* attracted attention.
3. The mechanic worked with the *assurance* that comes of long experience.
4. His cheerful *compliance* with the rules and regulations won him promotion.
5. We shall endeavor to merit the *continuance* of your patronage.
6. The employees' *entrance* is on Fifth Street.
7. The new stenographer was a *hindrance* rather than a help.
8. The quality of paper used for the envelopes is a matter of great *importance*.
9. A program of patriotic airs was presented in *observance* of Independence Day.
10. The *predominance* of bright colors distinguished the new streamlined models.
11. He gave his consent with great *reluctance*.
12. The *buoyancy* of the new salesman is proving a good influence on the entire staff.
13. I have no *hesitancy* whatsoever in recommending Miss Atkins.
14. I have the greatest *confidence* in my physician's ability.
15. For the *convenience* of our customers, we are opening a suburban office.
16. His *dependence* on his partner's judgment and discretion was absolute.
17. With his *experience*, he should make a great success in this field.
18. Tom's new friend has a desirable *influence* over him.
19. It should not be hard to prove his *innocence*.
20. Mr. Clark has expressed a *preference* for Model A-22.
21. The Board of Health feared a *recurrence* of the epidemic.
22. From his *reticence* on the subject, I suspect something serious is the matter.
23. We cannot tolerate *inefficiency* in this office.
24. Sam is a candidate for the *presidency* of the students' organization.

LESSON 18

Able and Ible Suffixes

The terminations *able* and *ible* signify able to, capable of, fit or worthy to be.

1. **acceptable** — Capable of being accepted; meeting the qualifications.
2. **advisable** — Proper to be done; prudent; expedient.
3. **capable** — Able; efficient; competent.
4. **available** — Accessible or attainable.
5. **conceivable** — Imaginable; thinkable.
6. **debatable** — Disputable; questionable.
7. **disagreeable** — Unpleasant; annoying; distasteful.
8. **desirable** — Expedient; advisable; acceptable.
9. **durable** — Permanent; lasting.
10. **practicable** — Capable of being done or used; useful.
11. **receivable** — Capable of being received.
12. **salable** — Capable of being sold; marketable.
13. **accessible** — Easy to reach or enter.
14. **admissible** — Capable of being conceded or allowed.
15. **audible** — Capable of being heard.
16. **collectible** — Capable of being gathered together.
17. **convertible** — Capable of being changed or transformed.
18. **feasible** — Capable of being done or brought about; practicable.
19. **incredible** — Surpassing belief; unlikely.
20. **legible** — Clear; readable.
21. **permissible** — Allowable; tolerable.
22. **possible** — Feasible; practicable.
23. **reversible** — Capable of going through a series of changes backward or forward; finished on both sides.
24. **susceptible** — Yielding; sensitive.

WORDS USED IN SENTENCES

1. Your proposal is not *acceptable* to our company.
2. Mr. Turner's physician does not think it *advisable* for him to make the trip at this time.
3. Miss Webster is proving to be a most *capable* bookkeeper.
4. Not one copy of the trade journal is *available*.
5. It is scarcely *conceivable* that an employee with his record could have done such a thing.
6. Whether or not this plan will bring any advantages is *debatable*.
7. It takes great tact to deal with a *disagreeable* customer.
8. A complete change of personnel is *desirable* in this case.
9. This brand of hosiery is extremely *durable*.
10. Radio communication has proved to be *practicable*.
11. The accountant asked for a list of the bills *receivable*.
12. These materials are *salable* even though slightly damaged in the fire.
13. The camp site must be in an *accessible* location.
14. The testimony was not *admissible* as it did not relate directly to the case.
15. He was so weak that his voice was scarcely *audible*.
16. How many of these past-due accounts do you estimate are *collectible?*
17. The X Corporation is planning a new issue of *convertible* 5 per cent bonds.
18. It is not at all *feasible* for us to attempt to maintain our own delivery system.
19. The *incredible* story of the cashier's embezzlement of company funds has just reached us.
20. A *legible* style of penmanship is a requirement for this record-keeping work.
21. His absence from the lecture is *permissible*.
22. This system makes it *possible* for the students to earn additional credits.
23. We are offering a special selection of *reversible* topcoats.
24. This instrument is most *susceptible* to changes in temperature.

LESSON 19

Ise, Ize, Yze; Tion, Sion Suffixes

The verb suffixes *ise, ize,* or *yze* mean to subject to, to make like, to act in the way of, to carry on.

1. **advertise** — To give notice of; to announce.
2. **despise** — To regard as contemptible; to scorn.
3. **exercise** — To exert; to perform; to employ actively.
4. **revise** — To improve; to reform; to amend.
5. **supervise** — To oversee; to superintend.
6. **comprise** — To consist of; to involve.
7. **apologize** — To make an excuse; to express regret.
8. **authorize** — To empower; to sanction.
9. **realize** — To comprehend; to attain.
10. **summarize** — To state briefly or concisely; to sum up.
11. **systematize** — To arrange in an orderly plan.
12. **analyze** — To examine closely and critically; to reduce to useful terms.

The noun suffixes *tion* and *sion* indicate state, action.

13. **compulsion** — Coercion; restraint; force.
14. **conclusion** — An inference; a judgment; a deduction; a closing.
15. **expression** — Diction; language; aspect.
16. **distinction** — A characteristic difference.
17. **persuasion** — Act or art of influencing or convincing.
18. **exhibition** — A showing or display of something, as of works of art, manufactured objects, etc.
19. **collection** — The act or process of assembling an aggregate; accumulation.
20. **communication** — A verbal or written message; also, a means of access.
21. **location** — Situation; place.
22. **conflagration** — An extensive and destructive fire.
23. **distribution** — The act or process of dealing out or dividing.
24. **opposition** — Resistance; hostility.

WORDS USED IN SENTENCES

1. Orcutt & Jones is *advertising* great sales of furniture.
2. Any honorable person would *despise* such trickery.
3. *Exercise* the greatest care not to violate the copyright law.
4. The spelling book is to be *revised* next year.
5. I have been asked to *supervise* the midyear examination.
6. A dictionary and an atlas *comprised* the entire reference library of that office!
7. The manager *apologized* for his curt reply.
8. I have been *authorized* to purchase a new desk for my office.
9. Do you *realize* the seriousness of this situation?
10. To *summarize:* our staff should be enlarged, our floor space increased, and our advertising doubled.
11. The new filing system makes it possible to *systematize* much of the data.
12. Have you *analyzed* the figures in the last financial statement?
13. I feel under no *compulsion* to purchase from that concern.
14. Our *conclusion* is that the whole affair is a farce.
15. We are allowing this extra discount as an *expression* of our appreciation of your patronage.
16. You have the *distinction* of being the first agent for our product in your state.
17. As a result of the salesman's power of *persuasion*, I signed on the dotted line.
18. Our products are on *exhibition* at the Chicago Merchandise Mart.
19. Here are the bills that are due for *collection*.
20. We have had no *communication* of any kind from the witness.
21. The new store is in an accessible *location*.
22. This *conflagration* is the result of a carelessly discarded cigarette.
23. The general manager will send orders for the *distribution* of new stock to the branch stores.
24. We hereby voice our *opposition* to the proposal.

LESSON 20

Er (Eer, Ier), Or Suffixes

The noun-forming suffixes *er*, *eer*, *ier*, and *or* indicate one who, that which. *Er* is also used to form the comparative degree of adjectives and adverbs.

1. **adviser** — A counselor.
2. **bookkeeper** — One who keeps accounts.
3. **builder** — One who constructs.
4. **debater** — A person who takes part in a formal argument.
5. **grocer** — One who sells groceries.
6. **manufacturer** — One who makes articles, usually on a large scale.
7. **messenger** — A bearer of a communication.
8. **farmer** — One who cultivates or tills the land.
9. **writer** — An author; a penman; one who writes.
10. **neater** — More trim; more tidy.
11. **smoother** — Having a more even surface or texture.
12. **auctioneer** — One who sells property or goods by public sale.
13. **engineer** — One who is skilled in the principles and practice of any mechanical science.
14. **profiteer** — A person who takes unfair advantage of a situation to make undue profits.
15. **cashier** — An employee whose duty it is to receive and pay out money.
16. **collector** — One who makes a practice of gathering objects of a certain class; an official whose duty it is to gather taxes, duties, debts, etc.
17. **competitor** — One who contends with others for the same object.
18. **consignor** — One who sends goods to another.
19. **contractor** — One of the parties to a written agreement; one who makes a business of supplying or constructing on a large scale for a stated sum.
20. **donor** — One who gives or presents a thing; a giver.
21. **doctor** — A licensed physician or surgeon; a holder of the highest degree of a university.
22. **indicator** — One who, or that which, points out.
23. **instructor** — A teacher.
24. **percolator** — A vessel fitted with a strainer that allows a liquid to filter through it, as a special type of coffeepot.

WORDS USED IN SENTENCES

1. I know of no better *adviser* on financial matters than your banker.
2. All incoming mail containing money or checks goes first to the *bookkeeper* for entry.
3. Can you recommend a reliable *builder* to do the work on my house?
4. The *debater* for the negative side presented his points convincingly.
5. The corner *grocer* has installed a full line of frozen foods.
6. This tag contains the *manufacturer's* guarantee.
7. Please send the package by special *messenger*.
8. The market reports given over the radio have been of great help to *farmers*.
9. He is a well-known *writer* of adventure stories.
10. See how much *neater* the office looks since the new files were installed.
11. This desk top is much *smoother* than the other.
12. "Sold!" cried the *auctioneer*.
13. The *engineer* in charge of the construction of the hydroelectric plant has had several similar projects.
14. *Profiteers* flourished during the difficult days of the World War.
15. The *cashier* stamped the bill "Paid."
16. I received a reminder from the tax *collector's* office today.
17. Our chief *competitor* has introduced a new line of refrigerators.
18. Whose name appears as *consignor* on the bill of lading?
19. This *contractor* is known for the quality of materials he uses.
20. The hospital sent out a call for blood *donors*.
21. It will be necessary to have your *doctor's* signature on this blank.
22. The *indicator* on the oil tank shows that the tank is half full.
23. The *instructor* assigned an alternative project.
24. We announce a sale of modern chromium-trim *percolators*.

LESSON 21

Words Often Misspelled

decisive	efficient	fortunate	increasing
defense	eighth	franc	indebtedness
deficiencies	elimination	frequent	independence
deliberately	emergency	frontage	indicate
deputy	emphasizes	garage	individual
desiccate	enervate	generally	industrial
design	enthusiasm	generation	inhabitant
desperate	entitle	grammar	initial
develop	equally	grievance	innocuous
difficulty	especially	grocery	innovation
dilemma	essential	guess	inoculate
disappear	etiquette	haphazard	inquire
disappoint	evidence	harass	installation
discrimination	exaggerate	hazard	insurance
discussion	excavation	heard	insure
disposal	exclusively	herd	interrupt
dissatisfied	existence	honest	intimidate
dissipate	expedition	horizon	intolerable
divide	extravagant	hosiery	investigation
division	favorable	idiosyncrasy	invitation
duteous	finally	illustration	iridescent
earliest	financial	imagine	janitor
ecstasy	foreign	immediately	jealous
edge	foresight	inadvertent	journey
editor	fortieth	incidentally	juice

Word Origin

Charge. "To charge" is, literally, "to load a car," from the Latin *carrus*, "a chariot." The implication of loading or weighing still survives in such expressions as "charge with responsibility," "charge a prisoner with guilt," "charge our account."

LESSON 22

Words Often Mispronounced

denunciate	dė nŭn′shĭ āt	February	fĕb′rōō ĕr′ĭ
derelict	dĕr′ĕ lĭkt	film	fĭlm
derisive	dė rī′sĭv	finance	fĭ năns′
despicable	dĕs′pĭ kȧ b'l	finesse	fĭ nĕs′
desultory	dĕs′ŭl tō′rĭ	flaccid	flăk′sĭd
detail (n.)	dė tāl′	flagrant	flā′grănt
dexterous	dĕk′stēr ŭs	forehead	fŏr′ĕd
dictionary	dĭk′shŭn ĕr′ĭ	gala	gā′lȧ
diminution	dĭm′ĭ nū′shŭn	genuine	jĕn′ū ĭn
direct	dĭ rĕkt′	gist	jĭst
discharge	dĭs chärj′	Gloucester	glŏs′tēr
drowned	dround	government	gŭv′ērn mĕnt
Dubuque	dȯȯ būk′	grievous	grēv′ŭs
duet	du̇ ĕt′	grimy	grīm′ĭ
Duquesne	dȯȯ kān′	guardian	gär′dĭ ăn
eczema	ĕk′zė mȧ	gubernatorial	gū′bēr nȧ tō′rĭ ăl
elaborate (adj.)	ė lăb′ō rĭt	Haverhill	hā′vēr ĭl
err	ûr	hearth	härth
escalator	ĕs′kȧ lā′tēr	heinous	hā′nŭs
every	ĕv′ēr ĭ	hoof	hōōf
exemplary	ĕg zĕm′plȧ rĭ	hospitable	hŏs′pĭ tȧ b'l
expert (adj.)	ĕks pûrt′	hundred	hŭn′drĕd
exquisite	ĕks′kwĭ zĭt	idea	ī dē′ȧ
extraordinary	ĕks trôr′dĭ nĕr′ĭ	illustrate	ĭl′ŭs trāt
factory	făk′tō rĭ	impious	ĭm′pĭ ŭs

Word Origin

Candidate. In ancient Rome, a man campaigning for office wore a white toga and was referred to as *candidatus*, "one clothed in white." From this word came our word *candidate*, meaning "one campaigning for office," but without the significance as to dress.

BRIEF TEST ON PART II

1. Name five prefixes and five suffixes and give the meanings of each.

2. Indicate the prefix in each of the following words and show how it affects the meaning of the word.

   correlate   describe   perceive   transgressor
   counterclaim   nonsense   semideveloped   uncollectible

3. Indicate the suffix in each of the following words and show how it affects the meaning of the word.

   legislative   librarian   miscellaneous   perception
   leniency   loveliness   necessity   periodical

4. Write sentences containing each of the following words.

   atomizer   barbarous   comparative   nullification
   attendance   characterize conversant   predicament

5. By referring to the dictionary, indicate the correct pronunciation for each of the following words.

   deliberate   demonstrative   formidable
   gratuitous   increment   pianist

6. Refer to a dictionary for the meaning of the prefixes *micro* and *thermo*. Give two words in which each occurs.

7. Write sentences containing the words you chose for Exercise 6.

8. List the following words, correcting any misspellings.

   changing   Britian   comparision
   begger   adequate   crystalize

9. What do the terminations *ant* and *ent* denote?

10. Write a short paragraph concerning the origin of *Portland cement;* of *bonus*.

44

PART III

Word Usage

Part III offers some of the most interesting and helpful material in the entire text. From the days of Mrs. Malaprop in Sheridan's "The Rivals" down to the "boners" of our contemporary college youths, readers have laughed over the blunders resulting from the confusion of words similar in sound and in appearance. But to the stenographer, such blunders are no laughing matter.

Careful attention is the secret of mastering these difficulties. For example, in studying Lessons 23–26, inclusive, which present words confused because they are pronounced just alike, take time to notice the exact difference in the spelling of each word in a group of words. Make the mental image of the distinction so sharp that, when you hear the word, you will *know* which spelling is meant. Also, when you have occasion to look up the spelling of other homonyms, do not glance too quickly at the definitions. Be sure that the definition you find fits the word your transcript calls for.

Likewise, with those words that look or sound somewhat alike (see Lessons 27–32), accurate pronunciation is the key to the difficulty. In short—to careful seeing, add careful speaking.

The study of synonyms and of antonyms (Lessons 33–36 and 37–39, respectively) will help you enlarge your vocabulary. Because the English language is derived from so many sources, it is exceedingly rich in synonyms. It is said, for example, that there are thirty-seven synonyms for "pure." Form the habit of reading the paragraphs on synonyms and antonyms following the definitions of many words in the dictionary.

Form the habit, also, when consulting the dictionary, of noticing the indication of the correct preposition to be used following certain words.

LESSON 23

Words That Sound Exactly Alike (Homonyms)

1. **aloud** — Audibly; with a loud voice.
   allowed — Permitted; sanctioned.

2. **calender** — A finishing machine used in the manufacture of paper or cloth; also, to smooth, finish, and give a glossy surface to paper or cloth by using this machine.
   calendar — A record of time.

3. **canvas** — Strong tent cloth.
   canvass — To solicit.

4. **capitol** — The official building of Congress or of a state legislature.
   capital — The seat of government of a state or country; money invested in a business or other enterprise.

5. **compliment** — A flattering speech or attention; also, to commend.
   complement — That which fills or completes.

6. **council** — An assembly of men summoned for deliberation.
   counsel — An attorney; advice; also, to advise.

7. **correspondence** — Letters.
   correspondents — Letter writers.

8. **coarse** — Rough; not fine.
   course — A way; part of a dinner; action.

9. **current** — A flowing; an onward motion; electricity; belonging to the present.
   currant — A small, acid berry.

10. **due** — Owed or owing, as a debt; proper.
    dew — Condensed moisture.

11. **dyeing** — Staining; coloring.
    dying — Ceasing to live.

12. **fare** — Cost of travel; food.
    fair — Beautiful; blonde; just; an exhibit.

WORDS USED IN SENTENCES

1. Miss Hale, please read that paragraph *aloud*. Smoking is not *allowed* in the shipping room.

2. The Eureka Paper Company has installed the latest model of *calender*. Our artist has designed an attractive *calendar* for next year.

3. The *canvas* used in army cots must be of a specified quality. Would you be willing to *canvass* this block for the Community Chest?

4. The gold dome of the state *capitol* in Boston, the *capital* of Massachusetts, is a familiar landmark. He started business with a *capital* of $5,000.

5. The officer received a *compliment* on the speed with which he obtained the *complement* of men needed for the cruise.

6. The city *council* admitted that the *counsel* of the specialist was sound.

7. Our *correspondence* with our foreign *correspondents* is unusually heavy just now.

8. The man in the canoe threw a *coarse* woolen jacket about his shoulders; then he continued his *course* upstream. It is quite unnecessary to serve an eight-*course* dinner on this occasion.

9. The *current* issue of the *Boy Mechanic* contains an informing article on the difference between alternating and direct *current*. This recipe for *currant* jelly is an excellent one.

10. The grass is wet *due* to the heavy *dew*.

11. We do not advise *dyeing* this garment, as it is cut in a style that is *dying* out rapidly.

12. We announce a reduced *fare* effective for the duration of the county *fair*. The *fare* at this inn is very good, and the prices are *fair*.

Word Origin

Investigate. The Latin verb *vestigare* means "to track or trace by footprints." The addition of *in* changed the meaning to a figurative one of "tracing facts or searching for information," which is the meaning of our *investigate*.

LESSON 24

Words That Sound Exactly Alike
(Homonyms—*Continued*)

1. **flour**   Finely ground meal.
   flower   A blossom; to bloom.

2. **forth**   Forward; onward.
   fourth   Next after the third.

3. **grate**   A frame of iron bars, as in a window or a coal-burning furnace; to produce a harsh sound; to reduce to small particles by rubbing.
   great   Eminent; very large.

4. **here**   In this place.
   hear   To listen to.

5. **whole**   Unimpaired; intact; entire.
   hole   An opening.

6. **instance**   An example; a step in an action.
   instants   Moments.

7. **led**   Guided.
   lead   A heavy metal.

8. **lesson**   An exercise assigned for study.
   lessen   To decrease; to impair.

9. **loan**   That which one borrows or lends.
   lone   Solitary.

10. **marshal**   An officer.
    martial   Military.

11. **miner**   A worker in a mine.
    minor   Under full age.

12. **muscle**   An organ that produces movement of the body.
    mussel   A mollusk.

WORDS USED IN SENTENCES

1. Please bring home 5 pounds of *flour*, and a dozen roses from the *flower* shop.

2. Today we go *forth* to the *fourth* campaign.

3. The *grate* for the new furnace is defective. I made a *great* effort not to let his shrill voice *grate* on my nerves.

4. We stopped *here* so as to *hear* the band concert.

5. The man spent a *whole* day in repairing the *hole* in the fence.

6. For *instance*, two shots were heard just a few *instants* apart.

7. The guide *led* the group of students through the exhibit of articles made of *lead*.

8. This *lesson* in mathematics *lessens* my enthusiasm for the subject.

9. The *loan* was negotiated for the education of the *lone* orphan.

10. The *marshal* announced that *martial* law was in force.

11. The *miner's* eldest son is still a *minor*.

12. It takes strong *muscles* to open this variety of *mussel*.

Word Origin

Dollar. In the sixteenth century, a very fine grade of silver was mined in Joachimsthal (Joachim's dale), in Bohemia. A silver coin, the equivalent of the German golden gulden, was first minted there and was called *Joachimsthaler*. This long word was shortened to *thaler* and came into general use throughout Europe, in England taking the form *dollar* about 1553.

Pay. Paying a bill originally meant pacifying a creditor, being derived from the Latin *pax*, "peace."

LESSON 25

Words That Sound Exactly Alike
(Homonyms—*Continued*)

1. **packed**   Arranged compactly.
   pact   An agreement.

2. **past**   The time gone by; also used as an adjective.
   passed   Moved along; transferred.

3. **piece**   A fragment.
   peace   Freedom from war; content.

4. **pedal**   A treadle.
   peddle   To hawk.

5. **plain**   Simple; prairie land.
   plane   A tool for smoothing a surface; a flat surface.

6. **presents**   Gifts
   presence   The state of being in a certain place; bearing; mien.

7. **principal**   Chief; the original sum; the head of a school.
   principle   A fundamental truth; a rule of action.

8. **raise**   To lift; to erect.
   raze   To level to the ground.
   rays   Beams of light.

9. **residents**   Those living in a place.
   residence   A house; dwelling place.

10. **write**   To inscribe by hand.
    rite   A ceremony.
    right   Correct; a privilege.

11. **rôle**   A part in a play; a function assumed by anyone.
    roll   To move onward by turning over and over; a list.

12. **sail**   A sheet of canvas on a ship arranged to catch the wind and propel the boat; to travel by water.
    sale   The act of selling.

WORDS USED IN SENTENCES

1. The assembly room was *packed* when the new trade *pact* was read.

2. In the *past*, few freshmen have *passed*.

3. The spoiled child was given another *piece* of cake just to keep *peace* in the family.

4. The boy asked the mechanic to repair the *pedal* on his bicycle promptly, as he used his wheel to *peddle* newspapers.

5. The family from the *plains* sent a mail order for some *plain* white cloth and a carpenter's *plane*.

6. The children unwrapped their *presents* in the *presence* of the entire family.

7. The *principal* factor to be considered in making this investment is the safety of the *principal*. The *principal* adhered strictly to the *principle* of equal opportunity for all.

8. We are *raising* money to *raze* the old post office. The *rays* of the sun are slanting in December.

9. We are now *residents* of Pittsburgh, having recently established a legal *residence* there.

10. Please *write* a short article on the coronation *rite*. The father claimed the *right* to educate his own son.

11. He took over the *rôle* of investment counselor last month. With a quick turn of the cylinder knob, *roll* the paper into the typewriter.

12. The *sail* is made of cloth purchased at a jobber's *sale*.

Word Origin

Magazine has its origin in an Arabic word, *makhzan*, meaning "a storehouse." The Spanish adapted the word as *magacén*, and the French, in turn, as *magasin*. The English word *magazine* first meant a "storehouse," especially for military supplies; then, figuratively, a "storehouse of information," first in book form, but now any periodical publication.

LESSON 26

Words That Sound Exactly Alike
(Homonyms—*Continued*)

1. **scene** — A landscape; view.
   seen — Perceived by the eye.

2. **cite** — To quote; to name.
   sight — Vision.
   site — A location.

3. **stake** — A pointed stick; a hazard; to wager.
   steak — A slice of meat or fish.

4. **stationery** — Writing supplies.
   stationary — In a fixed position.

5. **straight** — Not crooked or curved.
   strait — A water passageway; narrow.

6. **tear** — To rend; also, a rent.
   tare — The allowance for the weight of a container.

7. **they're** — Contraction for "they are."
   there — In that place.
   their — Belonging to them.

8. **two** — One plus one.
   too — More than enough; also.
   to — Toward.

9. **vain** — Proud; conceited.
   vein — A blood vessel.
   vane — A weathercock.

10. **weighed** — Determined the heaviness of.
    wade — To walk through water, snow, etc.

11. **ware** — An article of merchandise.
    wear — To have on.

12. **wave** — To swing back and forth; an undulation or swell on the surface, as of the sea.
    waive — To forgo; relinquish.

13. **waist** — That part of the body between the chest and the hips; a garment.
    waste — Needless destruction; useless consumption; to expend needlessly.

WORDS USED IN SENTENCES

1. The *scene* from my window is the most inspiring one I've ever *seen*.

2. Let me *cite* an instance of where *sight* has been restored to the blind. The *site* chosen for the new post office is entirely satisfactory.

3. Build a campfire near that *stake*, and in a few moments we'll be broiling *steak*.

4. The concern that sells office supplies and *stationery* should carry *stationary* storage cabinets.

5. We steered *straight* for the open sea. Bering *Strait* is 36 miles wide.

6. He complained that there was an unsightly *tear* in the upholstery and that the manufacturer had not allowed for the *tare* on the shipment.

7. *They're* going to drive *there* in *their* car.

8. I feel that *two* years is not *too* long a time to devote *to* this research.

9. The *vain* man was proud of the blue blood in his *veins*. He even had his coat of arms on his weather *vane!*

10. Although the Boy Scout carried a knapsack that *weighed* many pounds, he shouted, "I will *wade* that stream!"

11. We carry all types of merchandise from kitchen*ware* to men's *wear*.

12. With a *wave* of her hand, she said, "I *waive* all my claims to the fund."

13. Around her *waist* she wore a tawdry belt that was a *waste* of money.

Word Origin

Money is derived from the name of a Roman goddess, Juno Moneta, in whose temple in Rome money was coined. In the course of the Roman conquests, the word *moneta* was introduced into various countries with which the Romans came in contact. In France, it became *monnaie*, from which our word *money* is directly derived. In England, the word became *mint*.

LESSON 27

Words That Sound or Look Somewhat Alike

1. accede   ăk sēd′   To comply with.
   exceed   ĕk sēd′   To surpass.

2. except   ĕk sĕpt′   Omitted.
   accept   ăk sĕpt′   To take, receive.

3. access   ăk′sĕs   Admittance; admission.
   excess   ĕk sĕs′   Surplus.

4. adept   ă dĕpt′   Well skilled; proficient.
   adapt   á dăpt′   To adjust.
   adopt   á dŏpt′   To choose; to take as one's own.

5. averse   á vûrs′   Disinclined.
   adverse   ăd vûrs′   Opposing; unfavorable.

6. advise   ăd vīz′   To inform; to counsel.
   advice   ăd vīs′   Information; recommendation.

7. affect   ă fĕkt′   To act upon; to alter; to assume.
   effect   ĕ fĕkt′   To bring about; that which is brought about.

8. anecdote   ăn′ĕk dōt   An interesting incident; a brief story.
   antidote   ăn′tĭ dōt   A remedy to counteract the effects of a poison.

9. angel   ān′jĕl   A spiritual being.
   angle   ăng′g'l   A corner.

10. area   ā′rē á   Surface; extent.
    aria   ä′rĭ á   A melody.

11. arraign   ă rān′   To call into court.
    arrange   ă rānj′   To put in order.

12. essay   ĕs′ā   A thoughtful composition; to attempt.
    assay   ă sā′   To test an ore or a chemical; also used as a noun.

WORDS USED IN SENTENCES

1. I cannot *accede* to your proposal unless the appropriation for advertising does not *exceed* $5,000.

2. All the local contractors, *except* Rogers Brothers, will *accept* his offer to submit bids.

3. Despite the fact that he had *access* to the cash drawer at all times, no one seemed to mistrust his sudden buying to *excess*.

4. She was *adept* in *adapting* herself to conditions, but she would not *adopt* the country's customs.

5. He declared himself to be *averse* to taking any action on the *adverse* report.

6. The controller *advised* the applicant to seek the *advice* of the personnel manager.

7. The actor's *affected* mannerisms had a most unfavorable *effect* on the audience. In fact, they *affected* the critics also.

8. The *anecdote* about the interne's mistake in giving the wrong *antidote* for poison ivy was very amusing.

9. The artist's sketch shows plainly how the mural of *angels* will soften the sharp *angles* of the walls.

10. The exhibition *area* will be equipped with microphones so that all may hear the soprano sing the famous *aria*.

11. The charges against the *arraigned* prisoner were *arranged* in chronological order.

12. Each student in the metallurgical course was asked to write a term *essay* on the *assaying* of a certain ore.

Word Origin

Conclave. We use this word to indicate any type of private meeting. The word, literally, means "a locked room," from *con*, "with," and *clavis*, "key." In 1280, the populace, incensed over a delay of nearly three years in electing a successor to the Pope, locked the Cardinals in the Episcopal Palace and kept them there in strict seclusion until they came to a decision.

LESSON 28

Words That Sound or Look Somewhat Alike (*Continued*)

1. **attain**   ă tān′   To gain; achieve; accomplish.
   attend   ă těnd′   To care for; be present at.

2. **biannual**   bī ăn′ û ăl   Occurring twice a year.
   biennial   bī ěn′ĭ ăl   Occurring once in two years.

3. **boarder**   bōr′dēr   A person who pays for his meals.
   border   bôr′dēr   The edge; also, to touch at the edge.

4. **bouillon**   boō yôn′   A broth.
   bullion   boŏl′yŭn   Gold or silver metal.

5. **casual**   kăzh′û ăl   Unimportant; incidental.
   causal   kôz′ăl   Pertaining to a cause.

6. **cease**   sēs   To stop.
   seize   sēz   To lay hold of; grasp.

7. **salary**   săl′ȧ rĭ   Payment for services; wages.
   celery   sĕl′ēr ĭ   A vegetable.

8. **senses**   sĕns′ez   Mental faculties.
   census   sĕn′sŭs   Statistics of population.

9. **close**   klōz   To shut; the end.
   clothes   klōthz   Garments; wearing apparel.
   cloths   klŏthz   Fabrics.

10. **collusion**   kŏ lū′zhŭn   A secret scheme to defraud.
    collision   kŏ lĭzh′ŭn   A clash.

11. **comma**   kŏm′ȧ   A mark of punctuation.
    coma   kō′mȧ   A state of unconsciousness.

12. **commend**   kŏ mĕnd′   To intrust; to approve.
    command   kŏ mȧnd′   To order with authority; to lead; a mandate.

WORDS USED IN SENTENCES

1. Last week I *attained* an ambition of many years—I *attended* the opening exercises of the university.

2. The treasurer's four *biannual* reports are to be included in the *biennial* volume.

3. As the new *boarder* sat down at the table, he commented on the colorful *border* on the service plates.

4. A first course of *bouillon* aids digestion. A heavy shipment of *bullion* has recently been sent to Washington.

5. In a most *casual* manner the rhetoric teacher remarked that "because" and "therefore" are called "*causal* words" in grammar.

6. The practice of parking bicycles before the library must *cease*. Beginning tomorrow, the police will *seize* any parked bicycles.

7. The agriculturist received a good *salary* while he was conducting research studies into the various methods of cultivating and marketing *celery*.

8. "I would be bereft of my *senses* if we took a *census* oftener than every ten years," exclaimed the record clerk.

9. Toward the *close* of the spring sale of women's *clothes* and all types of *cloths*, it was necessary to *close* the store doors.

10. There was undoubtedly *collusion* between the witness and the arrested man not to reveal the true facts of the *collision*.

11. A *comma* should be inserted before and after the phrase, "the patient being in a *coma*."

12. The lieutenant was *commended* for the way in which he *commanded* his company.

Word Origin

Precipitate means, literally, "headfirst," being derived from the Latin, *prae*, "before," plus *caput*, "head." Therefore, a precipitate action is one into which a person dashes headlong.

Precipice has the same origin, through the French, *précipice*, meaning "a headlong fall"; or, a place from which one might take a headlong fall, or a cliff.

LESSON 29

Words That Sound or Look Somewhat Alike (*Continued*)

1. commence   kŏ měns′   To begin.
   comments   kŏm′ ěnts   Remarks.

2. courtesy   kûr′tĕ sĭ   Politeness; a favor.
   curtesy   kûr′tĕ sĭ   A husband's life interest in the landed estate of his deceased wife.
   curtsy   kûrt′ sĭ   A gesture of respect.

3. credible   krěd′ ĭ b'l   Believable.
   creditable   krěd′ ĭt á b'l   Worthy of praise.

4. diary   dī′ á rĭ   A record of daily events.
   dairy   dâr′ ĭ   A place where milk products are prepared or sold.

5. decease   dĕ sēs′   Death.
   disease   dĭ zēz′   Illness.

6. difference   dĭf′ ēr ěns   Distinction; controversy; dissimilarity.
   deference   děf′ ēr ěns   Courteous submission; respect.

7. devise   dĕ vīz′   To contrive; to convey real estate by will.
   device   dĕ vīs′   A contrivance.

8. dissimulate   dĭ sĭm′ û lāt′   To conceal by pretending.
   disseminate   dĭ sěm′ ĭ nāt   To spread widely.

9. divers   dī′věrz   Various or sundry.
   diverse   dī vûrs′   Different.

10. addition   ă dĭsh′ ŭn   An increase.
    edition   ĕ dĭsh′ ŭn   The form in which a literary work is published; the number of copies of a book printed at one time.

11. elusive   ĕ lū′ sĭv   Evasive; difficult to grasp mentally.
    illusive   ĭ lū′ sĭv   Unreal; imaginary; misleading.

12. emerge   ĕ mûrj′   To rise out of; to come into view.
    immerge   ĭ mûrj′   To sink into; to immerse.

WORDS USED IN SENTENCES

1. He *commenced* his talk with some appreciative *comments* on the work of the staff.

2. Out of *courtesy* to the aged man, I will call at his home to discuss *curtesy* rights with him. The young women to be presented at court must practice the *curtsy*.

3. The report of the landslide seemed *credible* in view of the torrential rains. The guide's conduct in the emergency was extremely *creditable*.

4. According to my kitchen *diary*, we ordered milk from the *dairy* every day.

5. We regret to inform you of Mr. Sheffield's *decease* resulting from heart *disease*.

6. There may be a *difference* of opinion on the matter, but out of *deference* to the widow's wishes no change of policy will be made.

7. It will be necessary to *devise* some more effective follow-up system than that clumsy tickler *device*.

8. By *dissimulating* their aims, they have been able to *disseminate* the dangerous propaganda.

9. For *divers* reasons, the appropriations will be used for *diverse* purposes.

10. In *addition* to the regular *edition* of the explorer's memoirs, a special de luxe *edition* will be published.

11. There's something *elusive* about that tune; its haunting motif fills me with *illusive* fancies.

12. The technician *emerged* from behind a screen holding a white-hot metal plate by a pair of pincers; he *immerged* the plate in a beaker of oil

Word Origin

Stationer. In Latin, *stationarius* referred to a person who occupied a station or stall in a market place or elsewhere for the sale of books. Then it came to mean a publisher of books as well as a bookseller. Gradually, *stationer* came to mean a person who sold materials used in writing.

LESSON 30

Words That Sound or Look Somewhat Alike (*Continued*)

1. emigrant — ĕm'ĭ grănt — A person who *goes from* one country to another to live.
   immigrant — ĭm'ĭ grănt — A person who *comes into* a country from another to live.

2. eminent — ĕm'ĭ nĕnt — Distinguished; outstanding.
   imminent — ĭm'ĭ nĕnt — Threatening to happen.

3. envelope — ĕn'vĕ lōp — A paper container or wrapper.
   envelop — ĕn vĕl'ŭp — To enclose in.

4. expend — ĕks pĕnd' — To spend; lay out.
   expand — ĕks pănd' — To extend; unfold.

5. extant — ĕks'tănt — Still existing.
   extent — ĕks tĕnt' — Space; compass.

6. for — fôr — A preposition.
   four — fōr — Next after three.
   fore — fōr — The front.

7. formerly — fôr'mēr lĭ — Heretofore.
   formally — fôr'măl lĭ — In a dignified way.

8. genius — jēn'yŭs — Extraordinary creative power; great talent.
   genus — jē'nŭs — In zoology and botany, a classification next above the species.

9. ingenious — ĭn jēn'yŭs — Clever; resourceful.
   ingenuous — ĭn jĕn'ū ŭs — Candid; frank.

10. later — lāt'ēr — At a subsequent time.
    latter — lăt'ēr — The second of two things or persons mentioned.

11. lathe — lāth — A machine for shaping material.
    lath — lăth — A strip of wood.

12. lightning — līt'nĭng — An electric flash from a cloud.
    lightening — līt''n ĭng — Making lighter or less dark.

WORDS USED IN SENTENCES

1. This man is an *emigrant* from Russia and an *immigrant* to the United States.

2. The death of the *eminent* jurist is *imminent*.

3. On opening the *envelope*, I drew out a beautiful sketch showing how the clouds *envelop* Mt. Washington.

4. We are willing to *expend* a fair amount in an attempt to *expand* our circulation.

5. Four authentic copies of his work are known to be *extant*. To what *extent* are they accessible?

6. *For four* months this office has been in the *fore* in sales.

7. *Formerly* the opening events were conducted most *formally*.

8. No one can deny that Thomas Edison was a *genius*. The lion and the domestic cat belong to the *genus* Felis.

9. This *ingenious* invention is the result of a chance remark made by an *ingenuous* young woman.

10. *Later* in the day, there is to be a contest between the juniors and seniors. The *latter*, in spite of their seniority, may not be victorious.

11. Behind the bench where the *lathes* are operating, the plaster has fallen, exposing the *laths* in the ceiling.

12. The house will be completed when the *lightning* rods have been installed and the window casings given a *lightening* coat of paint.

Word Origin

Accumulate is derived from the Latin *cumulare*, "to pile." The addition of the prefix *ad*, meaning "to," resulted in *accumulare*, "to pile together." Thus, to the ancient Romans, as to us, the person who was "making his pile" was accumulating a fortune.

Do you see any relation between *accumulate* and the mountainlike cloud formation called "cumulus"?

LESSON 31

Words That Sound or Look Somewhat Alike (*Continued*)

1. lose   lōoz   To mislay.
   loose   lōos   Unfastened; not restrained; to release.

2. magnate   măg′nāt   An influential or powerful person.
   magnet   măg′nĕt   A body that attracts iron.

3. mood   mōod   Disposition; feeling.
   mode   mōd   Fashion; method.

4. morale   mō răl′   State of mind; spirit or feeling.
   moral   mŏr′ăl   Ethical; just.

5. ordinance   ôr′dĭ năns   A law.
   ordnance   ôrd′năns   Military supplies, including equipment and ammunition.

6. persecute   pûr′sĕ kūt   To oppress; torment.
   prosecute   prŏs′ĕ kūt   To sue.

7. perpetrate   pûr pĕ trāt   To be guilty of.
   perpetuate   pēr pĕt′ū āt   To make lasting.

8. perquisite   pûr′kwĭ zĭt   An added privilege.
   prerequisite   prē rĕk′wĭ zĭt   Something required as a preliminary.

9. personal   pûr′sŭn ăl   Individual; private.
   personnel   pûr′sŏ nĕl′   Persons engaged in a certain service; the staff.

10. perspective   pēr spĕk′tĭv   A view, either mental or physical, in correct proportion.
    prospective   prŏ spĕk′tĭv   Anticipated; expected.

11. precedence   prē sēd′ĕns   The act of going before; superiority in rank.
    precedents   prĕs′ē dĕnts   Authoritative examples; usages.

12. precede   prē sēd′   To go before.
    proceed   prŏ sēd′   To advance.

WORDS USED IN SENTENCES

1. I cautioned him that he might *lose* the wrist watch because of the *loose* strap.

2. The steel *magnate* described the giant *magnets* used in the industry.

3. Whatever your *mood*, choose carefully your *mode* of expression both in speech and in writing.

4. The *morale* of the entire organization would be improved if a more *moral* group of men were in control.

5. According to a local *ordinance*, it is unlawful to ship *ordnance* through the city's streets.

6. I cannot bring myself to *persecute* that wretched man any further by *prosecuting* him in this case.

7. He *perpetrated* a crime that will be *perpetuated* through the pages of history.

8. I fear that the *perquisites* attached to the post weigh more heavily than the special training and other *prerequisites*.

9. My *personal* feeling in the matter is that their *personnel* is exceptionally well trained.

10. I must get a new *perspective* before I decide on the *prospective* position.

11. The etiquette that decides what *precedence* one official has over another is based on long-established *precedents*.

12. Mr. Allen's wife *preceded* him through the door and then both *proceeded* to the elevator.

Word Origin

Stimulate. The Latin *stimulus* meant "a goad." Hence the literal meaning of *stimulate* is "to excite or rouse as with a goad."

Stagnate, on the other hand, has its origin in the Latin *stagnum*, "a pool of standing water," and means, literally, "to lie still like a pool."

LESSON 32

Words That Sound or Look Somewhat Alike (*Continued*)

1. preposition — prĕp'ō zĭsh'ŭn — A part of speech.
   proposition — prŏp'ō zĭsh'ŭn — An offer; a business proposal.

2. prophesy — prŏf'ĕ sī — To foretell; predict.
   prophecy — prŏf'ĕ sĭ — A prediction.

3. quiet — kwī'ĕt — Calm; still; also, to calm.
   quite — kwīt — Completely; wholly.

4. receipt — rē sēt' — An acknowledgment of thing received; to mark as paid.
   recipe — rĕs'ĭ pē — A formula for mixing ingredients.

5. respectively — rē spĕk'tĭv lĭ — Severally.
   respectably — rē spĕk'tȧ blĭ — In a conventionally correct manner.
   respectfully — rē spĕkt'fool ĭ — With respect.

6. reverence — rĕv'ēr ĕns — Profound respect; also, to esteem.
   reference — rĕf'ēr ĕns — That which refers or alludes to something.

7. spacious — spā'shŭs — Roomy.
   specious — spē'shŭs — Apparently, but not actually, fair or just; plausible.

8. stature — stăt'ūr — The natural height of a man.
   statue — stăt'ū — A carved image.
   statute — stăt'ūt — An enacted law.

9. suit — sūt — A legal action; clothing; the act of wooing; also, to please, to satisfy.
   suite — swēt — A connected set of things; a retinue.

10. trial — trī'ăl — Examination; an experiment; hardship.
    trail — trāl — A footpath or track.

11. topography — tō pŏg'rȧ fĭ — The geographical or surface features of a region.
    typography — tī pŏg'rȧ fĭ — The arrangement of type; the art of printing.

12. weather — wĕth'ēr — The state of the atmosphere; to come through safely.
    whether — hwĕth'ēr — Indicating an alternative.

WORDS USED IN SENTENCES

1. A simple alteration in the contract—a mere change of a *preposition*—changed the nature of the *proposition* entirely.

2. The economist *prophesied* a marked upturn in business. Let us hope his *prophecy* comes true.

3. By her *quiet* manner she puts one *quite* at ease.

4. She wrote a gracious note to acknowledge *receipt* of the famous *recipe* for clam chowder.

5. Dear Sir: Our new models of cars are priced at $500, $750, and $990, *respectively*. Our installment methods are conducted most *respectably*. May we have the pleasure of serving you? *Respectfully* yours,

6. I have the greatest *reverence* for the opinions of the jurists quoted in this *reference* book.

7. The arguments that the office layout was not *spacious* enough were *specious* indeed.

8. The *stature* of the man was perfectly reproduced in the *statue*. The *Statute* of Frauds relates to contracts yet to be performed.

9. Bring a full-dress *suit* with you for the ball in the Royal *Suite* at the King's Hotel, to be given in honor of the Governor's *suite*.

10. As a *trial*, we will attempt to follow the Indian *trail* to the summit.

11. The *topography* of the region is most interestingly described in the new textbook on physical geography, which, by the way, is a beautiful example of *typography*.

12. The *Weather* Bureau forecasts clear *weather* tomorrow—let's see *whether* it will be true.

Word Origin

Eliminate. The Latin *limen*, "a threshold," plus *e*, a variant of *ex*, "from," formed the Latin verb, *eliminare*, "to put from one's threshold," "to put out of doors." *Eliminate*, in its modern meaning, "to get rid of, as by expulsion," is a direct descendant.

The same root, *limen*, survives also in **preliminary,** which means, literally, "before the threshold," but is now used figuratively as meaning "introductory."

LESSON 33

Words That Mean the Same Thing (Synonyms)

Note: Synonyms are seldom identical in meaning.

1. **colleague** — An associate in a profession or a civil office. Not used of partners in business.
   partner — A sharer, associate, joint owner in business.

2. **cite** — To mention a person or passage as an authority.
   quote — To repeat the exact words used by another.

3. **duty** — That which one is bound to do or perform.
   obligation — The agreement by which one is obligated or bound.

4. **fault** — Anything wanting or that impairs excellence.
   defect — Want of something necessary for completeness or perfection.
   blemish — A mark of deformity; a flaw.

5. **honor** — Esteem due to worth; integrity.
   glory — Praise; reputation; fame.

6. **eminent** — Standing high in one's calling.
   distinguished — Notable in excellence or refinement.
   celebrated — Famed.
   renowned — The state of being widely known for one's great achievements of merit.

7. **surprise** — To take unawares.
   astonish — To strike with sudden fear or wonder; to surprise greatly.

8. **discontinue** — To interrupt the continuance of; to stop.
   abandon — To give up or surrender utterly.

9. **ostensible** — Seeming; apparent; declared.
   plausible — Apparently reasonable; not quite convincing to good judgment.

10. **reciprocal** — Done by each to the other; interchanging.
    mutual — Joint interest or ownership in the same thing or person.
    common — The same use or ownership by many.

WORDS USED IN SENTENCES

1. The newly appointed judge greeted his *colleagues*, among whom was a former law *partner*.

2. The lawyer *cited* Blackstone as his authority and *quoted* at length from the famous "Commentaries."

3. As a citizen, he considered it his *duty* to contribute to the welfare fund, though he was under no actual *obligation* to do so.

4. The chief *fault* with this device is its great size. Actually, it has no mechanical *defect* and that *blemish* is merely a superficial scratch.

5. The *honor* of his reputation was at stake, and the *glory* of his achievement correspondingly lessened.

6. The after-dinner speakers were an *eminent* jurist, a *distinguished* economist, and a *celebrated* explorer, each *renowned* for his contribution to social progress.

7. I was *surprised* to have another visit from her so soon. We were all *astonished* at the size of the new ocean liner.

8. We will *discontinue* this publication in the spring, although it means that we must *abandon* our reform program.

9. The *ostensible* object of his search was a mislaid book. He gave a *plausible* excuse for his late arrival.

10. The *reciprocal* trade pact is of *mutual* advantage to the two countries because it protects the industries they have in *common*.

Word Origin

Finance developed from the Latin *finis*, meaning "the end." **Final** and **finish** are derived from the same root. In early days, *finance* meant "fine," "forfeit," or "ransom," implying the idea of "settling up." Its present meaning arose in the eighteenth century in France, especially in connection with the tax farmers, called *financiers*.

LESSON 34

Words That Mean the Same Thing
(Synonyms—*Continued*)

1. caution — To warn.
   advise — To give advice.

2. disparage — To dishonor by comparison with what is inferior; to undervalue.
   discredit — To destroy trust in.

3. contrary — Opposed; perverse.
   adverse — Detrimental; acting against.
   opposite — On different sides—one across from the other.

4. differ — To be of unlike opinion; to disagree.
   dispute — To argue pro and con; to discuss; to attempt to overthrow.
   quarrel — To dispute angrily or violently.

5. amateur — One who cultivates an art or is clever at a game simply for personal gratification; nonprofessional.
   novice — One new in any business, profession, or calling; one unacquainted or unskilled.

6. answer — To respond to a question or communication.
   reply — To answer—a more formal word, however, than "answer."

7. audience — An assembly of hearers.
   spectators — Lookers-on; bystanders.

8. allow — To grant license to; to consent to; to let one have.
   permit — To authorize; to give leave.

9. cure — To make well; to heal.
   remedy — To set right anything that has gone wrong.

10. balance — The difference between two sides of an account.
    remainder — The portion of a thing, usually the smaller part, left over.
    rest — Any portion, large or small, left over.

11. begin — To start; less formal and more frequently used than "commence."
    commence — To start or begin; restricted to a form of action.

12. error — A deviation from the right or from accuracy.
    mistake — An act resulting from misunderstanding or inadvertence.
    blunder — An act resulting from ignorance, heedlessness, or awkwardness.

WORDS USED IN SENTENCES

1. The foreman *cautioned* the men against carelessness in handling the machinery and *advised* them to be on the alert always.

2. At the risk of seeming to *disparage* their efforts, I must *discredit* the rumor that they have already exceeded their sales quota.

3. *Contrary* to our expectations, the manager made an *adverse* report regarding the proposal to buy the property on the *opposite* side of the street.

4. The two friends *differ* in their political views; but they do not *dispute* each other's right to his opinion, and they have never been known to *quarrel*.

5. He declared that he was only an *amateur*, not a professional. The many trophies he had won, however, proved him no *novice*.

6. I cannot *answer* the first two questions. This letter is in *reply* to your recent request for information on educational researches under way.

7. A large *audience* assembled for the lecture on Modern Art. The *spectators* cheered the football players as they entered the field.

8. We will *allow* you our regular discount, but we can *permit* no changes in our method of handling contract accounts.

9. Fresh air and sunshine will undoubtedly *cure* this disease. The purpose of this regulation is to *remedy* the waste of electric current in the plant.

10. Your account shows a credit *balance*. He sold the *remainder* of the stock at auction. A few members of the club approved of the new rules; the *rest* opposed them.

11. I will *begin* to read aloud now. The play will *commence* promptly at eight-thirty.

12. The clerk made an *error* in totaling the figures, but he discovered his *mistake*. To introduce a lady to a gentleman is a social *blunder*.

Word Origin

Clue. This word is derived from a Middle English word meaning a ball or skein. In myths, a ball of thread was used in guiding one's way out of a labyrinth or maze. Hence came the word to mean that which gives a hint to the solution of a problem.

LESSON 35

Words That Mean the Same Thing
(Synonyms—*Continued*)

1. **criticize** — To examine or judge the merits of, as of a book or picture; also, to find fault with.
   censure — To find fault with; to blame, to express disapproval of.

2. **address** — A formal, learned communication, either read or given from memory.
   speech — A less formal discourse.
   talk — An informal speech presupposing no preparation.

3. **bound** — Morally or legally constrained or compelled.
   obliged — Constrained by some imperious necessity.

4. **part** — A fraction of the whole.
   portion — Some rightfully assigned fraction of the whole.

5. **choose** — To select.
   prefer — To esteem above others.

6. **impossible** — Not possible at all.
   impracticable — Not possible under existing conditions.

7. **defamation** — Malicious and groundless injury done or attempted to be done to the reputation of another.
   slander — The malicious dissemination or spreading abroad by speech of false tales or suggestions to the injury of another.
   libel — Anything written, printed, or pictured tending to lessen or degrade another's reputation.

8. **detained** — Held back or restrained from proceeding; delayed.
   hindered — Impeded; obstructed.

9. **join** — To effect a junction with; connect, combine.
   unite — To be attached permanently; fuse, coalesce.

10. **remunerate** — To pay an equivalent for any service rendered or expense or loss sustained.
    compensate — To make up for; to recompense.

11. **majority** — More than half.
    plurality — An excess of votes over those for any other candidate for the same office, especially over the next opponent.

WORDS USED IN SENTENCES

1. The expert *criticized* the report thoroughly, but found nothing to *censure*.

2. Professor Scott is scheduled to give an *address* before the Science Club on Monday evening and an after-dinner *speech* on Wednesday. If possible, he will try to give a five-minute *talk* to your study group.

3. He is *bound* by his sense of honor to repay the loan he was *obliged* to accept from his friend.

4. The first *part* of the attorney's letter informs me that I am to receive a *portion* of my uncle's estate.

5. I shall *choose* the brown traveling case because it is very sturdily built, but I really *prefer* the light-tan one.

6. Although your sales plan is not *impossible*, it is *impracticable* because of our great distance from the market.

7. A spoken *defamation* of a man's character is *slander;* the same words in print constitute *libel*.

8. I was *detained* a few minutes by a telephone call; frequent interruptions during the day have *hindered* me in my work.

9. We *joined* hands and *united* in singing "Auld Lang Syne."

10. I can *remunerate* you for the time you spent in research for this project; but no amount can *compensate* you for your discriminating selection of data.

11. Of the 4,000 ballots cast for three candidates, Foster received 2,752 votes, which gave him a *majority*; James received 1,103; and Black trailed with 145. Foster's *plurality* over James was 1,649 votes.

Word Origin

Manufacture. This word comes from the Latin *manus*, "hand," and *facere*, "to make"—"to make by hand." While in modern industry manufactured goods are seldom made by hand, the word describing the process has remained unchanged.

LESSON 36

Words That Mean the Same Thing
(Synonyms—*Continued*)

1. **irritate** — To vex; to excite to impatience.
   aggravate — To intensify something that is already bad.
   exasperate — To provoke to intense anger.

2. **number** — The amount of units.
   quantity — Amount or portion; extent; size; degree.

3. **discovery** — That which is found out; disclosure; revelation.
   invention — A contrivance, plan, or device that did not exist before.

4. **sample** — Part of the thing itself.
   specimen — A part that shows the quality and character of the whole; a sample.

5. **adjoining** — In contact with.
   adjacent — Near.

6. **apt** — Habitually tending; inclined; customarily disposed.
   likely — Appearing like truth; in all probability; probably.
   liable — Exposed to a certain contingency or casualty.

7. **silent** — Making no noise or utterance.
   tacit — Implied, but not expressed in words.

8. **noted** — Famous; celebrated.
   notorious — Widely, but unfavorably, known.

9. **proposition** — A project or undertaking involving some action.
   proposal — That which is offered for consideration or acceptance.

10. **duplicate** — A counterpart of something else.
    copy — Something as nearly like the original as can be made.
    fascimile — An exact reproduction, implying an imitation of the original.
    transcript — A written or typewritten copy; as of a document or of shorthand notes.

11. **happen** — To occur; to come to pass by chance.
    transpire — To escape from secrecy; to leak out; to become known.

12. **character** — The sum of the qualities that constitute the true individuality of a person.
    reputation — What others think of a given person.

WORDS USED IN SENTENCES

1. The doctor was *irritated* to learn that his patient had exposed herself to the damp air, which only *aggravated* her cough. The patient's husband was *exasperated*, because it was so unnecessary.

2. Check the *number* of packages in this shipment, and verify the *quantity* in each package.

3. The *discovery* of radium revolutionized the treatment of many diseases. The *invention* of the steam engine was the leading factor in bringing about the Industrial Revolution.

4. From the *samples* of paper that accompanied the *specimens* of your art work, we have selected the one enclosed.

5. I bought two *adjoining* lots and later built a house and a garage *adjacent* to it.

6. An impulsive person is *apt* to make promises that are *likely* to prove difficult of fulfillment; however, he is sometimes *liable* for their accomplishment.

7. He remained *silent* throughout the discussion, thus seeming to give his *tacit* consent to the plan.

8. In his last motion picture the actor portrayed the part of a *noted* financier; in his next one he will be a *notorious* swindler.

9. Mr. Smith's housing *proposition* has been thoroughly considered, and a *proposal* has been drawn up for approval.

10. As the typist did not prepare enough *duplicates* of the contracts, Miss Green will have to type another *copy*. Please attach a *facsimile* of the application to the *transcript*.

11. Every precaution was taken to prevent the news of what *happened* at the meeting from *transpiring*.

12. We build our *characters;* we earn our *reputations*.

Word Origin

Ambition. When ancient Roman candidates for public office went about soliciting votes, the custom was called *ambitio*, "a going about." Since this custom indicated a desire for honor or power, the word came to have that meaning. The French and later the English adapted the word to mean a desire to achieve.

LESSON 37

Words That Mean the Opposite Thing (Antonyms)

Words Used in Sentences

1. ability / weakness — He has considerable *ability* as a draftsman. The student was not promoted because of his *weakness* in mathematics.

2. abundance / scarcity — We have an *abundance* of amateur talent for the school play, but there is a *scarcity* of professional talent.

3. include / exclude — The group *included* professional and semiprofessional players but *excluded* amateurs.

4. adopt / reject — We *adopted* the accounting system but *rejected* the other changes suggested.

5. concrete / abstract — Give a *concrete* example of the *abstract* statement, "Honesty is the best policy."

6. major / minor — The *major* part of the lecture was devoted to the works of *minor* nineteenth-century poets.

7. brilliant / dull — A *brilliant* conversationalist can make even a *dull* topic seem interesting.

8. positive / uncertain — I am *positive* that the purpose of the plan is right, but I am *uncertain* about the procedure.

9. introductory / concluding — An *introductory* phrase is usually set off by a comma from the *concluding* portion of the sentence.

10. expand / contract — Bridge engineers must take into consideration the fact that steel *expands* with heat and *contracts* with cold.

11. strange / familiar — The office routine, *strange* at first, soon became *familiar* to him.

12. artificial / natural — An *artificial* lake enhanced the *natural* beauty of the park.

13. lenient / strict — The instructor, ordinarily *lenient* with his pupils, was *strict* when the occasion required.

LESSON 38

Words That Mean the Opposite Thing
(Antonyms—*Continued*)

Words Used in Sentences

1. **oppose**
   support
   He consistently *opposed* any measure that was not *supported* by the popular vote.

2. **confusion**
   order
   There was no *confusion* in the stock room because the materials were always kept in *order*.

3. **local**
   universal
   This appliance has been adapted in order to meet *local* weather conditions. This form is not in *universal* use.

4. **defective**
   perfect
   We will replace this *defective* lens with a *perfect* one.

5. **superior**
   inferior
   Goods of *superior* quality, in the long run, prove less expensive than those of *inferior* quality.

6. **definite**
   vague
   Please make a *definite* recommendation to replace the present *vague* statement.

7. **previous**
   subsequent
   The *previous* rating still applies to *subsequent* sales.

8. **fictitious**
   real
   He used *fictitious* names to shield the *real* person.

9. **commend**
   disapprove
   I *commended* him for his generosity, though I *disapproved* of his extravagance.

10. **satisfaction**
    discontent
    Much to my *satisfaction*, the new regulations dispelled the *discontent* that had prevailed among the workers.

11. **unnecessary**
    indispensable
    In this position, previous experience is *unnecessary*; but physical endurance is *indispensable*.

12. **seldom**
    often
    He *seldom* missed a board meeting and *often* was asked to preside.

13. **create**
    destroy
    The favorable impression he had *created* on his audience was *destroyed* by his final remarks.

LESSON 39

Words That Mean the Opposite Thing
(Antonyms—*Continued*)

Words Used in Sentences

1. **exterior**
   interior
   The rough *exterior* of the coconut yields a valuable fiber; the nut in the *interior* is a widely used tropical food.

2. **collect**
   scatter
   He *collected* much valuable data from the books that were *scattered* on the library table.

3. **exposed**
   hidden
   The prospector *exposed* himself to countless perils in his search for the ore *hidden* deep within the earth.

4. **reduce**
   enlarge
   Now we can *reduce* the price of this article because we have *enlarged* our production department.

5. **radical**
   conservative
   This is a *radical* change in our system of distribution, but even a *conservative* estimate of its economy is amazing.

6. **remote**
   close
   We plan to leave our *remote* farm next year and live where we shall be *close* to a good school.

7. **cause**
   effect
   The *cause* of the explosion is not yet known, but its *effect* was felt for miles around.

8. **ignorance**
   knowledge
   Although I was in *ignorance* of the details, I had a general *knowledge* of the plan.

9. **pertinent**
   unrelated
   He included in his report not only *pertinent* details but also much *unrelated* data.

10. **fixed**
    changeable
    A *fixed* date for the departure of the expedition could not be set because of the *changeable* weather conditions.

11. **ample**
    inadequate
    We have an *ample* supply of canned goods, but the fresh vegetables obtainable are *inadequate* for our needs.

12. **valuable**
    worthless
    The rail and harbor facilities make this a *valuable* factory site, but the dilapidated buildings are *worthless*.

LESSON 40

Prepositions

Usage has decreed that certain prepositions shall follow certain words. Some of the most troublesome prepositional combinations in common use are listed here. The dictionary should be consulted whenever in doubt about the correct preposition.

adapted *to* (a thing or situation)

adapted *for* (a pursuit or course of action)

adapted *from* (a piece of literature)

agree *among* (themselves)

agree *to* (a proposal)

agree *on* (a course)

agree *with* (a person)

agreeable *to*

approve *of*

apply *for* (a position)

apply *to* (a person)

ask *of* or *from* (a person)

ask *for* (something desired)

bill *of* or *for*

buy *from*

charge *against* (a person)

charge *with* (a thing)

comply *with* (a request)

conform *to* or *with*

convenient *for* (a purpose or use)

convenient *to* (a place)

correspond *to* or *with* (a thing)

correspond *with* (a person)

credit *for*

depend *on*

different *from*

disappointed *in*

dispense *with*

employed *for* (a purpose)

employed *at* (a certain salary)

employed *in, on, upon* (a work or business)

enter *at* (a given point)

enter *in* (a record)

enter *into* (agreements)

enter *upon* (duties)

equivalent *to*

free *from*

identical *with*

impose *on*

independent *of*

inherent *in*

irrespective *of*

need *of* or *for*

part *from* (persons)

part *with* (things)

proceed *with* (a matter already begun)

proceed *to* (a place or matter not begun)

profit *by*

prior *to*

purchase *from*

rely *on*

LESSON 41

Words Often Misspelled

justifiable	minimum	o'clock	peaceable
justification	mining	official	people
Lackawanna	minority	ofttimes	persuade
languages	misappropriating	omit	philosopher
legacy	mite	opponents	physical
legend	moving	opportunity	physician
legitimate	museum	original	picnicking
liberal	mutilate	originate	pierce
linen	national	ought	planned
liquefy	nationalities	package	policy
loath	necessary	pageant	politician
loathe	negative	pain	possession
luncheon	nervousness	Palo Alto	possibility
machinery	nickel	pamphlet	practical
magnificent	ninetieth	pane	practice
maintain	notoriety	parade	precious
maneuver	notoriously	paragraph	preliminary
material	novelty	parallel	preparation
meanness	nucleus	parent	pressure
meant	nuisance	partially	prestige
meantime	obstacles	particularly	privilege
mediocre	obtainable	passage	professional
memory	occasionally	Paterson	prohibitory
merchant	occupy	patient	prominent
might	occurred	pattern	pronunciation

Word Origin

Coin. The origin of *coin* goes back to the Latin *cuneus*, "a wedge." The French adopted the word as *coin*, meaning "a die for stamping money." Later, the meaning shifted from the instrument to that which is stamped.

LESSON 42

Words Often Mispronounced

implacable	ĭm plā'kå b'l	mischievous	mĭs'chĭ vŭs
incognito	ĭn kŏg'nĭ tō	municipal	mū nĭs'ĭ păl
indefatigable	ĭn'dē făt'ĭ gå b'l	new	nū
inexplicable	ĭn ĕks'plĭ kå b'l	New Orleans	nū ôr'lē ănz
infamous	ĭn'få mŭs	nomenclature	nō'měn klā'tu̱r
inherent	ĭn hēr'ĕnt	obligatory	ŏb lĭg'å tō'rĭ
inquiry	ĭn kwīr'ĭ	often	ôf'ĕn
interesting	ĭn'tēr ĕs tĭng	onerous	ŏn'ēr ŭs
irate	ī'rāt	ordeal	ôr dē'ăl
iron	ī'ērn	partner	pärt'nēr
irrelevant	ĭr rĕl'ē vănt	patronage	pā'trŭn ĭj
irreparable	ĭ rĕp'å rå b'l	peculiar	pē kūl'yēr
irrevocable	ĭ rĕv'ō kå b'l	pecuniary	pē kū'nĭ ĕr'ĭ
juvenile	jōō'vē nĭl	penalize	pē'năl īz
kiln	kĭl	penury	pĕn'ū rĭ
laboratory	lăb'ō rå tō'rĭ	percolate (v.)	pûr'kō lāt
lamentable	lăm'ĕn tå b'l	perfume (n.)	pûr'fūm
latent	lā'tĕnt	perhaps	pēr hăps'
learned (adj.)	lûr'nĕd	picture	pĭk'tu̱r
liaison	lē'ā'zôN'	plagiarism	plā'jĭ å rĭz'm
long-lived	lŏng līvd'	poem	pō'ĕm
ludicrous	lū'dĭ krŭs	posthumous	pŏs'tu̱ mŭs
masseur	mă sûr'	Poughkeepsie	pō kĭp'sĭ
menu	mĕn'ū	Prague	präg
mercantile	mûr'kăn tĭl	preferable	prĕf'ēr å b'l

Word Origin

Calculate. The Romans did their adding and subtracting with the aid of little stones for counters. These were called *calculi*. The past participle of the verb *calculare*, "calculatus," is the origin of the English *calculate*.

BRIEF TEST ON PART III

1. Write sentences using the following pairs of homonyms.

medal	ate	cede	hire	made	your	board	bear
meddle	eight	seed	higher	maid	you're	bored	bare

2. For each of the following words: (*a*) after reference to a dictionary, indicate the proper pronunciation; (*b*) use in a sentence.

costume	salon	desert	venerable	recourse	poplar	breath
custom	saloon	dessert	vulnerable	resource	popular	breathe

3. Rearrange the following words, grouping synonyms together.

satire	give	analogy	grant	irony
peculiarity	frugal	economical	similarity	idiosyncrasy

4. Use each word in Exercise 3 in a sentence.

5. Give the antonym for each of the following words.

future	failure	obsolete	secret
busy	defend	recede	increase

6. Use each word in Exercise 5 in a sentence.

7. What preposition should be used after each of the following words?

pursuant	productive	prejudice
retroactive	adjust	devoid
satisfied	sensitive	immune

8. Use each word in Exercise 7 in a sentence.

9. List the following words, correcting any misspellings.

consientious	irrelevant	penatrate
statistical	interferred	souvenier

10. Write a short paragraph concerning the origin of *finance;* of *check.*

PART IV

New Words; Words of Foreign Origin; Geographic Names

The material in Part IV is particularly interesting in view of modern conditions.

Our changing industrial, political, and social life is bringing new words into our language almost daily. The radio, the daily newspaper, as well as weekly and monthly magazines, abound with such words as those listed in Lesson 43. Indeed, before this book is published, still others will probably have been added to the extremely large body of words that constitute the English language.

Then, international relations, which today interest the average American as never before in our country's history, have made us foreign-word-conscious. In addition to the more common words and phrases of foreign origin included in Lessons 44-46, the daily press makes use of many more. The student should form the habit of looking up the meaning of all foreign words and phrases he hears or reads that are not familiar to him.

The importance of spelling geographic names correctly need not be emphasized. The stenographer, especially, must make no mistakes in addressing mail, whether to foreign or to domestic cities. A United States Official Postal Guide and an up-to-date atlas are essential reference books in the modern office.

Here are two typing hints:

1. Foreign words and phrases, except those most commonly used, should be italicized in printed matter—indicated in typewriting by underscoring.

2. New words that are not fully accepted as recognized members of our language may be quoted.

LESSON 43

New Words and Old Words With New Meanings

1. arterial — är tēr′ĭ ăl — Of or pertaining to a main highway.
2. cellophane — sĕl′ō fān — A trade-marked name for thin, transparent, waterproof sheets of viscose (made from cellulose); used for wrappings.
3. close-up — klōs′ŭp′ — Any photograph taken at close range; a close or intimate view or examination of anything.
4. debunk — dē bŭngk′ — To divest of undiscriminating praise or flattery.
5. defeatism — dē fēt′ĭz′m — The policy of admitting defeat of one's country, party, etc., on the ground that the continuation of the contest is inadvisable.
6. extrovert (also extravert) — ĕks′trō vûrt (ĕks′trȧ vûrt) — One whose interest is centered in external objects and actions; opposite of *introvert*.
7. gadget — găj′ĕt — A contrivance or device—especially, a part of machinery.
8. ideology — ĭd′ē ŏl′ō jĭ — Visionary theorizing; manner of thinking characteristic of a class or an individual.
9. intelligentsia — ĭn tĕl′ĭ jĕnt′sĭ ȧ — Intellectuals collectively; the educated class.
10. plebiscite — plĕb′ĭ sīt — A direct vote of all the people on a measure, as to determine a form of government.
11. racketeer — răk′ĕ tēr′ — One who, either singly or with others, extorts money or advantages by threats of violence or of unlawful interference with business.
12. robot — rō′bŏt — An automatic device that performs functions usually ascribed to human beings; an automaton.
13. stratosphere — strā′tō sfēr — The upper portion of the atmosphere.
14. tabloid — tăb′loid — A small-sized daily newspaper containing chiefly photographs of current events.
15. totalitarian — tō tăl′ĭ târ′ĭ ăn — Pertaining to a highly centralized government that allows no recognition of other political parties.

LESSON 44

Commonly Used Words and Phrases of Foreign Origin

Note: Unless otherwise indicated, the words and phrases in Lessons 44–46, inclusive, are of French origin. The others are indicated as follows: *L.*, Latin; *I.*, Italian; *Gk.*, Greek. The diacritical markings indicate approximate pronunciations, as it is impossible to give the exact English equivalent of foreign pronunciations.

à la carte	ä lä kärt′	According to the bill of fare.
à la mode	ä lä mōd′	After the fashion.
ad infinitum (L.)	ăd ĭn′fĭ nī′tŭm	To infinity; without limit.
apropos	ăp′rŏ pō′	Suitably; with respect to.
au fait	ō′fĕ′	Expert; skillful; to the point.
au revoir	ō′rĕ vwär′	Till we meet again.
beau monde	bō′mônd′	World of fashion.
bête noire	bāt′ nwär′	Bugbear; an object of deep dread or aversion.
blasé	blä′zā′	Bored; indifferent.
bloc	blŏk	Combination of members of different parties for a common purpose.
bona fide (L.)	bō′nà fī′dĕ	In good faith.
bourgeois	boor zhwä′	A person of the middle class.
carte blanche	kärt′ blänsh′	Unlimited authority.
chic	shēk	Originality plus style.
coiffure	kwä′fūr′	Style of hairdress.
comme il faut	kô′mēl′fō′	As it should be.
connoisseur	kŏn′ĭ sûr′	One who knows well the details of a fine art.
coterie	kō′tĕ rĭ	A clique; a small, select circle of congenial persons.
dé classé	dā′klä′sā′	Separated or degraded from one's class in society.
de trop	dĕ trō′	Superfluous; out of place.
debris	dĕ brē′	Remains; fragments.
debut	dā bü′	First appearance before the public.
dilettante	dĭl′ĕ tăn′tĭ	An admirer of the fine arts; an amateur or a dabbler in art.
distrait	dĭs′trā′	Absent-minded.
diva (I.)	dē′và	A prima donna.
éclat	ā klä′	Striking effect; brilliancy of success.

LESSON 45

Commonly Used Words and Phrases of Foreign Origin (*Continued*)

elite	å lēt′	The select or choice part.
en masse	ĕn măs′	In the mass.
en passant	äN pä′säN′	In passing.
en rapport	äN rå′pôr′	In sympathy; congenial.
en route	än rōōt′	On the road.
ennui	äN′wē	Languor of spirit.
entourage	än′tōō räzh	The attendants of a person of prominence.
entre nous	äN′trē nōō′	Between ourselves.
entree	äN′trā	Permission or right to enter; a course between the soup and the main course.
esprit de corps	ĕs′prē′ dē kôr′	Animating spirit of a collective body.
exposé	ĕks′pō zā′	An exposure of something discreditable.
faux pas	fō′pä′	A false step; a mistake.
finesse	fĭ nĕs′	Cunning; delicate skill.
hoi polloi (Gk.)	hoi′ pŏ loi′	The populace.
hors d'œuvres	ôr dû′vr′	Relishes served at the beginning of a meal.
ibid. (L.)	ĭb′ĭd	In the same place (an abbreviation of *ibidem*).
laissez faire	lĕ′sā′ fâr′	Noninterference.
lese majesty	lēz maj′ĕs tĭ	Any offense violating the dignity of a ruler.
mal de mer	mȧl′ dē mâr′	Seasickness.
naïve	nä ēv′	Artless.
naïveté	nä ēv′tā′	Artlessness.
nee	nā	Born; used in introducing a woman's maiden name.
noblesse oblige	nŏ′blĕs′ ŏ′blēzh′	Rank imposes obligation.
nom de plume	nŏm′ dē plōōm′	Pen name.
outré	ōō′trā′	Bizarre; fantastic.

84

LESSON 46

Commonly Used Words and Phrases of Foreign Origin (*Continued*)

par excellence	pär ĕk′sĕ läns	Pre-eminently.
passé	pă′sā′	Past; gone by; behind the times.
penchant	päN′shäN′	Decided taste; strong mental leaning or attraction.
petite	pē tēt′	Small.
pièce de résistance	pyĕs′dĕ rā′zēs′täNs′	The main dish of a meal.
piquant	pē′kănt	Giving zest.
première	prē-myâr′	The first performance of a play, opera, etc.
prestige	prĕs tēzh′	Weight or influence derived from success.
protégé	prō′tĕ′zhā	One under the care and protection of another.
raison d'être	rā′zôN′ dâ′tr′	Reason of being.
regime	rā zhēm′	System of rule.
rendezvous	rän′dĕ voo	Appointed meeting place.
repertoire	rĕp′ĕr twär	List of dramas, songs, etc., ready for performance.
résumé	rā′zû′mā′	A summary.
revue	rĕ vū′	A burlesque on recent events.
sang-froid	säN′frwà′	Coolness in trying circumstances.
savoir-faire	så′vwår′fâr′	Presence of mind; tact.
séance	sā′äNs′	A session; exhibition by a medium.
table d'hôte	tà′blĕ dōt′	A course meal served at a fixed price.
tête-à-tête	tāt′à tāt′	An intimate conversation between two persons.
tout ensemble	too′täN′säN′bl′	The whole taken together.
valet	văl′ĕt	A male body servant.
vice versa (L.)	vī′sĕ vûr′så	Conversely.
visé	vē′zā	Indorsement on a passport.
voilà	vwà′là′	There! behold!

LESSON 47

Legal and Business Terms of Latin Origin

a posteriori	ā′pŏs tē′rĭ ō′rī	From effect to cause.
a priori	ā′prĭ ō′rī	From cause to effect.
ad valorem	ăd vȧ lō′rĕm	According to the value.
caveat emptor	kā′vḗ ăt ĕmp′tŏr	Let the buyer beware.
de facto	dē făk′tō	Actually.
de jure	dē jōō′rĕ	By lawful title.
del credere[1]	dĕl krĕd′ēr ĕ	Of trust, credit.
et al.	ĕt ăl	And others. (Abbreviation for *et alii*.)
ex officio	ĕks ŏ fĭsh′ĭ ō	By virtue of an office.
ex post facto	ĕks pōst făk′tō	From what is done afterwards.
habeas corpus	hā′bḗ ăs kôr′pŭs	A writ to produce a person before a court or judge.
in re	ĭn rē	Concerning.
ipso facto	ĭp′sō făk′tō	By the fact or act itself.
modus operandi	mō′dŭs ŏp ē răn′dī	Manner of operation.
per annum	pĕr ăn′ŭm	Annually.
per capita	pĕr kăp′ĭ tȧ	For each person.
per diem	pĕr dī′ĕm	By the day.
per se	pûr sē	By itself.
prima facie	prī′mȧ fā′shĭ ē	At first view.
pro forma	prō fôr′mȧ	As a matter of form.
pro rata	prō rā′tȧ	Proportionately.
pro tem.	prō tĕm′	Temporarily. (Short for *pro tempore*.)
proximo (prox.)	prŏk′sĭ mō	In the next month after the present.
status quo	stā′tŭs kwō	The state in which. The existing condition.
ultimo (ult.)	ŭl′tĭ mō	In the month preceding the present.
versus (v. or vs.)	vûr′sŭs	Against.

[1] This phrase is of Italian origin.

LESSON 48

States and Territories of the United States

State	Abbreviation	Capital
Alabama	Ala.	Montgomery
Arizona	Ariz.	Phoenix
Arkansas	Ark.	Little Rock
California	Calif.	Sacramento
Colorado	Colo.	Denver
Connecticut	Conn.	Hartford
Delaware	Del.	Dover
District of Columbia	D. C.	Washington
Florida	Fla.	Tallahassee
Georgia	Ga.	Atlanta
Idaho		Boise
Illinois	Ill.	Springfield
Indiana	Ind.	Indianapolis
Iowa		Des Moines
Kansas	Kans.	Topeka
Kentucky	Ky.	Frankfort
Louisiana	La.	Baton Rouge
Maine		Augusta
Maryland	Md.	Annapolis
Massachusetts	Mass.	Boston
Michigan	Mich.	Lansing
Minnesota	Minn.	St. Paul
Mississippi	Miss.	Jackson
Missouri	Mo.	Jefferson City
Montana	Mont.	Helena
Nebraska	Nebr.	Lincoln
Nevada	Nev.	Carson City
New Hampshire	N. H.	Concord

States and Territories of the United States (*Continued*)

State	Abbreviation	Capital
New Jersey	N. J.	Trenton
New Mexico	N. Mex.	Santa Fe
New York	N. Y.	Albany
North Carolina	N. C.	Raleigh
North Dakota	N. Dak.	Bismarck
Ohio		Columbus
Oklahoma	Okla.	Oklahoma City
Oregon	Oreg.	Salem
Pennsylvania	Pa.	Harrisburg
Rhode Island	R. I.	Providence
South Carolina	S. C.	Columbia
South Dakota	S. Dak.	Pierre
Tennessee	Tenn.	Nashville
Texas	Tex.	Austin
Utah		Salt Lake City
Vermont	Vt.	Montpelier
Virginia	Va.	Richmond
Washington	Wash.	Olympia
West Virginia	W. Va.	Charleston
Wisconsin	Wis.	Madison
Wyoming	Wyo.	Cheyenne

Territories and Dependencies

Alaska		Juneau
Canal Zone		
Guam		Agaña
Hawaii		Honolulu
Philippine Islands	P. I.	Manila
Puerto Rico	P. R.	San Juan
Samoa		Pago Pago, Island of Tutuila
Virgin Islands		Saint Thomas

LESSON 49

Other North and South American Countries and Their Capitals

CANADA

Edmonton, Alberta (Alta.)
Victoria, British Columbia (B. C.)
Winnipeg, Manitoba (Man.)
Fredericton, New Brunswick (N. B.)
Halifax, Nova Scotia (N. S.)
Toronto, Ontario (Ont.)
Charlottetown, Prince Edward Island (P. E. I.)
Quebec, Quebec (Que.)
Regina, Saskatchewan (Sask.)
St. John's, Newfoundland (NF.)[1]

SOUTH AMERICA

Buenos Aires, Argentina
La Paz and Sucre, Bolivia
Rio de Janeiro, Brazil
Santiago, Chile
Bogotá, Colombia
Quito, Ecuador
Asunción, Paraguay
Lima, Peru
Montevideo, Uruguay
Caracas, Venezuela

CENTRAL AMERICA

Belize, British Honduras
San José, Costa Rica
Guatemala, Guatemala
Tegucigalpa, Honduras
Managua, Nicaragua
San Salvador, Salvador

WEST INDIES

Hamilton, Bermuda
Havana, Cuba
Santo Domingo, Dominican Republic
Port-au-Prince, Haiti
Kingston, Jamaica

MEXICO [2]

Chihuahua, Chihuahua
Saltillo, Coahuila
Monterrey, Nuevo León
Hermosillo, Sonora
Ciudad Victoria, Tamaulipas

[1] Newfoundland is an island colony, not a province.
[2] Northern-border states only.

LESSON 50

Fifty Largest Cities of the United States [1]

City	Population	City	Population
New York, N. Y.	7,454,995	Columbus, Ohio	306,087
Chicago, Ill.	3,396,808	Portland, Oreg.	305,394
Philadelphia, Pa.	1,931,334	Atlanta, Ga.	302,288
Detroit, Mich.	1,623,452	Oakland, Calif.	302,163
Los Angeles, Calif.	1,504,277	Jersey City, N. J.	301,173
Cleveland, Ohio	878,336	Dallas, Tex.	294,734
Baltimore, Md.	859,100	Memphis, Tenn.	292,942
St. Louis, Mo.	816,048	St. Paul, Minn.	287,736
Boston, Mass.	770,816	Toledo, Ohio	282,349
Pittsburgh, Pa.	671,659	Birmingham, Ala.	267,583
Washington, D. C.	663,091	San Antonio, Tex.	253,854
San Francisco, Calif.	634,536	Providence, R. I.	253,504
Milwaukee, Wis.	587,472	Akron, Ohio	244,791
Buffalo, N. Y.	575,901	Omaha, Nebr.	223,844
New Orleans, La.	494,537	Dayton, Ohio	210,718
Minneapolis, Minn.	492,370	Syracuse, N. Y.	205,967
Cincinnati, Ohio	455,610	Oklahoma City, Okla.	204,424
Newark, N. J.	429,760	San Diego, Calif.	203,341
Kansas City, Mo.	399,178	Worcester, Mass.	193,694
Indianapolis, Ind.	386,972	Richmond, Va.	193,042
Houston, Tex.	384,514	Fort Worth, Tex.	177,662
Seattle, Wash.	368,302	Jacksonville, Fla.	173,065
Rochester, N. Y.	324,975	Miami, Fla.	172,172
Denver, Colo.	322,412	Youngstown, Ohio	167,720
Louisville, Ky.	319,077	Nashville, Tenn.	167,402

[1] From the Bureau of the Census, Washington, D. C., Sixteenth Census of the United States: 1940.

LESSON 51

Fifty Large Cities of the World

(OUTSIDE OF NORTH AMERICA)

City	Population
London (Greater), England	8,202,818
Chengtu, China	8,000,000
Tokyo, Japan	6,085,800
Berlin, Germany	4,242,501
Moskva (Moscow), Soviet Union	3,663,300
Shanghai, China	3,259,100
Osaka, Japan	3,101,900
Paris, France	2,829,746
Leningrad (Petrograd), Soviet Union	2,776,400
Buenos Aires, Argentina	2,290,731
Wien (Vienna), Germany	1,843,173
Rio de Janeiro, Brazil	1,700,500
Hamburg, Germany	1,647,000
Tientsin, China	1,389,000
Cairo, Egypt	1,311,200
Sydney, Australia	1,235,367
Warszawa (Warsaw), Poland	1,220,000
Bombay, India	1,161,383
Calcutta, India	1,193,651
São Paulo, Brazil	1,151,200
Barcelona, Spain	1,148,129
Nagoya, Japan	1,119,500
Kyoto, Japan	1,107,400
Glasgow, Scotland	1,088,417
Roma (Rome), Italy	1,062,861
Budapest, Hungary	1,051,804
Madrid, Spain	1,048,072
Mexico, Mexico	1,029,068
Birmingham, England	1,012,700
Istanbul and Suburbs, Turkey	1,003,486
Praha (Prague), Czechoslovakia	945,000
Hong Kong (Island Colony), China	944,492
Kobe, Japan	938,200
Marseille (Marseilles), France	914,232
Canton, China	861,000
Liverpool, England	856,850
Santiago, Chile	829,240
Peiping (Peking), China	811,000
Amsterdam, Netherlands	781,665
Hankow, China	778,000
Manchester, England	758,140
Napoli (Naples), Italy	757,251
Köln (Cologne), Germany	756,605
Yokohama, Japan	738,400
München (Munich), Germany	736,000
Nanking, China	726,711
Leipzig, Germany	717,000
Milano, Italy	712,844
Baku, Soviet Union	709,500
Alexandria, Egypt	699,400

LESSON 52

Words Often Misspelled

proprietor	sacrilegious	structure	troupe
punctual	sandwich	subsidy	typing
punish	sanitary	successor	unchangeable
purchasing	Sault Sainte Marie	sufficient	unconscious
qualified	saving	sugar	undoubtedly
quality	Schenectady	suing	unfortunate
questionnaire	scrutinizing	summoning	unique
racing	sectional	superintendent	unprecedented
reasonable	securing	suspicious	unusually
receive	senate	sympathize	urban
receiving	senator	tailor	urbane
recent	sensational	taking	urge
recipient	separate	taxation	various
recognition	series	telephone	vegetable
recommendation	session	temerity	vengeance
recruit	shoulder	temporary	vicinity
reduction	sincerely	tempt	vicious
referred	society	testimony	victim
reliability	solemn	therefor	village
relief	specially	therefore	volume
religious	specialty	timidity	welcome
repetition	standard	topic	wherever
represent	strategy	toured	Wilkes-Barre
require	strenuous	tragedy	Ypsilanti
responsible	strictly	troop	zinc

Word Origin

Bank. The humble Teutonic word *benc*, meaning "a bench," was the origin of our *bank*. It was adopted in Italian as *banca*, to describe a money-changer's bench, the forerunner of modern banking.

When these benches broke, they were *banca rotta*—in French, *banque route*—resulting in our *bankrupt*.

LESSON 53

Words Often Mispronounced

prerogative	prē rŏg'a tĭv	Spokane	Spō kăn'
pretense	prē tĕns'	spurious	spū'rĭ ŭs
pretty	prĭt'ĭ	squalor	skwŏl'ēr
primarily	prī'mĕr ĭ lĭ	stipend	stī'pĕnd
probably	prŏb'a blĭ	strength	strĕngth
program	prō'grăm	stupendous	stū pĕn'dŭs
qualitative	kwŏl'ĭ tā'tĭv	subsidiary	sŭb sĭd'ĭ ĕr'ĭ
quantitative	kwŏn'tĭ tā'tĭv	subtle	sŭt''l
quay	kē	succinct	sŭk sĭngkt'
quintuplet	kwĭn'tū plĕt	superfluous	sū pûr'floo ŭs
recuperate	rē kū'pēr āt	surreptitious	sûr'ĕp tĭsh'ŭs
refutable	rĕf'ū ta b'l	tedious	tē'dĭ ŭs
regular	rĕg'ū lēr	telegrapher	tĕ lĕg'ra fēr
reptile	rĕp'tĭl	temperature	tĕm'pēr a tūr
reputable	rĕp'ū ta b'l	tenacious	tĕ nā'shŭs
research	rē sûrch'	tepid	tĕp'ĭd
respite	rĕs'pĭt	theater	thē'a tēr
ridiculous	rĭ dĭk'ū lŭs	toward	tō'ērd
routine	roō tēn'	tremendous	trē mĕn'dŭs
salmon	săm'ŭn	tube	tūb
secretary	sĕk'rē tĕr'ĭ	Tuesday	tūz'dĭ
senile	sē'nīl	umbrella	ŭm brĕl'a
Sioux City	soō sĭt'ĭ	vehicular	vē hĭk'ū lēr
sonorous	sŏ nō'rŭs	versatile	vûr'sa tĭl
soot	soŏt	yellow	yĕl'ō

Word Origin

Asset. This word is derived directly from the French *assez*, meaning "enough," which, in turn, came from the Latin *ad* and *satis*, "enough." It implied originally that one's possessions were sufficient to meet demands.

BRIEF TEST ON PART IV

1. Look up the definitions of the following new words.

    streamline   gangsterism   Babbitt   tourism

2. Pronounce, define, and use in a sentence each of the following commonly used foreign words and phrases.

    nonchalance   dénouement   viva voce
    bagatelle   sub rosa   in toto
    trousseau   in statu quo   verbatim
    bon voyage   ex cathedra   extempore

3. Name five states of the United States whose names should not be abbreviated.

4. From an atlas ascertain the largest city in each of the Canadian provinces, and indicate its pronunciation.

5. Give the correct spelling for the principal city of the province of New Brunswick and for the capital of Newfoundland.

6. List, in order of population, the five largest cities of the United States. Write in full the name of the state in which each is located.

7. Write the names of the two largest cities of the world.

8. List the following words, correcting any misspellings.

    wonderous   suing   soothe
    ninteenth   renewel   practicaly

9. Indicate the correct pronunciation of the following words.

    precedence   poem   inquiry
    route   hospitable   economical

10. How did *chinaware* get its name? *Russia leather?*

PART V

Words Used in Business

Part V brings you to the bread-and-butter words of business, for here you will study the spelling, definition, pronunciation, and use of many of the words that stenographers encounter daily no matter what type of office they work in. Many of these words will probably be unfamiliar to you at first; but by the time you complete this text, you should be able to recognize them instantly in dictation and be familiar with their meaning.

Do not, however, get the impression that this is a *complete* list of business terms. A complete dictionary of business terms would be an extremely large volume, indeed. In your personal notebook, which by this time should be growing into a sizable reference book, record additional business words as you encounter them. Review them and the words in these lessons frequently.

LESSON 54

General Business Terms [1]

1. **account sales (A/S or A/s)** — An account sent by one person to another, showing the sales, charges, etc., made by the sender on the other's account or in his behalf.
2. **acknowledgment (ack.)** — A declaration before a duly qualified public officer, by one who has executed a document, that the execution was his free act.
3. **advances** — Money or value supplied beforehand.
4. **agent (agt.)** — One having the authority to represent another person in a business transaction with a third person.
5. **allocation** — Apportionment, as of funds.
6. **allotment** — A share or part granted or distributed.
7. **allowance** — A sum granted as a reimbursement or repayment; a deduction from the gross weight or value of goods.
8. **arbitration** — The submitting of a dispute to an impartial person, board, or tribunal.
9. **arrears** — That which is behind in payment or remains unpaid.
10. **articles of agreement** — A written statement of the terms or conditions of a contract or an agreement.
11. **assignment (assigt., asgmt.)** — The act of transferring or allotting; the instrument by which the transfer is made; transfer of property of a debtor to an assignee for benefit of his creditors.
12. **back order (b.o.)** — An order made when goods are out of stock, for shipment when the goods arrive.
13. **bankruptcy** — The state of being legally unable to pay one's debts.
14. **barometer (bar.)** — Figuratively, that which indicates or determines the probable changes in business conditions.
15. **barter** — The act of exchanging goods for goods.
16. **bid** — An oral or written offer, as of a price.
17. **bill of goods** — A list of merchandise; an invoice.
18. **bonus** — Money or something of value paid in addition to a stated compensation; an extra dividend.
19. **boycott** — A combination to prevent dealing in a commodity or with a person or a group.
20. **brand** — A trade-mark; a quality, grade, class, or make of goods.
21. **by-product** — Something produced during a manufacturing process that is secondary to the original product.
22. **calendar year** — The year beginning January 1 and ending December 31.
23. **capitalization** — The face value of the stocks and bonds of a business.
24. **cartage (ctg.)** — The charge made by a public carrier for transporting goods; also, the conveyance of goods.

---

[1] For additional abbreviations of business terms, see page 148.

WORDS USED IN SENTENCES

1. We enclose the *account sales* covering your last consignment of potatoes to us.
2. These papers will be delivered to you as soon as an *acknowledgment* before a notary has been obtained.
3. The statement was rendered to show the cash *advances* made to the author on his royalty account.
4. Mrs. Lenox has appointed Mr. Chalmers *agent* to sell the land she owns in Clark County.
5. The chairman of the Finance Committee urged that the *allocation* of funds be made in accordance with his recommendations.
6. The *allotment* of space in the exhibit hall will be made next Monday.
7. We will make you an *allowance* for the imperfect bag.
8. The strike was settled by *arbitration*.
9. When may we expect payment of your account, which is very much in *arrears?*
10. The *articles of agreement* have not yet been drawn up by our lawyer.
11. The court approved an *assignment* of the property of the debtor to a trust company, so that all his creditors might be protected.
12. All *back orders* will be filled by the end of the week.
13. The demands of his creditors became so insistent that he was forced into involuntary *bankruptcy*.
14. The stock exchange has always been considered a *barometer* of business conditions.
15. The use of money has almost eliminated the practice of *barter*.
16. Sealed *bids* for the construction of the tunnel will be opened at 2:00 p.m. today.
17. The *bill of goods* you mailed us on January 10 was filled yesterday.
18. Each employee received a 10 per cent cash *bonus* as a Christmas present from the firm.
19. Edmonds & Company said that they had been the victims of a *boycott*.
20. Our store carries only the best *brands* of canned goods.
21. Often the value of a manufacturer's *by-products* exceeds the value of his main product.
22. Enclosed is a profit and loss statement for the *calendar year* just ended.
23. The *capitalization* of the firm is $50,000,000.
24. The *cartage* from the depot to the warehouse must be included in the cost price.

LESSON 55

General Business Terms (*Continued*)

1.	certify	To testify to in writing; to verify.
2.	charter	A document granting a corporation rights or privileges.
3.	client	One who engages a lawyer; a customer or patron.
4.	clientele	Body of clients of a business firm or of a professional person.
5.	commerce	Trade or traffic on a large scale.
6.	commission broker	One who buys or sells for another, receiving a certain percentage in payment for his work.
7.	commodity	Anything movable (except animals) that is bought or sold.
8.	competition	The effort of rival businesses to obtain custom.
9.	compromise	An arrangement for settlement by mutual concession.
10.	concession	A grant by a government of land or property or a right to use such for some specified purpose; a thing yielded.
11.	confirmation	Verification or proof.
12.	consideration	A recompense, as for a service; a compensation.
13.	consign	To forward or deliver goods to someone to be sold or called for.
14.	consolidate	Unite; combine; merge.
15.	consumer	One who buys a commodity for his own use.
16.	corporation (corp.)	A group of persons treated by law as an artificial person, with rights or liabilities apart from those of the persons in the group.
17.	cost plus	Pertaining to a method of determining the total cost of contract work, which involves adding to the actual cost a certain percentage of the cost as profit.
18.	credentials	Testimonials showing that the holder is entitled to credit or has the right to exercise some official power.
19.	credit memorandum (cr. memo.)	A statement showing the credit given the buyer for goods returned, allowance made, etc.
20.	custody	The care and keeping of property for another.
21.	customs	Duties levied by a government upon imported or exported commodities.
22.	cycle	A recurring succession of business conditions.
23.	decentralize	To divide and distribute that which has been brought together, as the administration of public affairs.
24.	defaulter	One who misappropriates funds entrusted to him.
25.	defray	To provide for the payment of.

WORDS USED IN SENTENCES

1. When a bank *certifies* a check, it assures that sufficient money is on deposit to meet the obligation and guarantees payment of the check.
2. A corporation *charter* may be obtained more easily in some states than in others.
3. The lawyer had many prominent citizens among his *clients*.
4. It took several years for the broker to build up his *clientele*.
5. Our *commerce* with South America is growing rapidly.
6. The *commission broker* lost heavily on the last shipment of melons he received.
7. Cotton is a *commodity* that often causes labor disputes.
8. It is said that *competition* is the life of trade.
9. The strike was settled by a *compromise*.
10. Our company has the *concession* for all restaurants at the State Fair.
11. Please wire us a *confirmation* of the order that you gave us over the telephone.
12. A *consideration* is required in order to legalize a contract.
13. The shipment of automobiles was *consigned* to a well-known Philadelphia dealer.
14. The two corporations will *consolidate* at the close of the fiscal year.
15. The price to the *consumer* was reduced by eliminating the middleman's profit.
16. The purpose could be accomplished better by a *corporation* than by an individual or a partnership.
17. The contracts are to be awarded on a *cost-plus* basis.
18. The stranger was asked to present his *credentials*.
19. Enclosed is our *credit memorandum* covering goods returned by you on July 10.
20. The assets of the bankrupt are in the *custody* of the receiver.
21. The Federal Government collects millions of dollars in *customs* annually.
22. A business *cycle* consists of four distinct periods; namely, prosperity, crisis, depression, and recovery.
23. Several large corporations have voted recently to *decentralize* their method of operation.
24. The cashier proved to be a *defaulter*.
25. The chairman asked for contributions to *defray* the expense of printing the programs.

LESSON 56

General Business Terms (*Continued*)

1. depletion — The exhaustion of, as of resources.
2. deteriorate — To impair; to make worse; to grow worse.
3. director (dir.) — One of a body of persons selected to manage the affairs of a corporation or a company.
4. disbursements — Funds that have been expended or paid out.
5. discount (dis.) — Deduction from a gross sum; an allowance on an account, usually given for prompt or cash payment. Interest on a loan deducted when the loan is made.
6. discrepancy — A disagreement, variance, difference.
7. discretionary — Unrestrained except by discretion or judgment.
8. discrimination — A distinction in treatment, especially an unfair or injurious one.
9. dissolution — Disorganization; separation into parts; the final liquidation of a business.
10. document — A paper containing an authoritative record.
11. domestic trade — Internal, native trade—not foreign trade.
12. drawing account — An allowance made a salesman or other employee for salary or expenses, especially in advance of future sales and commissions earned.
13. dun — To make insistent demands for payment.
14. dutiable goods — Imports or exports subject to duty.
15. duty — A governmental tax on the importation or exportation of goods.
16. efficiency — The competency with which the desired result is produced or the maximum effect is obtained.
17. embarrass — To encumber with debt; to beset with demands or claims.
18. enterprise — An important project, involving energy and courage.
19. equitable — Fair; unbiased; just; reasonable.
20. establish — To cause to be accepted as true; to set up in business.
21. estimate (est.) — To form an opinion of; to fix the worth, value, size of; to calculate the price of approximately.
22. exchange (ex., exc., exch.) — The process of settling accounts without the actual transfer of money, by interchanging drafts or bills of exchange; a place where things are exhibited, as a cotton exchange.
23. excise (ĕk sīz′) — A duty or tax on the manufacture, sale, or consumption of articles or commodities within the country.
24. exempt — Free from some burden or limitation to which other persons or things are subject.
25. expedite — To hasten; to facilitate.

WORDS USED IN SENTENCES

1. The *depletion* of certain mineral ores has had serious consequences.
2. A building *deteriorates* rapidly if it is not cared for.
3. Mr. Owens was a *director* of the local bank as well as of several other large organizations.
4. The treasurer reported heavy cash *disbursements*.
5. We will allow you a *discount* of 2 per cent if this bill is paid within ten days.
6. The annual audit disclosed a serious *discrepancy* in the books of the company.
7. You have been given *discretionary* powers in connection with this transaction.
8. A public service corporation can show no *discrimination* in its treatment of customers.
9. The partners announced a *dissolution* of the partnership effective December 31 of this year.
10. A will is a valuable *document* and should be safeguarded.
11. Our product is suitable for *domestic trade* only.
12. The salesman was allowed a liberal *drawing account*.
13. We dislike to *dun* you, Mr. Winthrop, but your account is now five months overdue.
14. Among the *dutiable goods* declared by the importer was a diamond necklace.
15. By an act of Congress, the *duty* on imported jewelry has been increased.
16. The increase in the output of Factory A is due to the *efficiency* of the production methods in effect there.
17. He was financially *embarrassed* because of the failure of his crops.
18. There is some doubt as to whether or not the new *enterprise* can succeed.
19. His creditors were willing to settle their outstanding claims on an *equitable* basis.
20. The firm has been *established* for 105 years.
21. He *estimated* that this year's business would exceed last year's by 10 per cent.
22. The terms *domestic* and *foreign* as applied to kinds of *exchange* are self-explanatory.
23. The Government derives a considerable revenue from *excise* taxes on tobacco.
24. Churches and educational institutions are *exempt* from taxation.
25. This improved machinery will greatly *expedite* the manufacturing process.

LESSON 57

General Business Terms (*Continued*)

1. **exports** — Merchandise sent out of a country.
2. **extension (ext.)** — Additional time for payment; the total cost of each article itemized, with its unit price, on an invoice.
3. **facilities** — Means for making possible the performance of any action.
4. **financier** — One skilled in, and usually engaged in, money matters.
5. **fiscal year** — The year by which accounts are reckoned. It may or may not coincide with the calendar year.
6. **fixed charges** — Established claims on the revenue of a concern, as interest on debts, rental, taxes, etc.
7. **forecast** — A prophecy or estimate of a future happening.
8. **franchise** (frăn′chĭz) — A particular privilege conferred by a government or a sovereign; the right to vote.
9. **frank** — The privilege, granted by a government to public officials, of mailing matter relating to official business without charge.
10. **fraudulent** — Dishonest; obtained by unfair methods.
11. **freight (frt.) in** — Freight paid on merchandise purchased and received. (Freight paid on merchandise sold and shipped is called *freight out*.)
12. **goods in process** — In manufacturing establishments, merchandise partially completed.
13. **gross profit** — The excess of gross receipts over the expenditures.
14. **guarantee (gu., guar.)** — That which is given by way of security. (May also be spelled *guaranty*.)
15. **imports** — Merchandise brought into a country.
16. **incorporated (inc., incorp.)** — Formed into a legal body with special functions, rights, duties, and liabilities.
17. **infringement** — Violation, breach; an encroachment on a right.
18. **inheritance** — The acquisition of property by one person as heir to another; that which has been inherited.
19. **insolvency** — Condition of a person or firm unable to pay debts.
20. **installment** — A portion of a debt or a sum of money to be paid at a particular time.
21. **integrity** — Honesty; moral soundness.
22. **interlocking** — Connected into one system or organization so that one cannot be worked independently of another.
23. **investment (inv.)** — Money expended for any kind of property purchased for income; also, the property so purchased.
24. **invoice (inv.)** — A written document listing goods sent to a purchaser, and including prices, quantities, and charges.

WORDS USED IN SENTENCES

1. The value of our country's *exports* to South America is increasing steadily.
2. The retailer pointed out to the wholesaler that the total of the *extensions* on the invoice did not agree with the amount on the trade acceptance.
3. The increased *facilities* of the plant will enable us to care for double our present business.
4. I should like to consult a reliable *financier* before we proceed with so far-reaching an enterprise.
5. The financial statement covers the *fiscal* year, which ended on June 30.
6. The *fixed charges* of the company are entirely too large in comparison with its liquid assets.
7. The business *forecast* for the year was most optimistic.
8. The new bus company has just been granted a *franchise* by the City Council.
9. Congressmen may *frank* only correspondence that is of an official nature.
10. That company obtained the contract by *fraudulent* means.
11. *Freight-in* charges last month amounted to nearly $1,000.
12. We have a large inventory of *goods in process*.
13. Although the *gross profit* was enormous, unexpected administrative expenses reduced the net profit to 5 per cent.
14. The typewriter was sold with a year's *guarantee* against mechanical defects.
15. The excess of *imports* over exports during the first quarter resulted in an unfavorable trade balance.
16. The company was *incorporated* under the laws of Delaware.
17. The new battery is an *infringement* on our patent.
18. This 10-acre farm came to him as an *inheritance* from his grandfather.
19. The *insolvency* of the concern brought great losses to many persons.
20. Many high-priced articles of merchandise are sold on the *installment* plan.
21. The banker's *integrity* was unquestioned.
22. These corporations are known to have *interlocking* directorates.
23. His *investment* in Oklahoma oil properties made him wealthy.
24. Our *invoices* are typed in triplicate on special machines.

LESSON 58

General Business Terms (*Continued*)

1. **itemized statement** — A statement listing individually all transactions during a certain period.
2. **jobber** — One who buys goods in bulk from manufacturer or importer to sell again to other dealers without changing the form of the goods. A middleman.
3. **license** — Authoritative permission to do that which otherwise would be illegal; a document granting such permission.
4. **limited liability** — That liability of each shareholder which is limited to the amount of his stock or share, or to an amount fixed by a guarantee or by law.
5. **line of credit** — Amount of credit extended to a person or firm, usually by a manufacturer or wholesaler.
6. **liquidation** — The settling of accounts and the distribution of assets in winding up an estate or business.
7. **lucrative** — Profitable; gainful.
8. **managerial** — Of, pertaining to, or characteristic of, a manager.
9. **margin of profit** — Difference between cost and selling price.
10. **marketability** — Quality or state of being salable.
11. **mercantile agency** — A concern that procures information relating to the financial standing and credit of merchants.
12. **merchandise** — Goods, wares, or articles bought and sold.
13. **middleman** — One who buys in bulk and sells in smaller lots for resale; a jobber.
14. **minute book** — A book in which the proceedings at the meetings of a board of directors, company, or society are kept.
15. **monopoly** — Sole command of the manufacturing, distributing, or selling of anything.
16. **net** — Remaining after deducting all charges, loss, etc.
17. **notary public** — A public officer who attests or certifies documents.
18. **note** — A written agreement to pay a certain sum of money at a fixed date, or on demand, to a certain person.
19. **option** — A stipulation whereby a party in a time contract may demand its fulfillment within a specified limit.
20. **overhead** — The general expenses of a business as distinct from the direct costs of manufacturing and selling.
21. **paper profits** — Profits unrealized, existing only on paper.
22. **partnership** — The relationship between persons who have contracted to join in business.
23. **patent (pat.)** (păt′ĕnt) — The granting to an inventor, for a term of years, of the right to the exclusive control over his invention.

WORDS USED IN SENTENCES

1. Your *itemized statement* for May agrees with our record of the month's transactions.
2. Few wholesalers buy anything from that *jobber* now.
3. The physician's *license* to practice medicine was prominently displayed in his office.
4. Investors have *limited liability* for the debts of those corporations in which they hold stock.
5. In our opinion, their financial statements warrant our increasing their *line of credit*.
6. Settlement of the estate was complicated by the fact that the heirs desired the *liquidation* of the business.
7. The venture proved to be most *lucrative*.
8. His son has been promoted to a *managerial* position.
9. The *margin of profit* on this article is entirely too low.
10. Consider the *marketability* of the device carefully before you invest.
11. The *mercantile agency* sent us a confidential report on the financial standing of the concern.
12. Shopworn *merchandise* should never be offered for sale.
13. The *middleman's* profit affects retail prices.
14. Please keep the company's *minute book* in the safe.
15. That company is attempting to obtain a *monopoly* in the envelope-manufacturing field.
16. Our *net* income last year was $148,715 and our gross income, $340,000.
17. Please have this document acknowledged before a *notary public*.
18. Enclosed is my check for $50 and a 60-day *note* for the balance of the account.
19. He holds a valuable *option* on the oil land.
20. Our *overhead* must be reduced next year.
21. The decline of the stock market today wiped out thousands of dollars in *paper profits*.
22. Many law firms are *partnerships*.
23. The inventor was unable to obtain a *patent* on his article.

LESSON 59

General Business Terms (*Continued*)

1. **personal property** — Property that is not real estate—clothing, furniture, jewelry, etc.
2. **port of entry** — A district or locality where foreign goods may be entered for import.
3. **postdated** — Bearing a future date.
4. **potential** — Existing in possibility.
5. **power of attorney** — A document giving one person authority to act for another, generally in the absence of the latter.
6. **preferential** — Having priority or preference.
7. **procedure** — A course of action or of conduct.
8. **proceeds** — The amount realized from the sale of property.
9. **prorate** — To divide, distribute, or assess proportionately.
10. **prospect** — A possible customer or client.
11. **proxy** (prŏk′sĭ) — A person empowered to represent another in a given matter; the instrument by which he is so empowered.
12. **public utilities** — Companies supplying some service indispensable to the general public, as gas, water, power.
13. **quota** — A proportional part or share.
14. **rebate** — A discount or deduction from; an unlawful discrimination.
15. **recapitulation** — A concise summary of principal points or facts.
16. **recoup** — To regain, as a loss; to reimburse oneself.
17. **redeemable** — Recoverable by a fulfillment of some obligation.
18. **referee (ref.)** — One to whom a matter is referred; an arbitrator.
19. **renewal** — An extension granted, as of a note or lease.
20. **rescind** — To annul; cancel.
21. **resources** — Funds, money, or any property that can be converted into supplies; available means.
22. **retail** — To sell in small quantities direct to the consumer.
23. **retrench** — To economize; curtail expenses.
24. **royalty** — A share of proceeds paid, as to an author or inventor, by those doing business under some right belonging to him.
25. **schedule** — A written or printed formal list.
26. **sight draft** — A draft payable upon presentation.
27. **silent partner** — A partner who shares in the profits and losses of a business but takes no part in its management.
28. **speculate** — To engage or invest in a hazardous business transaction in the hope of making a large profit.

WORDS USED IN SENTENCES

1. His *personal property* included many valuable paintings and a collection of priceless gems.
2. The city of New York is one of the most important *ports of entry* of North America.
3. This check is *postdated*, so do not deposit it until the date given on the check.
4. The *potential* sales of this product are limited because of local conditions.
5. He gave his secretary a *power of attorney* to be used during his absence.
6. Creditors presenting *preferential* claims were given first consideration.
7. We should be glad to have your advice on the *procedure* to be followed in this matter.
8. The *proceeds* from the forced sale of his belongings will not meet his debts.
9. The cost of the expedition will be *prorated* among the members.
10. The salesman has some excellent *prospects* in his territory.
11. Enclosed is my duly signed *proxy* to be used at the stockholders' meeting.
12. The new law places further restrictions on *public utilities*.
13. A bonus was given to each salesman who exceeded his sales *quota* for the quarterly period.
14. The practice of giving a *rebate* on such bills has been discontinued.
15. In office practice a *recapitulation* is frequently referred to as a "recap."
16. He is attempting to *recoup* some of his losses by investing in this stock.
17. The preferred stock is *redeemable* at 55 on demand.
18. The court named a *referee* to take charge of the bankrupt concern.
19. Our lease comes up for *renewal* next spring.
20. The contract was *rescinded* before the expiration date.
21. Mr. Adams has exhausted his financial *resources*.
22. This book will *retail* at $2.
23. In order to conform to the budget, it will be necessary to *retrench* considerably next year.
24. The *royalty* was figured on the gross amount of the annual sales of the book.
25. The new price *schedule* will be ready next week.
26. We have placed with our bank for collection a *sight draft* for the past-due balance of your account.
27. Mr. Eliot's elder brother is a *silent partner* in the real estate firm.
28. Do not *speculate* unless you are in a position to lose.

LESSON 60

General Business Terms (*Continued*)

1. **substantial** — Of real worth and importance; valuable.
2. **sundries** — Various small things.
3. **surety** — A guaranty or security against loss, or for the carrying out of some agreed promise or act; one who makes a pledge in behalf of another and accepts certain responsibilities.
4. **surplus** — More than sufficient; undistributed profits.
5. **symbol** — A letter, abbreviation, or mark that stands for something else.
6. **syndicate (synd.)** — A group of capitalists organized to carry out, on their own account, a financial project.
7. **tariff** — A system of duties imposed by a government on goods imported; also, a schedule of charges for freight or passenger transportation.
8. **terminology** — The technical or special terms or words used in any business, art, or science.
9. **tracer** — An inquiry following up something that has gone astray, generally used with regard to shipments.
10. **trade acceptance** — A draft drawn by the seller directly on the purchaser of goods, and accepted by the purchaser for payment at a definite time.
11. **trade discount** — A deduction from the list price, made generally to other dealers in the same line of business.
12. **trust** — A combination of business interests to effect a monopoly in special lines; property held by a person or company, called the trustee, for the benefit of another.
13. **turnover** — A cycle of purchase, sale, and replacement of a stock of goods; also, the rate at which this process takes place.
14. **validity** — In law, having strength, force, or authority.
15. **verification** — Confirmation by evidence.
16. **voucher** — Receipt showing payment, as paid checks or receipted bills.
17. **warehouse receipt** — A receipt for goods stored in a warehouse.
18. **wholesale (whlse.)** — The buying and selling of goods in large quantities only.
19. **without recourse** — These words added to the indorsement of a negotiable instrument protect the indorser from liability to the indorsee and holders.
20. **workmen's compensation** — Compensation given workmen accidentally injured while employed.

WORDS USED IN SENTENCES

1. The indications are that there will be a *substantial* increase in prices of raw materials next fall.

2. The neighborhood drugstore carries a large stock of *sundries*.

3. The young man had to obtain a *surety* bond before he could be appointed cashier.

4. The *surplus* goods will be placed on sale at reduced prices.

5. % is the *symbol* for "per cent."

6. *Syndicates* flourish during boom times.

7. Our country has a high protective *tariff*.

8. Legal *terminology* is difficult for the layman to understand.

9. We have started a *tracer* to ascertain why you have not yet received the merchandise shipped to you on January 10.

10. A bill for the goods always accompanies a *trade acceptance*.

11. We will allow you a *trade discount* of 10 per cent from the list price.

12. Such a *trust* would eliminate private enterprise in that field. He receives a large income from a *trust* fund left him by an uncle.

13. As a result of its new advertising policy, the store increased its *turnover* from three times to five times a year.

14. The *validity* of the document has been proved beyond doubt.

15. It will be necessary to obtain a *verification* of the promoter's statements.

16. The *vouchers* were examined by an official auditor.

17. These goods will be delivered to you on presentation of the *warehouse receipt*.

18. He can buy that lamp for you at *wholesale*.

19. He indorsed the check *without recourse*, for he did not know the maker very well.

20. The state had no *workmen's compensation* law in effect at the time of the accident.

LESSON 61

Accounting Terms

1. account (acct.) — The debits and credits pertaining to a particular phase of the business, grouped under a specific name.
2. account current — An open account.
3. accrual — A sum that accumulates gradually.
4. administrative expense — Expense incurred in the management of a business, estate, or property.
5. amortization (á môr'tĭ zā'shŭn) — The gradual reduction and extinction of a debt by means of periodic contributions to a special fund.
6. assets — Anything of value owned by a person, firm, or estate.
7. auditor (aud.) — A person authorized to examine and verify accounts.
8. balance (bal.) — The equality between two sides of an account; also, the excess on either side.
9. balance sheet — A statement of the assets, liabilities, and capital of a business.
10. book of original entry — An account book in which a transaction is first recorded and from which that entry is copied into a ledger.
11. budget — An estimate of the revenues and expenditures for a given future period.
12. capital (cap.) — The value of a business as measured by the excess of its assets over its liabilities.
13. certified public accountant — A person who has passed a state examination qualifying him to act as an accountant and auditor.
14. closing the books — Transferring at regular intervals to the proprietorship accounts the adjusted balances of the income and expense accounts.
15. contingent liability — A debt that may have to be paid if certain circumstances occur.
16. controlling account — An account that summarizes the balances in a subsidiary ledger.
17. credit (cr.) — An entry on the right side of an account; financial standing.
18. creditor (cr.) — One to whom a debt is owed.
19. current asset — Cash or any other asset that will be turned into cash within a comparatively short time.
20. debit (dr.) — An entry on the left side of an account; opposed to credit.
21. debtor (dr.) — One who is under obligation to another.

WORDS USED IN SENTENCES

1. The Cash *account* is debited for cash received and credited for cash paid out.

2. The *account current*, when analyzed, revealed the number of transactions still open.

3. The *accrual* of unpaid wages amounted to a large sum.

4. The manager's salary is properly chargeable to *administrative expense*.

5. The *amortization* of the debt was provided for in the certificate of indebtedness.

6. The bank is requesting a copy of our statement of *assets* and liabilities.

7. All the books are in readiness for the *auditor*.

8. When an account has entries on one side only, the total of such entries is the *balance* of the account.

9. A *balance sheet* describes the condition of the business at a specified date.

10. The sales journal is a *book of original entry*.

11. A well-planned *budget* should include a regular sum for emergencies.

12. The recent losses have greatly reduced the company's working *capital*.

13. The comptroller of that corporation is a *certified public accountant*.

14. Assemble these figures preparatory to *closing the books*.

15. The customer's discounted note was shown on the balance sheet as a *contingent liability* of the firm.

16. The balance of the Customers *Controlling account* is the total that customers owe.

17. We have verified the *credits* to your account and find that our records agree with yours.

18. There will be a meeting of the *creditors* of the bankrupt concern on January 15.

19. *Current assets* are also known as "liquid assets."

20. The largest *debit* in this column is for $10,000.

21. Here is a list of our *debtors* as of March 1.

LESSON 62

Accounting Terms (*Continued*)

1. **fixed asset** — An asset required for transacting business but not for sale, such as machinery, furniture, etc.
2. **footing** — The adding of a column of figures; the sum so obtained.
3. **good will** — The patronage that a business has earned because of its reputation for fair dealing.
4. **imprest fund** — A fund or sum of money earmarked for a specific purpose, as a petty cash fund.
5. **intangible assets** — Assets the value of which can be only estimated, such as good will; opposed to tangible assets.
6. **inventory (invty.)** — A list of items, usually with estimated value; a periodic account of stock.
7. **journal (jour.)** — A book of original entry in which is entered, in chronological order, a condensed record of each transaction.
8. **ledger (led.)** — A book of final entry to which are transferred, under account names, the sums entered in the journal.
9. **liabilities (lia.)** — Debts or money obligations; opposed to assets.
10. **liquid asset** — An asset that can be readily converted into money.
11. **net profit** — Excess of gross profit over total expenses.
12. **nominal account** — An account whose balance represents an expense or income.
13. **obsolescence** — The state or condition of passing out of usefulness.
14. **posting** — The act of transferring debit and credit items from books of original entry to accounts in the ledger.
15. **profit and loss statement** — A statement showing the income and expenses of a business for a certain period.
16. **proprietorship** — The excess of assets over liabilities; the equity of the owner in the business.
17. **reserve** — A sum set aside to meet an emergency, to pay a debt at maturity, or to replace assets.
18. **sinking fund** — Cash set aside to be used, with its accumulated interest, to pay a debt at maturity.
19. **solvent** — Able to pay just debts or claims.
20. **subsidiary ledger** — A ledger containing certain accounts that are summarized by a controlling account in the general ledger.
21. **tangible assets** — Assets that exist physically, as machinery and buildings; opposed to intangible assets.
22. **transaction** — A business event, as buying goods.
23. **trial balance** — A list of the balances of the accounts in a double-entry ledger.
24. **undivided profits** — Profits that have not been distributed as dividends or otherwise allocated.

WORDS USED IN SENTENCES

1. The most common *fixed assets* are machinery, furniture and fixtures, land, and buildings.
2. Penciled *footings* in accounts are used in the preparation of a trial balance.
3. The *good will* of a business very often represents its most valuable asset.
4. The auditor simplified the system of recording petty cash disbursements from the *imprest fund*.
5. *Intangible assets* play an important part in determining the selling price of a business.
6. In determining the gross profit, the merchandise *inventory* must be taken into account.
7. Miss Smith's entries in the *journal* are very neat.
8. Monthly statements are usually prepared from information furnished by the accounts in the *ledger*.
9. When the *liabilities* of a concern exceed its assets, the concern is insolvent.
10. The most *liquid asset* is cash.
11. Notwithstanding the large business we did last year, the books show that we made only $28,000 *net profit*.
12. The balances of *nominal accounts*, representing consumed expenses, as rent and salaries, appear in the profit and loss statement.
13. Due to *obsolescence*, the machinery was replaced.
14. If a *posting* has been omitted, it should be made as soon as the omission is discovered.
15. It is interesting to compare the *profit and loss statement* for the year ending December 31 with that for the six months ending June 30.
16. *Proprietorship* increases when an asset is sold or exchanged for another asset of greater value.
17. It is necessary to increase our *reserve* for taxes.
18. A *sinking fund* provided for the retirement of the bonds.
19. Their balance sheet showed that they were both *solvent* and prosperous.
20. As their name implies, *subsidiary ledgers* are subsidiary to controlling accounts in the general ledger.
21. Anything that has physical existence, as merchandise, furniture, etc., is considered a *tangible asset*.
22. The business of the bookkeeper is to record *transactions*.
23. A *trial balance* is a check of the arithmetical accuracy of the ledger accounts.
24. *Undivided profits* represent earnings of a business that have not been distributed to its owners.

LESSON 63

Advertising, Publishing, and Printing Terms

1. addenda — Appendixes or other matter added to a book.
2. arabic figures — 1, 2, 3, etc., as distinguished from I, II, III, etc.
3. Ben Day — A process for shading the background of a line engraving.
4. bibliography — A list of books of an author or of the literature on a particular subject.
5. blurb — A laudatory announcement of a book, often printed on the jacket or outer paper cover. (Slang or colloquial.)
6. boldface (b.f.) — Type in which the lines are very thick.
7. brochure (brō shūr′) — A pamphlet or booklet, usually above the average in the quality of its workmanship.
8. caption — A heading, especially the title of an illustration.
9. caret — A sign (∧) placed below a line to indicate where new or omitted words or letters are to be inserted.
10. cartoon — A humorous drawing; also, a design drawn as a model.
11. colophon — An emblem used by a publisher on title pages or on book covers, formerly, a design used as a tailpiece.
12. copyright — The exclusive right to reproduce or publish.
13. die — A hard metal device for stamping or cutting out an illustration, design, or title.
14. dummy — A set of sheets so bound as to represent a projected book, folder, or other unit of printing.
15. electrotype — A duplicate plate of a type form or engraving made from a wax or metal mold.
16. emboss — To represent in relief or raised work.
17. encyclopedia — One or more volumes containing information on all branches of knowledge, in alphabetic order.
18. engraving — The process of producing designs on wood, metal, or stone; the block so prepared; a picture printed from such a block.
19. errata slip (ĕ rā′tȧ) — The sheet on which are listed the errors in a publication, together with their corrections.
20. folio — The page number; a publication composed of sheets each folded once, making four pages to the sheet; a book of the largest dimensions—more than 11 inches high.
21. font — A full assortment of type of one design and size.
22. format — Shape, style, and size of a book.
23. frontispiece — An illustration in the front of a book, usually facing the title page.

WORDS USED IN SENTENCES

1. The *addenda* in this economic geography are useful to research students.
2. The illustrations in this book are to be numbered in *arabic figures*.
3. The reproductions of the forms will be much more attractive if *Ben Day* backgrounds are used.
4. Ordinarily, all works cited in a book are listed in the general *bibliography*.
5. The advertising manager will have copy for the *blurb* tomorrow.
6. The center headings in this circular are to be set in *boldface*.
7. We plan to publish a handsome *brochure* in recognition of the company's fiftieth anniversary.
8. Notice that each illustration in this text has both a main *caption* and a *subcaption*.
9. Please indicate in the margin what is to be inserted at the point marked by the *caret*.
10. A more vivid impression can be conveyed by a clever *cartoon* than by a long descriptive paragraph.
11. The initials of the firm name were interlaced in an intricate fashion to form a *colophon*.
12. The author protected his rights by renewing the *copyright* when it expired.
13. Please order a brass *die* for the design on the front cover of the book.
14. The *dummy* for the catalogue will be ready tomorrow.
15. All the *electrotypes* will be delivered to the printer tomorrow.
16. The craftsman displayed great skill in *embossing* the seal.
17. The information desired can be easily compiled from the *encyclopedia*.
18. The book will be profusely illustrated by both line and half-tone *engravings*.
19. Because of the errors discovered, it will be necessary to print an *errata slip* for this mathematics text.
20. Notice that in this *folio* edition the *folios* are at the foot of the pages.
21. We consider Granjon a most readable *font*.
22. In all respects, follow the *format* of the preceding edition.
23. The *frontispiece* is to be the only colored illustration in the book.

LESSON 64
Advertising, Publishing, and Printing Terms (*Continued*)

1. **half tone** — A plate for reproducing varying degrees of lights and shadows, as of photographs.
2. **italic (ital.)** — A style of type in which letters slope to the right.
3. **layout** — Process of planning a book, periodical, or advertisement in detail; also, the plan of what is laid out.
4. **leaders** — A row of dots used in tables, etc., to lead the eye across a space to the right word or number.
5. **linotype** — A machine for casting type in lines for printing.
6. **lithography** (lĭ thŏg′rȧ fĭ) — The process of putting printing or designs on stone or metal and producing printed impressions therefrom.
7. **logotype** (lŏg′ō tīp) — A single type plate containing two or more letters or a word or words of common occurrence, as *the*.
8. **lower case (l.c.)** — Small letters; letters that are not capitals. (Capital letters are known as *upper case*.)
9. **manuscript (ms.)** — A copy, in handwriting or typewriting, as submitted for printing or editorial consideration.
10. **mat** — Short for *matrix*, a die or mold for a type face.
11. **monotype** — A machine that casts and sets single types.
12. **octavo (8vo.)** (ŏk tā′vō) — A sheet folded into eight leaves, which are about 6 by 9½ inches; hence, a book of about that size.
13. **offset** — A smudge or transfer of ink from a freshly printed sheet upon another sheet; also, a kind of lithography.
14. **pagination** — The sequence of page numbers in a book.
15. **photogravure** (fō′tō grȧ vūr′) — A process of making prints from a depressed, engraved surface prepared photographically.
16. **pica** — Standard of measure for type composition; 12-point type.
17. **proofreader** — One who reads printed matter, indicating corrections by the use of conventional proofreading marks.
18. **quad** (kwŏd) — A square piece of type metal used in spacing and in blank lines in typesetting. Abbreviation of *quadrat*.
19. **rotogravure** (rō′tō grȧ vūr′) — A picture, design, or type matter etched on a cylindrical printing surface and printed by a rotary press.
20. **script** — Type, printing, or engraving in handwritten form.
21. **stereotype** — A plate cast from a matrix in type metal.
22. **superior figure** — A small figure appearing at the top of a line of type, serving as a reference figure.
23. **vignette** — An engraving finished with a cloud effect.
24. **watermark** — Identifying translucent letters or designs in a sheet of paper, visible by holding the sheet to the light.
25. **woodcut** — An engraving in wood; a print from such a block.

WORDS USED IN SENTENCES

1. Because of the large number of *half tones* that this book contains, it will be necessary to print it on smooth-finished paper.

2. For the sake of emphasis, set in *italics* the words that illustrate the definitions.

3. Enclosed is a *layout* of the ad for the evening papers.

4. The *leaders* in these tables do not align.

5. As this job is set in *linotype*, please avoid corrections.

6. We can produce a most pleasing result by *lithography*.

7. Company names and trade-marks are often made as *logotypes*.

8. Notice that "company" is to be set in *lower case* throughout this article.

9. Here is the complete *manuscript* for the English book.

10. It will be necessary to order new *matrixes* of this linotype font.

11. Complicated material, such as tables, is usually set in *monotype*.

12. The art collection will be published in *octavo* size.

13. We cannot accept this job because of the large number of *offset* pages. Children's books are often printed by *offset* lithography.

14. The *pagination* of each volume will begin with 1.

15. This edition contains an excellent *photogravure* portrait of the author.

16. The page size is to be 24 *picas* wide by 36 *picas* deep.

17. Please return the proofs bearing our *proofreader's* corrections.

18. Insert *quad* spaces between each item of the table.

19. The picture section of the Sunday newspaper is printed by *rotogravure*.

20. Many of the illustrations in the bookkeeping text are in beautiful *script*.

21. *Stereotypes* for use on rotary presses are curved to fit the cylinder.

22. Footnotes in this chapter are to be indicated by *superior figures*, not by asterisks.

23. The added cost is due to the expense of the *vignette* cuts.

24. The writer of the letter was traced through the *watermark* in the letterhead.

25. All the *woodcuts* in this book bear the artist's signature.

LESSON 65

Banking and Investment Terms

1. **acceptance (acc.)** — A draft on which the drawee has formally written "Accepted" and his signature.
2. **accrued** — Earned or accumulated but not yet paid, as interest.
3. **appreciation** — Increase in property value through a rise in price.
4. **bearer** — The person in possession of a bill or note that is payable to "bearer."
5. **Big Board** — The New York Stock Exchange.
6. **bill of exchange (B/E or b.e.)** — A draft. The term usually refers to an order for money payable in a foreign country; "draft," to an order in connection with a domestic transaction.
7. **bond** — An interest-bearing certificate of indebtedness issued by a government or by a corporation; also, a writing under seal by which a person binds himself to do a certain thing.
8. **broker** — One who makes both sales and purchases for others on commission, known as "brokerage."
9. **call money** — Borrowed money repayable on call or on demand.
10. **canceled check** — A check paid by the bank and stamped with the proper mark of cancellation—generally, by perforation.
11. **capital stock** — The investment in a corporation for which shares of stock have been issued.
12. **cashier's check** — A check drawn upon a bank by its cashier.
13. **certified check** — A check that has been guaranteed as to payment by the bank on which it is drawn.
14. **check protector** — A machine that stamps the amount of a check into the paper so that the amount cannot be altered.
15. **clearinghouse** — A meeting place where the banks in a city may daily exchange checks, drafts, notes, etc.
16. **collateral (coll.)** — Property pledged as security for payment of a debt.
17. **commercial paper** — Negotiable instruments arising out of commercial transactions calling for the payment of money.
18. **commitment** — The act of agreeing to buy or sell stock.
19. **common stock** — Ordinary capital stock.
20. **comptroller** (kŏn trōl′ẽr) — A controller; the official who supervises all phases of accounting procedure.
21. **convertible** — Any security that may be exchanged for another class of security in the same corporation.
22. **counterfeit** — To copy or imitate with fraudulent purposes; money manufactured in imitation of real money.
23. **coupon** (kōō′pŏn) — Small certificates, attached to a bond, representing the interest due for a certain period.

WORDS USED IN SENTENCES

1. The *acceptance* could not be rediscounted with a Federal Reserve bank.
2. The bonds were sold at 101 plus *accrued* interest.
3. Over the twenty-year period his security holdings showed a worth-while *appreciation*.
4. A check that is made payable to *"bearer"* is readily negotiable.
5. The quotations on the *Big Board* appear immediately on the ticker.
6. Because of recent European developments, we have temporarily discontinued issuing *bills of exchange*.
7. These municipal *bonds* pay $3\frac{1}{2}$ per cent.
8. Can you recommend a reliable *broker?*
9. The rate for *call money* has advanced.
10. He offered a *canceled check* as proof that the bill had been paid.
11. The new corporation has a *capital stock* of $100,000.
12. Since he has no checking account, I suggest that he remit by *cashier's check*.
13. We enclose our *certified check* for $25,000 and shall expect early delivery of the bonds purchased from you yesterday.
14. Most of the larger business houses use *check protectors*.
15. As soon as your check has passed through the *clearinghouse*, you may draw against it.
16. We will accept the stock certificates offered as *collateral* for the loan you desire.
17. This broker specializes in gilt-edge *commercial paper*.
18. They realized a huge profit on previous *commitments*.
19. The *common stock* of our company is selling at 51 on the Exchange.
20. The teller was promoted to the office of *comptroller*.
21. This issue offers an attractive investment in *convertibles*.
22. The Treasury Department issued a warning that there were many *counterfeits* in circulation.
23. *Coupons* on this bond should be clipped on January 1 and July 1.

LESSON 66

Banking and Investment Terms (*Continued*)

1. Curb — A market (once actually on the curb) trading in securities not listed on the New York Stock Exchange.
2. currency — Coins and bank notes.
3. debenture — An unsecured certificate of debt issued by a corporation.
4. defalcation — Fraudulent appropriation of money held in trust.
5. denomination — The face value of a bond, note, coupon, coin, bank note, etc.
6. deposit slip — The slip, showing details of the deposit, presented to the bank when a deposit is made.
7. depositor — One who places funds in a bank.
8. depository — A concern accepting funds on deposit; a company or warehouse for storing property for safekeeping.
9. dishonor — To refuse to accept a duly presented check, draft, or note; also, to refuse to pay one so presented.
10. diversification — Variation; modification.
11. dividend (div.) — The stockholders' share of corporation earnings.
12. draft (dft.) — An order signed by one person (the drawer) directing another (the drawee) to pay a sum of money to a third person (the payee), on demand or on a certain date.
13. Federal Reserve bank — One of twelve banks created under the Federal Reserve Act to serve as bankers for member banks of the Federal Reserve System.
14. fiduciary — A person or corporation to whom property is entrusted.
15. forgery — A false or counterfeit document or signature.
16. futures — Contracts for future deliveries.
17. greenback — A note issued by the United States Government, so called because the back is printed in green.
18. hypothecation — The pledging of a security for the payment of a loan.
19. indorse — To write one's name on the back of a note, check, etc., as evidence of its legal transfer.
20. inflation — Unsound expansion, especially of currency.
21. irredeemable — Not convertible; as, paper money not exchangeable for gold or silver coins.
22. issue — The stock or bonds of a company put out at one time.

WORDS USED IN SENTENCES

1. Trade on the *Curb* was quiet yesterday.

2. *Currency* should be carefully sorted in the cash drawer.

3. This issue of *debenture* bonds is convertible into stock.

4. Our former employee was bonded for a sufficient amount to cover fully the amount of his *defalcation*.

5. He exchanged several small bills amounting to $50 for a single bill of that *denomination*.

6. A duplicate *deposit slip* should accompany deposits made by mail.

7. The *depositor* could not reconcile his bank statement.

8. The First National Bank was named as one of the *depositories* for the fund.

9. The check was *dishonored* because of an erasure.

10. The *diversification* of investments is a protection against security losses.

11. The Board of Directors declared a 6 per cent *dividend*.

12. We hope you will honor this *draft* on presentation.

13. The *Federal Reserve banks*, their branches, and agencies serve the banks of the entire country.

14. The Second National Bank acted as *fiduciary* for the estate.

15. The *forgery* was very skillfully done.

16. July *futures* in the Kansas City market were $1\frac{1}{8}$ to $1\frac{5}{8}$ cents higher.

17. *Greenbacks* were first issued in 1862 as a war-revenue measure.

18. The *hypothecation* of these securities for the repayment of the loan is satisfactory.

19. Please *indorse* this check in full as a protection against loss.

20. *Inflation* was an issue in the last political campaign.

21. Portions of less than one-half of a piece of paper money are *irredeemable*.

22. A new *issue* of debenture bonds will be placed on the market next month.

LESSON 67

Banking and Investment Terms (*Continued*)

1. **joint account (J/A)** — An account kept in the names of two or more persons, any one of whom may claim the benefits therefrom.
2. **legal tender** — Money that is legally acceptable in paying a debt.
3. **letter of credit** — A written notice by a bank that the person named is entitled to draw on the bank up to a certain amount.
4. **listed stocks** — Stocks included in the list of those that can be bought and sold at an exchange.
5. **loan** — A sum of money lent at interest.
6. **margin** — The money deposited with a broker by a customer to protect the broker against loss in transactions for the customer.
7. **maturity** — The time fixed for the payment of a note or bond; the date on which a debt is legally collectible.
8. **monetary** — Pertaining to money or coinage.
9. **negotiable instruments** — Checks, notes, drafts, or other commercial paper that may be transferred to another by the owner's indorsement.
10. **no-par stock** — Stock having no par value.
11. **nonassessable** — Not liable to the imposition of a tax or fine.
12. **odd lot** — A smaller unit of trade than the standard unit on an exchange, such as less than 100 shares of stock.
13. **over the counter** — A term referring to dealings in securities that are not listed on any stock exchange.
14. **overdraw** — To draw a draft or a check on an account for a greater amount than one has on deposit in the bank.
15. **par value** — The face value of a share of stock.
16. **passbook** — A small book in which a bank enters deposits and sometimes withdrawals made by a customer.
17. **payee** — The one to whom a check or note is made payable.
18. **point** — The unit of fluctuation on the stock market; usually $1.
19. **preferred stock** — Stock that receives a preference in the distribution of dividends or assets.
20. **profit taking** — The selling of securities at a price greater than the purchase price.
21. **promissory note** — A written agreement by one person to pay to another a certain sum of money on demand or at a specified time.
22. **promoter** — One whose business it is to start new companies, encourage sales of securities, etc.
23. **protest** — To declare in an affidavit that a note or check was presented for payment and payment was refused.

WORDS USED IN SENTENCES

1. Husbands and wives often have *joint* bank *accounts* or *joint* investment *accounts*.
2. Because of their low denomination, these coins are not *legal tender* for the amount due.
3. This *letter of credit* will enable you to obtain the funds you need on your coming tour.
4. The broker suggested several *listed stocks* to his customer.
5. He applied for a *loan* at the bank.
6. Brokers are demanding that *margins* of 50 per cent of the purchase price be maintained.
7. The company bought its own bonds in the open market before they had reached *maturity*.
8. We regret to inform you that this stock has now no *monetary* value.
9. *Negotiable instruments* perform much the same function as currency.
10. The directors usually determine the amount for which each share of *no-par* stock shall be sold.
11. The fact that this stock is *nonassessable* makes it an attractive investment.
12. Some brokers specialize in trading in *odd lots*.
13. Sales *over the counter* were large yesterday.
14. In some states, knowingly *overdrawing* one's bank account is against the law.
15. This stock is selling for more than its *par value*, which is $100 a share.
16. His *passbook* showed no entries between September 1 and November 15.
17. The Hill Finance Corporation is the *payee* in this note.
18. Steel closed with a net gain of 2 3/8 *points*.
19. The holders of *preferred stock* recovered their original investment, but the holders of common stock took a heavy loss.
20. *Profit taking* on Saturday morning caused a decline in several stocks.
21. He discounted the *promissory note* at the bank.
22. The *promoter* was unsuccessful in his attempt to organize an investment company.
23. The cashier asked, "Do you wish to *protest* this note?"

LESSON 68

Banking and Investment Terms (*Continued*)

1. **quotations** — The published market prices of securities.
2. **rails** — Stocks or bonds of railroad companies.
3. **raise** — To increase fraudulently the original amount of a check.
4. **reconciliation** — An adjustment of differences.
5. **redemption** — Payment of a debt, particularly one covered by a bond issue, by discharging the financial obligation represented by such bonds.
6. **right** — A privilege offered to stockholders to purchase shares of a new stock issue in proportion to their holdings.
7. **scrip** — A provisional document certifying the holder's right to receive something else, as stock or bonds.
8. **seat** — Membership in a stock exchange.
9. **security** — Something of value pledged for the fulfillment of a contract; also, a stock or bond.
10. **specie** — Gold and silver coins as distinct from bills and notes.
11. **spot** — On hand for immediate delivery after sale.
12. **sterling** — The standard of monetary value established by the British Government; a general designation for English money.
13. **stock dividend** — A dividend payable by the distribution of additional stock of the company.
14. **stop-loss order** — An order to a broker authorizing him to sell at the market when a stock is at or below a specified quotation, or to buy when it is at or above a specified price.
15. **stop payment** — Notice to a bank not to honor a specific check.
16. **stub** — In a checkbook, receipt book, etc., the small part of each leaf that is fastened in the binding and remains in place as a memorandum of the part torn out.
17. **teller** — The clerk in a bank who pays out money (paying teller) or who receives deposits (receiving teller).
18. **ticker** — A telegraphic receiving instrument that prints stock quotations on a paper ribbon or "tape."
19. **traveler's check** — A check for a specific amount issued by a bank or company and payable at virtually all banks throughout the world.
20. **usury** — Interest at a higher rate than is allowed by law.
21. **vault** — A room in which money and valuables are kept.
22. **voucher check** — A check bearing upon it, or upon a detachable stub, a notation of the items covered by the check.
23. **withdrawal** — Removal, as from a place of deposit or investment.
24. **yield** — Percentage of return in interest or dividends.

WORDS USED IN SENTENCES

1. The *quotations* of leading stocks appear in daily newspapers.
2. *Rails* were quiet today.
3. The clerk was discovered in his attempt to *raise* the check.
4. My secretary prepares the *reconciliation* of my bank statement.
5. The *redemption* date of this issue of bonds is January 2, 1950.
6. In most cases, *rights* are negotiable and can be transferred like stock.
7. *Scrip* was issued to all holders of the common stock as of December 31.
8. At one time *seats* on the New York Stock Exchange sold for as high as $625,000.
9. I can offer ten shares of the common stock of the American Telephone and Telegraph Company as *security* for this loan.
10. In times of financial trouble, payment in gold *specie* is often suspended.
11. *Spot* cotton was quoted 50 points higher after the unfavorable weather reports were received.
12. Because of conditions abroad, the price of *sterling* exchange is fluctuating from day to day.
13. The company declared a *stock dividend* of one share of common stock for each ten shares held.
14. Stock sales resulting from *stop-loss orders* hastened the decline.
15. Notify the bank to *stop payment* on this check.
16. The *stubs* should be filled in before the corresponding checks are torn out.
17. There was a long line at the paying *teller's* window.
18. In the great speculative days of 1929, it was not uncommon for the *ticker* to be an hour late.
19. *Traveler's checks* are the safest method of carrying money when traveling.
20. An interest rate of 15 per cent is *usury*.
21. These records should be stored in our *vault*.
22. Details on the *voucher check* were used as evidence in the suit.
23. Your passbook shows few *withdrawals* from your account in the savings bank.
24. This investment will *yield* you 4 per cent.

LESSON 69

Insurance Terms

1. **actuarial** — Pertaining to the calculation of insurance risks.
2. **adjuster** — One who determines the amount payable under a policy for a fire loss, a shipping loss, etc.
3. **annuity** — An amount payable yearly—in practice, usually paid quarterly or semiannually.
4. **appraiser** — One who estimates the value of property.
5. **arson** — Malicious burning of property.
6. **attained age** — The age that the insured has reached at a particular birthday.
7. **beneficiary** (bĕn′ė físh′ĭ ĕr′ĭ) — The person to whom the value of a policy is payable at the death of the insured.
8. **blanket policy** — A policy that covers a group or class of things.
9. **burglary** — The felonious taking of the property of another through breaking into his house or building.
10. **casualty** — An accident.
11. **claimant** — One who makes a claim or asserts a right.
12. **commuted value** — A single sum payable at once in lieu of a number of smaller sums payable in the future.
13. **contingency** — A possible event or condition.
14. **conversion** — Changing from one type of policy to another.
15. **coverage** — The extent and kind of protection afforded under an insurance policy.
16. **deceased, the** — The dead person.
17. **employer's liability insurance** — An insurance contract by which the employer of laborers is protected against claims for damages from injuries sustained by employees.
18. **endowment** — Insurance in which the policy provides for the payment of a fixed sum to the insured at the expiration of a term of years.
19. **expiration** — A coming to a close; cessation; termination.
20. **fidelity bond** — Insurance against loss by dishonesty of employees.
21. **forfeiture** — That which is lost by way of penalty.
22. **fraternal** — Brotherly. A fraternal association organized for the pursuit of some common object by working together.
23. **general average (g. a.)** — In maritime insurance, the proportionate distribution of loss or expense arising from a sacrifice or an expenditure made for the benefit of all.
24. **incendiary** — Pertaining to the malicious burning of property.
25. **incontestability** — Quality or state of being indisputable.

WORDS USED IN SENTENCES

1. Special training in mathematics is necessary in order to do *actuarial* work.
2. Nothing must be moved until the *adjuster* makes his report of the damage caused by the fire.
3. Under the *annuity* policy I have just taken out, payments begin at the age of 55.
4. It will be necessary to call in an expert *appraiser* to value the collection of jade.
5. It is incredible that he should have been guilty of *arson*.
6. Please state the policyholder's *attained age* on February 1 next.
7. The *beneficiary* of an annuity insurance policy usually is the assured.
8. The manufacturer took out a *blanket policy* covering his buildings and equipment.
9. It is advisable to carry *burglary* insurance if one's house is unoccupied for long periods.
10. *Casualty* insurance protects from loss through damage caused by windstorms, earthquakes, and floods.
11. The *claimant* failed to file a proof of loss within the time specified under the policy.
12. The wife decided that she would take the *commuted value* of her husband's insurance rather than the yearly payments.
13. In the *contingency* of a collision, shatterproof glass is a good investment.
14. In case you are considering *conversion*, bear in mind the cash-surrender value and the loan value of the other policy.
15. The *coverage* in this particular policy exceeds that of any similar policy.
16. The *deceased* left his widow well protected by insurance.
17. Because of the recent introduction of the high-speed lathes, we suggest that you increase your *employer's liability insurance*.
18. I expect my fifteen-year *endowment* policy to pay for my son's college education.
19. I have decided not to renew my fire insurance policy at its *expiration*.
20. Our company has never carried a *fidelity bond*.
21. Nonpayment of the premium will result in *forfeiture* of the protection under this policy.
22. His membership in various *fraternal* organizations provides him with substantial insurance benefit.
23. Most shippers by water cover their goods with *general-average* insurance.
24. There is no doubt whatsoever that the fire was of *incendiary* origin.
25. As my life insurance is more than two years old, I am sure of its *incontestability*.

LESSON 70

Insurance Terms (*Continued*)

1. **indemnity** — That given as compensation for loss or damage.
2. **inflammable** — Easily set on fire.
3. **lapse** — To pass away slowly; to be or become void.
4. **Lloyd's** — A London corporation insuring the commercial and maritime interests of its members.
5. **longevity** — Length of life.
6. **marine insurance** — Insurance against loss or damage to ship, cargo, or freight by perils of the sea.
7. **maritime** (măr′ĭ tīm) — Having to do with navigation or shipping and commerce by sea.
8. **mortality** — The proportion of deaths in a specified number of the population.
9. **mutual** — Owned by the policyholders.
10. **paid-up policy** — A policy on which premiums have been paid in full.
11. **peril** — The hazard against which a policy insures.
12. **perpetuity** (pûr′pē tū′ĭ tĭ) — Quality or state of being continuous; duration without limitations as to time.
13. **policyholder** — One to whom an insurance policy has been granted.
14. **premium** — The amount paid for insurance; periodical payments.
15. **registrar** — An officer of an insurance company who keeps the records of policies issued.
16. **reinstate** — To reinstall; to restore.
17. **rider** — A clause to a policy to cover matters that do not form a part of the policy proper.
18. **risk** — The probability of loss to an insurance company by virtue of a contract; an applicant for a policy.
19. **social insurance** — Insurance, under the auspices of the government, covering masses of workers.
20. **suicide** — Self-murder.
21. **surrender value** — The value that the insurance company will allow on a policy when the payment of the premiums is discontinued and the policy returned.
22. **survivor** — One who outlives another person or any time, event, or thing.
23. **tontine** (tŏn′tēn) — An arrangement whereby certain benefits under a policy shared by a group of persons pass at the death of any one member of the group to the other members.
24. **underwriter** — An insurance company.
25. **waiver** — A written relinquishment of an insurance claim.

WORDS USED IN SENTENCES

1. Liability insurance provides *indemnity* against liability for injuries to or death of other persons.
2. Under the terms of this policy the storage of *inflammable* materials renders the policy void.
3. Unfortunately, he has allowed his policy to *lapse*.
4. According to *Lloyd's*, no information has been received about the "Santa Louisa."
5. Many factors, including heredity and environment, must be considered in estimating probable *longevity*.
6. Some *marine insurance* policies cover loss from theft as well as from perils at sea.
7. Naturally, midwestern agencies are not large *maritime* underwriters.
8. All life insurance is based on *mortality* tables.
9. Many of the large life insurance companies are *mutual* companies.
10. I am going to buy a *paid-up policy* with my inheritance.
11. After the New England hurricane in 1938, no one can deny the *peril* of such storms even in the North Atlantic states.
12. The *perpetuity* of life insurance principles in the United States is assured.
13. The agency numbers among its *policyholders* many professional people.
14. The *premiums* for an ordinary life policy are lower than the premiums for other kinds of insurance.
15. A vast army of clerks is employed in the *registrar's* office of any of the big insurance companies.
16. We are gratified, indeed, to *reinstate* your name on our list of policyholders.
17. The policy, with *rider* attached, is ready for your signature.
18. His medical history indicates that he will be a good *risk*.
19. The theory of *social insurance* has received a great deal of publicity recently.
20. Will the fact that his death was a *suicide* have any effect on his insurance?
21. In most cases, the cash-*surrender value* of a limited-payment policy is greater than that of ordinary life policies.
22. A policy covering two lives will be paid to the *survivor*.
23. The forfeiture clause makes this contract, in effect, a *tontine* policy.
24. Our company is one of the largest *underwriters* in the East.
25. Please sign this *waiver* of your rights.

LESSON 71

Legal Terms

1. abscond — To flee secretly.
2. acquittal — A verdict of not guilty; the act of setting free.
3. adjudicate — To hear and decide a case in court.
4. adjure — To charge or command solemnly.
5. administrator (admr.) — One appointed by a court to settle the estate of a person who dies intestate.
6. affidavit (afft.) — A written statement under oath.
7. alias — An assumed name.
8. alimony — The separate maintenance payable to a wife by her husband under court order after commencement of suit for divorce or legal separation.
9. allegation — That which is alleged or asserted.
10. ambiguity — Vagueness of expression.
11. annulment — The act of making void.
12. appellate (ă pĕl′ăt) — Relating to or dealing with appeals; vested with the power to review and affirm, modify, or reverse the decision of another tribunal.
13. apprehend — To seize; to arrest.
14. appurtenance — That which belongs to something else; adjunct.
15. attachment — A seizure by legal process; also, the instrument authorizing such seizure.
16. attestation — The act of witnessing the execution of any instrument; proof thereof by testimony.
17. bailee — A person who, other than as owner, receives the custody of goods for a specific purpose.
18. bequeath — To give property by will—usually said of personal property.
19. chancery (chăn′sẽr ĭ) — A court of equity; law based on natural principles of justice.
20. chattel — Any item of movable or immovable property except real estate, or the freehold, or things that are parcel of it. *Chattels personal* may be goods, furniture, etc. *Chattels real* may be rights in land, such as leases, mortgages, etc.
21. clemency — Compassion; leniency.
22. codicil — A supplement to a will.
23. contributory negligence — The negligence of an injured person that, combined with the negligence of another, was the proximate cause of the injury.
24. covenant — A promise under seal; to enter into a contract.
25. culprit — One guilty of a crime or fault.

WORDS USED IN SENTENCES

1. The pay-roll clerk *absconded* with the week's pay roll.
2. His attorneys are confident of an *acquittal*, as he has a perfect alibi.
3. The case was *adjudicated* in the lower court.
4. I *adjure* you to consider all implications in this matter.
5. The *administrator* of the estate was fair in all his dealings.
6. This bill must be accompanied by an *affidavit* duly executed.
7. The criminal was discovered in spite of the *alias* he had used.
8. The court decreed that an *alimony* of $200 a month was a reasonable amount.
9. The plaintiff's complaint contained an *allegation* of criminal negligence.
10. The answer to Question 1 was stricken from the records because of *ambiguity*.
11. *Annulment* of the contract was sought on the grounds of a technical error.
12. As soon as the adverse decision was announced, the plaintiff declared he would take the case to the *appellate* court.
13. He was *apprehended* in the raid on the gambling house.
14. The property was sold with all the *appurtenances*, including the right of way to the state highway.
15. The loan company obtained an *attachment* on the borrower's salary to meet the past-due payments.
16. The will is now ready for signature and *attestation*.
17. The tailor, the *bailee* in the case, declared he had exercised reasonable care in handling the cloth.
18. Mr. Rich told his attorney that he wished to *bequeath* $10,000 to his lifelong friend.
19. The case was referred to *chancery* for adjudication.
20. None of the *chattels* removed from the house were of substantial value.
21. The judge recommended *clemency* because it was the prisoner's first offense.
22. A *codicil* to the will upset their plans.
23. The plaintiff's carelessness in crossing the street against the traffic light was considered *contributory negligence*.
24. The two brothers entered into a *covenant* binding each to do his full share of the road-construction work.
25. The *culprit* was sentenced to two years in the penitentiary.

LESSON 72

Legal Terms (*Continued*)

1. **decedent** — A deceased person.
2. **defendant (dft.)** — One who is sued in a legal action.
3. **demise** (dĕ mīz′) — In law, the conveyance of an interest in real property for a term of years; however, the interest may be for life or in full. Also, to convey, as an estate.
4. **demurrer** (dĕ mûr′ẽr) — A pleading by a party to an action that, assuming the truth of the matter alleged by the opposite party, sets up that it is insufficient in law to sustain his claim.
5. **deponent (dep.)** (dē pō′nĕnt) — One who makes an affidavit or testifies in writing under oath.
6. **docket** — An abridged entry of legal proceedings; also, the book or register in which such entries are listed.
7. **domicile** — A person's legal and presumably permanent residence.
8. **duress** (dū′rĕs) — That degree of restraint, by threats or actual violence, sufficient in severity or apprehension to overcome the mind and will of a person of ordinary firmness.
9. **easement** — Any of several rights that one may have over another's land; as, a right of way.
10. **embezzlement** — Appropriation to one's own use of anything belonging to another, especially an employer's money.
11. **equity** — A body of laws based on natural principles of justice; the value of property in excess of liens against it.
12. **escrow** (ĕs′krō′) — A sealed instrument given to one not a party thereto, for delivery to the grantee on stated conditions, the instrument having no effect until delivered.
13. **estoppel** — A bar to the proof of some fact, because it is contrary to one's prior acts or admissions.
14. **executor (exec.)** (ĕg zĕk′ū tẽr) — One appointed by will to administer the estate of the testator in accordance with the terms of the will.
15. **felony** — Any crime above a misdemeanor, as murder, treason.
16. **garnishee** — To attach salary, wages, or income to pay a debt.
17. **hereditaments** — Any property that can be inherited.
18. **homicide** — The killing of a human being by another.
19. **impanel** — To enroll upon a panel or list, as for jury duty.
20. **inchoate** — Elementary, incipient, or incomplete.
21. **incorporeal** (ĭn′kôr pō′rē ăl) — Existing in contemplation of law and enjoyable as a right; intangible.
22. **indenture** — A written instrument under seal, as a mortgage.
23. **indictment** — A formal charge of crime.

WORDS USED IN SENTENCES

1. All the securities in the *decedent's* estate are sound.
2. The attorney for the *defendant* will now summarize.
3. The house was *demised* to him for a period of ten years.
4. The court upheld the *demurrer* of the defendant.
5. The *deponent's* testimony was clearly and concisely worded.
6. The court *docket* showed the cases that awaited judicial decisions.
7. Notice that the form asks you to state where you have your *domicile*.
8. He insisted that he had joined the organization of his own free will and not under *duress*.
9. The *easement* was expressly granted in the deed transferring the property.
10. The cashier of the silk mill was guilty of *embezzlement*.
11. The ownership of the picture was determined by a court of *equity*.
12. All papers relating to the sale of the property were placed in *escrow* at the mortgage company's office.
13. By the principle of *estoppel*, he was prevented from collecting his share of the profits.
14. The State Trust Company is the *executor* of the estate.
15. The prisoner was indicted for *felony* by the grand jury.
16. The creditor threatened to *garnishee* the wages of the unfortunate man for the balance due.
17. The right to use the lake is one of the *hereditaments* that has been attached to the property since 1860.
18. The driver of the car was found guilty of *homicide*.
19. A grand jury has been *impaneled* to inquire into the charges.
20. The *inchoate* testimony offered by the defendant confused the issues of the case.
21. One of the *incorporeal* rights attached to the property purchased was the use of the wagon road through the woods.
22. The *indenture* provided for the repayment of the loan when the construction work was completed.
23. The *indictment* charged the defendant with grand larceny.

LESSON 73

Legal Terms (*Continued*)

1. **injunction** — A court order usually requiring a person to refrain from doing a certain thing.
2. **intestate** — Not having made a will; also one who dies without having made a lawful will.
3. **judicial** — Pertaining to the administration of justice.
4. **jurisprudence** — System of laws of a country.
5. **larceny** — Theft. "Grand larceny" is used when the value of the thing stolen exceeds an amount fixed by statute; "petty larceny," when it is less than that amount.
6. **legatee** — One to whom personal property is given by will.
7. **lien** (lē′ĕn) — A legal claim or charge on property for the satisfaction of a debt or obligation.
8. **litigation** — A contest in a court of justice.
9. **lunatic** — An insane person.
10. **malfeasance** (măl fē′zăns) — Wrongful misconduct, especially the performance of an illegal act by a public official.
11. **mandamus** (măn dā′mŭs) — A writ served to compel a person, corporation, or inferior court to perform some official duty.
12. **mandate** — A judicial command.
13. **misdemeanor** — An offense less serious than felony.
14. **mittimus** (mĭt′ĭ mŭs) — A warrant for commitment to prison; a writ for removal of records from one court to another.
15. **negligence** — Failure to exercise that degree of care required of a prudent person under the circumstances.
16. **negotiate** — To endeavor to effect an agreement; to effect a valid transfer of a negotiable instrument.
17. **nominal** — Existing in name only; not real or actual.
18. **outlawed** — Deprived of the benefit and protection of law.
19. **plaintiff** — One who brings suit.
20. **plea** — The answer of a defendant; a proceeding in court.
21. **probate** — To prove legally and officially, as a will; also, having jurisdiction over wills.
22. **quasi** (kwā′sī) — A quality or status attributed to something that it does not really possess in its own right.
23. **ratification** — The formal sanctioning of something already done.
24. **recognizance** (rē kŏn′ĭ zăns) — An undertaking or promise in court to be responsible for the performance of an act; as, to answer charges, keep the peace, or pay a debt.
25. **replevin** (rē plĕv′ĭn) — An action to recover the possession of chattels unlawfully taken.

WORDS USED IN SENTENCES

1. The *injunction* forbade the picketing of the plant.
2. The court appointed an administrator to settle the estate of Mr. White, who died *intestate*.
3. A *judicial* decree was issued by court in favor of the corporation.
4. The English system of *jurisprudence* is the basis of our common law.
5. He was convicted of grand *larceny*.
6. The chief *legatee* under the will was a minor boy.
7. The mortgage constituted a *lien* on the property.
8. The boundary-line dispute was settled only after prolonged *litigation*.
9. The *lunatic* escaped from the state insane asylum.
10. The surrogate was charged with *malfeasance*.
11. The corporation's plea for a writ of *mandamus* was denied on the grounds that the owner of the property was well within his rights in refusing the corporation a right of way.
12. The latest *mandate* of the Supreme Court attracted country-wide comment.
13. Passing a red light on a public highway is a *misdemeanor*.
14. It will be necessary to obtain a *mittimus* in order to take these records out of the county.
15. The collision at the crossroads was caused by the *negligence* of the truck driver.
16. To put this plan into operation, it will be necessary to *negotiate* a loan from the bank.
17. The lawyer charged only a *nominal* fee for his services because the man had been unemployed.
18. Although a debt may be *outlawed* under the Statute of Limitations, it still remains a moral obligation.
19. The *plaintiff* was suing only for the amount of the property damage.
20. The counsel for the defense made a strong *plea* for his client.
21. The will is to be *probated* next week.
22. The investigation assumed a *quasi*-scientific character when an eminent scientist accepted the chairmanship.
23. It will be necessary to receive *ratification* by the legislatures of three-fourths of the states.
24. The driver of the van was released on his own *recognizance* as he had no previous record of a traffic violation.
25. The attorney recovered his client's goods by serving a writ of *replevin* on the owners of the warehouse.

LESSON 74

Legal Terms (*Continued*)

1. **residuary** (rĕ zĭd′ū̇ ĕr′ĭ) — Pertaining to that which remains of an estate after prior provisions of a will are satisfied.
2. **restitution** — Restoration of anything to its rightful owner; act of giving an equivalent for loss, damage, etc.
3. **revert** — To return to the former owner or his heirs.
4. **status** — State; condition of a person for legal purposes.
5. **subpoena** (sŭb pē′ná) — A writ requiring a person to appear at a certain time and place.
6. **subrogation** (sŭb rō gā′shŭn) — The substitution of one person for another, the former acquiring the rights of the latter.
7. **subscribe** — To sign one's name at the end of an instrument.
8. **summons** — A legal command to appear in court on or before a certain day.
9. **surrogate** (sûr′ō gāt) — A judge who has jurisdiction over the probate of wills and the administration of estates.
10. **tender** — An offer in legal currency of the exact amount due upon a debt.
11. **testator** — A person who makes a will.
12. **tort** — A civil wrong independent of a contract for which a civil suit can be brought.
13. **trespass** — A violation of legal right; also, especially, to enter the premises of another without proper authority.
14. **trustee (tr.)** — One who holds the legal title to property for the benefit of another.
15. **ultra vires** — In excess, or beyond the scope, of authority.
16. **unilateral** (ū′nĭ lăt′ẽr ăl) — One-sided; said of a contract in which only one of the parties makes a promise.
17. **vagrancy** — The condition, quality, or fact of being a vagabond.
18. **vendor** — A seller—one who sells property.
19. **venire** (vē nī′rē) — A judicial writ used in summoning persons to serve as jurors.
20. **venue** (vĕn′ū) — The place in which the events that have occasioned a court action happened; also, the place from which the jury is taken, and where the trial in the action is held.
21. **verdict** — The finding of a jury; decision.
22. **voidable** — Capable of being adjudged invalid or of no force.
23. **warrant** — A writ by a magistrate authorizing an officer to make an arrest, a seizure, or a search.

WORDS USED IN SENTENCES

1. The *residuary* estate of Mr. Warner proved to be smaller than was expected.
2. We demand *restitution* for our losses occasioned by the strike.
3. As Mr. Black died intestate, his property will *revert* to the state unless lawful heirs can be located and identified.
4. Your son's *status* in the case is that of an infant, since he is not twenty-one years of age.
5. A *subpoena* will be duly issued and served upon him, as his testimony is required in the case.
6. Upon payment of the debt, the surety was entitled to *subrogation* with respect to the collateral held by the bank.
7. He will *subscribe* the document, thus giving it his official sanction.
8. The clerk of the court issued a *summons* to be served on Mr. Bell, whose presence was required as a material witness.
9. The case comes up before the *surrogate* soon.
10. His *tender* of $50 was not accepted because the amount due in the note is $75.
11. The intention of the *testator* was to give the amount to his nephew.
12. His grounds for suit was the *tort* of libel because of the newspaper article.
13. You are warned not to *trespass* on this property.
14. The bank has been appointed *trustee* for the children until they become of age.
15. The decision of the board of directors to enter the real estate business constituted an *ultra vires* act as being contrary to the constitution of the corporation.
16. The matter was finally settled by the drawing up of a *unilateral* contract, to be signed by the assignees.
17. The beggar was arrested on a charge of *vagrancy*.
18. The *vendor* of the property is now abroad.
19. The sheriff received the *venire* in ample time to summon the persons from whom the jurors were selected.
20. On the grounds of local prejudice, the defendant demanded a change of *venue*.
21. To the judge's question, "What is your *verdict?*" came the answer, "Not guilty."
22. The contract was *voidable* on the ground that no consideration had been agreed upon.
23. Without a search *warrant*, even an officer of the law cannot enter the premises of another.

LESSON 75

Office Supplies and Equipment Terms

1. **Addressograph** — A machine that prints names and addresses from metal plates.
2. **adhesive** — A sticky, tenacious substance for cementing or sticking materials together.
3. **alphabetic** — Pertaining to, or in the order of, the letters of the alphabet.
4. **billhead** — A printed form used for making out bills or accounts of charges.
5. **binder** — A set of durable covers for loose-leaf records.
6. **Bristol board** — Paper made stiff and given a special surface, glazed or unglazed; cardboard.
7. **calculator** — A machine or set of tables for facilitating computations.
8. **cardboard** — A stiff pasteboard for making cards, etc.
9. **catalogue** — An extensive printed enumeration and description of products, usually illustrated.
10. **collapsible** — Capable of being flattened or reduced to a more compact form.
11. **Comptometer** — The trade name of a calculating machine.
12. **copyholder** — A device for holding copy.
13. **costumer** — A piece of furniture having pegs or hooks around the top for holding hats and coats.
14. **crayon** — A drawing or writing implement made in various colors of clay, chalk, or other material.
15. **deckle edge** — The rough, untrimmed edge of a paper sheet as it comes from the papermaking machine.
16. **duplicator** — A device for making copies, as of typewriting.
17. **eradicator** — A preparation, usually a fluid, that erases or wipes out ink or stains.
18. **eyelet** — A small metal ring used for strengthening the holes punched into papers for binding such papers.
19. **fastener** — A device for attaching or stapling papers.
20. **file** — A folder or cabinet in which papers are preserved.
21. **glue** — A brownish gelatin used for adhesive purposes.
22. **hectograph** — A duplicator that uses a gelatin pad for reproducing the original copy.
23. **indelible** — That cannot be removed, blotted out, or effaced.
24. **label** — A slip to be attached to an object to give certain descriptive details and information.
25. **letterhead** — Letter paper having a printed or engraved heading.

WORDS USED IN SENTENCES

1. Our *Addressograph* operator can easily address all these envelopes tomorrow morning.
2. The package was neatly and securely fastened with *adhesive* tape.
3. Please arrange these names in *alphabetic* order.
4. Our new telephone number is to be placed on our *billheads*.
5. I need a three-ring *binder* that will hold 200 sheets and an index.
6. Use a high-quality *Bristol board*.
7. We have ordered a *calculator* for the use of our cost clerk.
8. This *cardboard* is obtainable in several colors.
9. The prices in this *catalogue* are net.
10. *Collapsible* corrugated files are often used as transfer files.
11. The *Comptometer* is operated by the touch method.
12. *Copyholders* are indispensable in billing, report, statistical, and payroll work.
13. There is a *costumer* in the office of each executive.
14. As you weigh each of these cartons, mark the weight plainly in black *crayon*.
15. We will feature a special sale on monogrammed *deckle-edged* stationery before Christmas.
16. Please run off a hundred copies of this notice on the *duplicator*.
17. A one-fluid ink *eradicator* is most convenient.
18. These *eyelets* come in three sizes—short, medium, and long.
19. Our paper *fasteners* are made from drawn-steel wire, carefully plated.
20. A subject *file* is of great help to a research student.
21. The shipping department uses large quantities of *glue*.
22. By reproducing this sheet on the *hectograph*, you can include the drawings.
23. Be sure to use an *indelible* pencil in obtaining the signatures.
24. The box bore a "Fragile" *label*.
25. What an attractive *letterhead* the company has!

LESSON 76

Office Supplies and Equipment Terms (*Continued*)

1. manifold paper — A lightweight paper, used in producing multiple copies.
2. Manila paper — A brown, durable wrapping paper made from Manila hemp, native to the Philippine Islands.
3. memorandum — An informal written record of some fact or agreement.
4. Mimeograph — A stencil device for duplicating letters, forms, etc.
5. mucilage (mū′sĭ lĭj) — A solution of gum used as an adhesive on envelopes, etc.—less strong than glue.
6. Multigraph — A machine that prints copy resembling typewritten copy.
7. onionskin — A thin, translucent paper with a glossy finish.
8. parchment — Sheepskin, goatskin, etc., dressed and prepared for writing purposes; today, often any of various fine writing papers in imitation of the original.
9. perforation — A hole made by boring or punching.
10. photostat — A trade-marked device for making photographic copies.
11. portfolio — A portable case for holding loose papers.
12. post binder — A loose-leaf covering device fitted with metal posts that pass through holes punched into the sheets that are to be placed in the binder.
13. precancel — To cancel postage stamps in advance of use.
14. pushpin — A steel-pointed tack, with a glass or metal head.
15. quadrille ruled — Designating a style of horizontal and vertical ruling that intersects uniformly to form squares.
16. quire — Unit of measure for paper—twenty-four (sometimes twenty-five) sheets of paper of the same size and quality.
17. ream — A quantity of paper, usually twenty quires (480 sheets).
18. requisition — A formal application made by one officer or department to another for things needed in business.
19. sealing wax — A resinous composition, plastic when warm, used to seal letters and documents.
20. stapler — A device for fastening papers together.
21. stencil — A piece of material capable of being perforated so that desired patterns or writing can be reproduced.
22. stylus (stī′lŭs) — A sharp-pointed instrument for writing—commonly, for making impressions on stencils.
23. T square — A ruler having a crosspiece at one end, used in making parallel lines.
24. thumbtack — A short, steel point with a broad, flat head for pressing, with the thumb, into a board.

WORDS USED IN SENTENCES

1. This grade of *manifold paper* will make as many as twelve clear carbon copies.
2. This is the heaviest weight of *Manila paper* manufactured.
3. Enclosed is a *memorandum* just received from our cashier.
4. This *Mimeograph* stencil should be cut immediately.
5. Our *mucilage* is guaranteed to stick wherever used.
6. Our *Multigraph* operator has several important advertising letters to run off.
7. *Onionskin* is often used when several carbon copies are desired.
8. The resolutions were engrossed on *parchment*.
9. Each sheet in the pad has a *perforation* at the left.
10. The library will make *photostats* of any pages in the book.
11. Artists use *portfolios* for carrying their sketches.
12. In ordering a new *post binder*, specify that it be bound in corduroy and have leather corners.
13. The use of *precanceled* stamps saves much time in the mailing department.
14. On this map, the gilt-headed *pushpins* indicate the cities and towns using our product.
15. We suggest that you use *quadrille-ruled* paper in preparing these graphs.
16. For a limited time only, this stationery is selling for 50 cents a *quire*.
17. We cannot estimate how many *reams* of paper we shall need until we figure approximately our next year's production of notebooks.
18. The accounting department has sent in a *requisition* for six-column work paper.
19. *Sealing wax* is so called because in medieval times it was made of bees' wax.
20. On this *stapler*, a slight pressure of the palm is sufficient to fasten forty sheets of paper.
21. This *stencil* is guaranteed to give clear reproductions and long runs.
22. The *stylus* that belongs with this duplicating set is worn out.
23. The *T square* is a fundamental piece of equipment for the mechanical draftsman.
24. These solid-head *thumbtacks* come in six sizes.

LESSON 77

Real Estate Terms

1. **abstract of title** — A summary showing the history of the ownership of a piece of real estate and any claims or charges against it.
2. **appraisal** — An expert's opinion of the value of real property.
3. **assessed valuation** — The appraisal of real estate for taxation purposes.
4. **assessment** — A charge against real estate for a municipal improvement.
5. **building and loan association** — An organization in which savings of members are lent to finance the purchase and building of houses.
6. **conveyance** — The act of transferring real property to another.
7. **dower** (dou′ẽr) — The interest that the law gives a widow in the realty of her deceased husband.
8. **ejectment** — Removal, under the direction of a court, of an occupant of real estate.
9. **encumbrance** — A claim, lien, or other factor that in some respect qualifies the absolute ownership of real estate.
10. **foreclosure** — A legal proceeding to compel the sale of real estate to satisfy a financial claim against it.
11. **frontage** — The length (or part) of a boundary line on a street.
12. **installation** — The setting up for use or service, as of a heating plant.
13. **lease** — An agreement for the use and occupancy of real estate for a definite consideration (known as "rent") for a definite term.
14. **lessee** — A tenant under a lease.
15. **lessor** — One who rents property to another.
16. **metes and bounds** — The boundary lines of a piece of property.
17. **mortgage** (môr′gĭj) — The conditional conveyance of property as security for the payment of a debt.
18. **mortgagee** — The holder of a mortgage.
19. **mortgagor** — The person who gives a mortgage.
20. **occupancy** — The dwelling in or taking possession of real estate; also, the time during which the property is occupied.
21. **premises** — A distinct portion or parcel of real estate.
22. **realty** — Landed property as distinguished from personal property.
23. **suburban** — Pertaining to, or living in, the outlying districts of a city or town.
24. **tenant** — An occupant of lands or buildings of another.

WORDS USED IN SENTENCES

1. The *abstract of title* disclosed a mortgage on the property.
2. The City Council has recently ordered an *appraisal* of the properties owned by the city.
3. The records showed the *assessed valuation* of the property to be $15,000.
4. The projected street improvement will mean a heavy *assessment* on the property owners.
5. By becoming a member of a *building and loan association*, Mr. Gray has been able to finance the purchase of a house and lot.
6. By a *conveyance* from his father, the young man became an owner of a large fruit farm.
7. In addition to her *dower*, Mrs. Henry received a bequest of $50,000.
8. The tenant's conduct is suitable grounds for *ejectment*.
9. The premises are free from all *encumbrances*.
10. Interest on the mortgage is so much in arrears that *foreclosure* seems inevitable.
11. The corner lot has a 40-foot *frontage* on Main Street and 100 feet on Broadway.
12. The *installation* of an air-conditioning system has increased the value of the property.
13. Read the terms of your *lease* carefully and keep a copy for your files.
14. The *lessee* must be responsible for repairs not caused by ordinary wear and tear.
15. Mr. Ames, the *lessor* of the house you rented, owns the entire block.
16. The description, by *metes and bounds*, shows that there are $5\frac{1}{4}$ acres in the property.
17. The holder of the first *mortgage* has greater protection than the holder of the second.
18. The *mortgagee* had the title to the property carefully investigated.
19. The *mortgagor* will pay the indebtedness provided by the mortgage terms.
20. The building will be ready for *occupancy* on October 1.
21. No loitering on these *premises!*
22. Many persons consider *realty* a particularly sound investment during an inflation period.
23. *Suburban* trains leave from the lower level of the Grand Central Terminal in New York.
24. The *tenant* of the third-floor apartment has renewed his lease for another year.

LESSON 78

Transportation and Shipping Terms

1.	air brake	A device or apparatus for stopping a vehicle or train by means of compressed air.
2.	ballast	Heavy material put in the hold of a ship to steady it; broken stone, etc., placed under a railroad track for support.
3.	bill of lading (B/L)	A written acknowledgment of the receipt, by a railroad, a steamship company, or other carrier, of goods for transportation.
4.	block signal	A signal that regulates the movement of trains along a definitely limited length of track, called a "block."
5.	boatswain	An under officer on a ship, in charge of rigging, anchors, etc.
6.	breakage	An allowance made by a shipper for loss by the destruction of merchandise.
7.	bulkhead	A transverse partition in a vehicle or ship to divide the interior into sections.
8.	caboose	A car fitted for the use of a freight-train crew.
9.	captain	The commander of a vessel.
10.	carload	A load that fills a car (distinguished from less-than-carload).
11.	classification	Sorting of freight into groups by destination or rate.
12.	commissary	An officer in charge of food supply or equipment.
13.	common carrier	One who undertakes to carry persons or goods for hire, as a transportation company.
14.	commuter	A passenger who travels daily back and forth between a city and a suburban residence.
15.	consignee	The person to whom goods are shipped.
16.	day coach	An ordinary railroad passenger car.
17.	demurrage (dē mûr′ĭj)	The detention of a vessel or car beyond the allotted time; payment therefor.
18.	derailment	The act of leaving or running off the rails.
19.	drayage	A charge for cartage between stations or vessels by trucks.
20.	embargo	Prohibition of movement of goods or vessels.
21.	fathom (fath.)	A measure of 6 feet, used in measuring cordage or for sounding the depth of water.
22.	forecastle	Forward part of a vessel, where the crew lives.
23.	freight (frt.)	Goods transported; also payment therefor.
24.	gangplank	A portable bridge by which to board or leave a ship.
25.	interstate	Going between states, as a passenger or freight movement.

WORDS USED IN SENTENCES

1. Our entire fleet of motor trucks is equipped with *air brakes*.
2. The shifting of *ballast* during a voyage may imperil the vessel.
3. *Bills of lading* are usually issued in triplicate.
4. The adoption of *block signals* has cut down the number of train wrecks tremendously.
5. The *boatswain's* whistle was a signal to lower the anchor.
6. Our annual *breakage* expense is less than 1 per cent a year.
7. The closing of the *bulkhead* prevented the spread of the fire that occurred in the ship's hold.
8. Before attempting passage over the flooded tracks, the engineer and trainmen held a conference in the *caboose*.
9. The *captain* sailed under sealed orders.
10. The purchasing agent has ordered a *carload* of paper for the forthcoming publications.
11. For purposes of establishing freight rates, the United States is divided into towns of three *classifications*—official, western, and southern.
12. The *commissary* has removed several items from the order list on the ground of extravagance.
13. A *common carrier* may demand payment in advance.
14. The *commuter* missed his regular train.
15. Who was the *consignee* on that last order for castings?
16. The modern air-conditioned *day coaches* make traveling a pleasure.
17. If you do not call for the goods at our freight depot before Friday, you must pay *demurrage*.
18. The *derailment* was caused by an open switch.
19. *Drayage* in your city is at your own expense.
20. Because of the Japanese beetle, there is an *embargo* on shipments of flowers and plants from this state.
21. The harbor was plumbed to the depth of 20 *fathoms*.
22. Conditions in the *forecastle* were subjected to daily inspection.
23. The *freight* was heavily insured.
24. He will be served with a warrant the moment he steps from the *gangplank*.
25. *Interstate* transportation is regulated by the Federal Government.

LESSON 79

Transportation and Shipping Terms (*Continued*)

1. interurban — Connecting cities or towns, as electric railways or bus lines.
2. intrastate — Wholly within the boundaries of one state.
3. itinerary — A listing of routes to be taken or places to be visited on a journey.
4. jettison (jĕt′ĭ sŭn) — The act of throwing overboard of goods, especially to lighten the load of a vessel in danger of being wrecked.
5. locomotive — An engine used for hauling trains of cars.
6. longshoreman — A dock laborer.
7. maintenance — The work of keeping equipment in repair.
8. manifest — A document listing the cargo on board a ship.
9. passport — A document permitting a person to enter a country or port.
10. Pullman — A sleeping car or parlor car, specifically one owned by the Pullman Company.
11. refrigerator car — A freight car equipped with cooling apparatus and used for transportation of perishable foods, etc.
12. right of way — The land over which the tracks of a railroad are laid or a road or highway is built; also, the right of precedence in passing another in traffic.
13. roadbed — Prepared ground on which a railroad or highway is built.
14. route (root) — A course to be followed, as in dispatching freight or passengers.
15. steerage (stēr′ĭj) — Part of a passenger vessel for which the lowest fare is charged; third class.
16. stevedore (stē′vĕ dōr′) — One who contracts or undertakes to load or unload a vessel.
17. steward (stū′ẽrd) — An employee on a ship who waits on table or attends staterooms.
18. stopover — A break in a journey; permission for such a break.
19. terminal — The end of a transportation line, usually having special facilities; terminus.
20. timetable — A tabulated statement of the time of departure and of arrival, as of trains, busses, etc.
21. trainman — A subordinate employee on a train; a brakeman.
22. via — By way of.
23. waybill (W.B. or W/B) — A statement of the contents of a consignment and shipping directions.
24. wharfage (hwôr′fĭj) — The fee for using a wharf or pier.

WORDS USED IN SENTENCES

1. That company operates a network of *interurban* bus lines.
2. Because distribution was wholly *intrastate*, Interstate Commerce Commission regulations did not apply.
3. Mr. Anderson's *itinerary* requires stopping first in Topeka, Kansas.
4. When *jettison* is necessary, the owners of the goods have certain reimbursement rights.
5. The development of the streamlined *locomotive* has made it possible to save a great deal of time.
6. The *longshoremen's* strike has tied up the steamship piers.
7. Their *maintenance* crew is far from adequate.
8. This *manifest* must be presented at the customhouse.
9. The retouching of photographs to be used for *passport* purposes is not permissible.
10. The observation car is open to anyone holding a *Pullman* ticket.
11. The modern *refrigerator car* has made possible the shipment of many seasonal foods formerly considered luxuries.
12. You are hereby informed that your trucks are daily encroaching on our *right of way*.
13. From the jostling I received during the night, I judge the *roadbed* needs rebuilding.
14. Do you plan to take the northern or the southern *route?*
15. Many of our country's most eminent men came here in the *steerage*.
16. *Stevedores* contracted with the various steamship companies for the unloading of their vessels.
17. The *steward* answered our call very promptly.
18. Please arrange a *stopover* in Chicago for me.
19. The New York Central's passenger *terminal* in New York City is the Grand Central Station.
20. Do you wish a full or a condensed *timetable?*
21. The *trainman* failed to remind me of the change of time.
22. Please ship *via* Union Pacific.
23. The *waybill* did not indicate that the contents were fragile.
24. The bookkeeper opened a special ledger account to record the amounts paid out for *wharfage*.

LESSON 80

Abbreviations Used in Business [1]

A 1	First class	f. o. b., FOB	Free on board
adv., advt.	Advertisement	frt., fgt.	Freight
Afft.	Affidavit	fwd.	Forward
amt.	Amount	h. p.	Horsepower
approx.	Approximately	I. B.	Invoice book
assn., assoc.	Association	I. C. C.	Interstate Commerce Commission
att., atty.	Attorney		
av., avg.	Average		
B/—	Bag, bale	int.	Interest, internal, interior, international
bbl.	Barrel		
bldg.	Building		
B/P, B. pay.	Bills payable	inv.	Invoice
B/R, B. rec.	Bills receivable	l. c. l.	Less than carload lot
B/S	Bill of sale		
C/B	Cashbook	l. f.	Ledger folio
ctf.	Certificate	ltd.	Limited
cf.	Compare	mdse.	Merchandise
chgd.	Charged	memo.	Memorandum
c. i. f.	Cost, insurance, freight	mfg.	Manufacturing
		misc.	Miscellaneous
c/o	Care of	N. P.	Notary Public
com.	Commerce	O. D.	Overdraft
con.	Consolidated	orig.	Original
C. P. A.	Certified Public Accountant	P/L, P&L	Profit and loss
		prin.	Principal
ctge.	Cartage	reg.	Registered
cwt.	Hundredweight	rev. a/c	Revenue account
ea.	Each	S. D. B. L.	Sight draft, bill of lading attached
Enc.	Enclosure		
ex div.	Ex dividend	shpt.	Shipment
ff.	And following pages	T/B	Trial balance
		W. R.	Warehouse receipt

[1] These abbreviations are in addition to those given in connection with the business terms, Lessons 54–79. They conform to business usage and are those that the stenographer or clerk is called on to use most frequently.

PART VI

Words Used in Special Businesses and Industries

Like the menu of a large, well-patronized restaurant, Part VI offers a great variety of dishes (of words) from which you may choose. It is not expected that any diner in a restaurant will order *all* dishes listed on the menu; neither is it expected that you will study *all* the lessons in this part.

If you are fortunate enough to be preparing for a definite position, or for some particular business or industry, confine yourself to the lessons dealing with the terms used in that business or industry. (Do not overlook the references to lessons on allied businesses or industries given in the footnotes.)

After you have mastered the words in the lessons you have studied, further prepare yourself for the vocabulary you will encounter by supplementary reading in technical and trade magazines and books to be found in any public library, making lists of words as suggested on page 95.

If you are not fortunate enough to have a definite position under consideration, then select the lessons that interest you most and pursue a similar course of study.

Always and systematically keep reviewing the general business terms in Part V.

Your study of words will not end with the last lesson in this text. In fact, it will never end, for it is limitless—and therefore unequaled in attention-holding value.

LESSON 81

Agricultural Terms [1]

1. acreage — ā′kēr ĭj — Acres collectively.
2. alluvial — ă lū′vĭ ăl — Relating to soil deposits made by flowing water.
3. brooder — brōōd′ẽr — A heated enclosure for chicks hatched in incubators.
4. citrus — sĭt′rŭs — Pertaining to fruits containing citric acid, as oranges, lemons, etc.
5. creamery — krēm′ēr ĭ — An establishment where dairy products are made or sold.
6. fallow — făl′ō — Untilled or unsowed land.
7. fertilizer — fûr′tĭ līz′ẽr — Any material put in or on the ground to enrich it.
8. fleece — flēs — The coat of wool that covers sheep.
9. fodder — fŏd′ẽr — Coarse feed for horses, cattle, etc.—especially, cornstalks.
10. forage — fŏr′ĭj — Vegetable food for animals; to gather food.
11. forestry — fŏr′ĕst rĭ — The science and art of developing or managing forests.
12. fowl — foul — Commonly, the domestic cock or hen, especially when considered as an article of food.
13. fungicide — fŭn′jĭ sīd — Any substance that destroys fungi.
14. furrow — fŭr′ō — A trench made in the ground by a plow.
15. ginning — jĭn′ĭng — Separating cotton fibers from the seeds by using a machine called a "gin."
16. grafting — grȧf′tĭng — The process of inserting buds or scions taken from one plant within the bark of another, effecting a permanent union.
17. granary — grăn′ȧ rĭ — A storehouse for grain.
18. grazing — grāz′ĭng — Feeding on growing herbage; browsing.
19. greenhouse — grēn′hous′ — A glass house artificially heated for growing tender plants.
20. harrow — hăr′ō — A cultivating implement for pulverizing and smoothing the soil.
21. hedge — hĕj — A thicket, especially when planted as a fence.
22. horticulture — hôr′tĭ kŭl′tūr — The art of growing fruits, vegetables, and other plants.

---

[1] See also "Grocery Terms," pages 189–191.

23. huckster	hŭk′stẽr	A peddler of small articles, provisions, and the like.
24. incubator	ĭn′kû bā′tẽr	An apparatus for hatching eggs artificially.
25. insecticide	ĭn sĕk′tĭ sīd	A poisonous preparation for destroying insects.
26. irrigation	ĭr′ĭ gā′shŭn	Artificial watering of farm land by canals, ditches, flooding, etc.
27. legume	lĕg′ūm	Any plant of the bean family.
28. maize	māz	Indian corn.
29. meadow	mĕd′ō	A tract of low, level land producing grass for hay.
30. motor plow	mō′tẽr plou	A motorized implement for turning up the earth to prepare it for sowing.
31. orchard	ôr′chẽrd	A field containing fruit trees.
32. pasture	pȧs′tů̄r	Grassland for grazing.
33. planter	plăn′tẽr	One who owns or cultivates a plantation; also, a planting machine.
34. plowshare	plou′shâr′	The blade of a plow.
35. poultry	pōl′trĭ	Domestic fowl reared for the table.
36. prairie	prâr′ĭ	A level or rolling tract of treeless land covered with coarse grass.
37. reaper	rēp′ẽr	A man or a machine that gathers a harvest by cutting.
38. rotation	rō tā′shŭn	Change by alteration; order of sequence.
39. scythe	sīth	A long-handled implement for cutting grass.
40. seepage	sēp′ĭj	Slow percolation of a fluid through porous soil.
41. separator	sĕp′ȧ rā′tẽr	A device for separating cream from milk.
42. sheaves	shēvz	Stalks of cut grain laid lengthwise and bound into bundles.
43. silage	sī′lĭj	Fodder, grain, or other food for winter use, cut, compressed, and preserved in an airtight chamber called a "silo."
44. spading	spād′ĭng	Digging with a spade.
45. stubble	stŭb′'l	The stubs of grain stalks covering a field after a crop has been cut.
46. stumpy	stŭmp′ĭ	Abounding in stumps.
47. thresher	thrĕsh′ẽr	A machine for separating grain from its stalks.
48. tractor	trăk′tẽr	An automotive vehicle used to draw a plow or other implement.
49. truck farm	trŭk färm	A farm on which vegetables are raised for the market.
50. vehicle	vē′ĭ k'l	Any kind of conveyance.

LESSON 82

Architectural and Building Terms [1]

1. aisle	īl	A passageway, as in a church, theater, or other audience room.
2. arcade	är kād′	A series of arches; a long, arched building; an arched or covered way or avenue, as between rows of shops.
3. asphalt	ăs′fôlt	Black mineral pitch used for waterproofing, paving, and roofing.
4. balcony	băl′kŏ nĭ	A platform projecting from the side of a house, usually enclosed with a balustrade, and more or less embellished; also, a projecting gallery in an auditorium.
5. balustrade	băl′ŭs trād′	A handrail supported by balusters (small pillars).
6. bas-relief	bä′rĕ lēf′	Sculpture in which the figure projects slightly from the background.
7. blueprint	bloō′prĭnt′	A photographic contact print, white on a bright-blue ground, used for copying architectural plans.
8. bonding	bŏn′dĭng	The act of laying brick so that each course will strengthen the one below it and assist in binding the wall together.
9. buttress	bŭt′rĕs	A projecting support that adds to the strength of a wall.
10. calcimine	kăl′sĭ mīn	A white or tinted wash for plaster walls, etc.
11. canopy	kăn′ŏ pĭ	An ornamental roof above a niche, statue, or door.
12. cantilever	kăn′tĭ lē′vēr	A beam that projects to form a support, and extends back far enough over its own support to carry its load safely.
13. casement	kās′měnt	A window sash that opens on hinges affixed to the upright side of the frame.
14. clapboard	klăp′bōrd	Narrow, beveled boarding used as outside covering of frame buildings.

[1] See also "Civil Engineering Terms," pages 164–167; "Hardware and Cutlery Terms," pages 191–194; "Machinery Terms," pages 197–199.

15.	column	kŏl′ŭm	A support for roofs, ceilings, etc.—composed of base, shaft, and capital—and generally cylindrical in section.
16.	cornice	kôr′nĭs	The horizontal projecting moldings at the top of a building or of a room.
17.	façade	fȧ säd′	Front view, or elevation, of an edifice.
18.	finial	fĭn′ĭ ăl	An ornament that forms the finish for the top of a tower or the point of a pitched roof; hence, any crowning ornamental architectural detail.
19.	flue	floo	Any channel or passage in a chimney for smoke or gases.
20.	gable	gā′b'l	The vertical triangular end of a building from the eaves to the apex of the roof.
21.	gargoyle	gär′goil	A projecting stone spout, grotesquely carved.
22.	Gothic	gŏth′ĭk	A style of architecture with high pointed arches, clustered columns, etc. Used extensively for churches.
23.	grille	grĭl	A grating or ornamental screen of wood or metal.
24.	jamb	jăm	Side post or trim of a doorway, window, etc.
25.	joists	joists	Horizontal timbers supporting a floor or ceiling.
26.	keystone	kē′stōn′	The uppermost and last-set stone of an arch, which completes the arch and locks its members together.
27.	lacquer	lăk′ẽr	To coat or varnish with a shellac.
28.	lattice	lăt′ĭs	Openwork of metal or wood, formed by crossing or interlacing bars or strips.
29.	lintel	lĭn′tĕl	Horizontal supporting piece above a door or window opening.
30.	macadamize	măk ăd′ăm īz	To pave a roadway with small broken stones.
31.	mansard	măn′särd	A roof with a double pitch on all sides.
32.	mantel	măn′t'l	The facing about a fireplace, including the shelf above it.
33.	masonry	mā′s'n rĭ	The art or work of building with brick or stone.

34.	mortar	môr′tẽr	Masonry bonding material of lime or cement, sand, and water.
35.	mortise	môr′tĭs	A hole to receive a correspondingly shaped piece called a tenon; to fasten by means of mortise and tenon.
36.	mosaic	mṓ zā′ĭk	Inlaid decoration composed of bits of stone, glass, etc., forming a pattern or design.
37.	mullion	mŭl′yŭn	The construction between the openings of a window frame made to accommodate two or more windows.
38.	mural	mū′răl	Pertaining to a wall; a wall painting.
39.	newel	nū′ĕl	The principal post at the foot of a staircase; also the central support of a winding flight of stairs.
40.	niche	nĭch	A recessed space or hollow; specifically, a recess in a wall.
41.	panel	păn′ĕl	A rectangular piece set into a frame, as in a door or wall.
42.	partition	pär tĭsh′ŭn	A wall or other barrier dividing one part from another.
43.	patio	pä′tĭ ō	The open inner court of a Spanish-style dwelling.
44.	pavilion	pȧ vĭl′yŭn	A structure not fully enclosed with walls.
45.	plastering	plȧs′tẽr ĭng	A mixture of lime (or gypsum) and sand to cover lathing.
46.	portico	pōr′tĭ kō	A colonnade at the entrance of a building.
47.	proscenium	prṓ sē′nĭ ŭm	That part of a modern theater or similar building immediately in front of the curtain.
48.	rotunda	rṓ tŭn′dȧ	A circular building or interior hall surmounted by a dome.
49.	specifications	spĕs′ĭ fĭ kā′shŭnz	The written instructions supplementing an architect's working drawings.
50.	stucco	stŭk′ō	Exterior plaster work of Portland cement, lime, and sand.

LESSON 83

Automobile Terms [1]

1. accelerator — ăk sĕl'ẽr ā'tẽr — A pedal-actuated throttle valve for regulating the speed of the engine and of the automobile.
2. assembly — ă sĕm'blĭ — A set of parts that, together, form one unit of a machine; as, a hub assembly.
3. axle — ăk's'l — A transverse bar extending through the hubs of road wheels on opposite sides of a vehicle.
4. bearing — bâr'ĭng — A support for a shaft, which can turn freely therein.
5. bore — bōr — The inside diameter of a cylindrical hole.
6. bushing — boŏsh'ĭng — A lining inserted in a cylindrical hole; as, the bore of a bearing.
7. cam — kăm — A part usually attached to a rotating shaft in such a way that at intervals it will engage and move some other part.
8. camber — kăm'bẽr — An arrangement of the axle of a wheel so that the spindles are slightly inclined toward each other.
9. carburetor — kär'bŭ rĕt'ẽr — A device that forms a combustible mixture of vapor.
10. casing — kās'ĭng — The outer covering of a pneumatic tire.
11. choke — chōk — A throttle valve in the air inlet to a carburetor.
12. clutch — klŭch — A mechanism used to couple the engine to the driving gear of the car.
13. compression ratio — kŏm prĕsh'ŭn rā'shō — The ratio of the sum of the total volume displaced by a piston while moving one full stroke, and the volume of the clearance space, to the volume of the clearance space.
14. connecting rod — kŏ nĕk'tĭng rŏd — A link connecting the piston with the crankshaft.
15. cowl — koul — Portion of an automobile body to which the windshield and instrument board are attached.
16. crankcase — krăngk'kās' — A metal housing, enclosing the crankshaft and containing the bearings.
17. crankpin — krăngk'pĭn' — A pin that forms the connecting member between the piston and the connecting rod.

---

[1] See also "Electrical and Radio Terms," pages 171–177.

18.	crankshaft	krăngk′shȧft′	A shaft to which connecting rods are attached and that serves to convert linear piston motion into rotary motion.
19.	cylinder	sĭl′ĭn dẽr	The engine chamber in which the piston moves.
20.	cylinder block	sĭl′ĭn dẽr blŏk	That part of the engine comprising the cylinders.
21.	cylinder head	sĭl′ĭn dẽr hĕd	That part of the engine covering the cylinders.
22.	differential	dĭf′ẽr ĕn′shăl	A mechanism that transmits power to wheels on opposite sides of a vehicle, thus permitting one wheel to turn faster than the other while the automobile is moving in a curve.
23.	distributor	dĭs trĭb′ů tẽr	A device connecting the spark coil in turn to spark plugs in the different cylinders of an engine.
24.	exhaust	ĕg zôst′	Gases of combustion escaping from the cylinders of an engine.
25.	flywheel	flī′hwēl′	A wheel mounted on an engine crankshaft and intended to keep down fluctuations in engine speed.
26.	freewheeling	frē′hwēl′ĭng	Motion forward of an automobile under such conditions that it is neither driven by the engine nor retarded by it.
27.	gasket	găs′kĕt	A piece of material inserted between adjacent metallic surfaces to effect a sealed joint.
28.	generator	jĕn′ẽr ā′tẽr	A machine that produces electric current.
29.	governor	gŭv′ẽr nẽr	A device for limiting speed to a predetermined maximum.
30.	horsepower	hôrs′pou′ẽr	A unit of measurement equivalent to the power required to lift 33,000 pounds at the rate of 1 foot a minute.
31.	housing	houz′ĭng	A covering or enclosure for working parts.
32.	ignition	ĭg nĭsh′ŭn	The general term for the component parts of the electrical system used to explode the fuel charge in the engine combustion chamber.
33.	magneto	măg nē′tō	A machine that generates electrical energy for ignition purposes and whose magnetic field is due to permanent magnets.

34.	manifold	măn′ĭ fōld	A pipe with two or more outlets through which water or gases are conducted into or out of the engine.
35.	muffler	mŭf′lẽr	A chamber through which exhaust gases are passed to diminish the noise accompanying their release.
36.	packing	păk′ĭng	Compressible material inserted between adjoining parts to provide a seal.
37.	piston	pĭs′tŭn	A member adapted to move back and forth in a cylinder.
38.	piston ring	pĭs′tŭn rĭng	A flexible split packing ring fitted in a groove on the outside of the piston to effect a gastight seal between the cylinder and piston.
39.	propeller shaft	prŏ pĕl′ẽr shȧft	A shaft that transmits power from the transmission to the rear axle.
40.	radiator	rā′dĭ ā′tẽr	A nest of pipes for cooling circulating water.
41.	safety glass	sāf′tĭ glȧs	Glass made with an inner layer of plastic material that prevents the glass from splintering.
42.	shim	shĭm	A piece of metal or other suitable material used to make small adjustments between surfaces.
43.	stroke	strōk	Total distance traveled in one direction by the piston in the engine cylinder.
44.	supercharger	sū′pẽr chär′jẽr	A device that permits more air to be supplied to an engine cylinder than can be drawn in by the pumping action of the piston.
45.	thermostat	thûr′mŏ stăt	A temperature-regulating device.
46.	throttle	thrŏt′′l	A valve by means of which the inlet passage of the engine can be controlled.
47.	toe-in	tō′ĭn′	An adjustment of the front wheels of an automobile so as to bring them closer together at the front than at the back.
48.	transmission	trăns mĭsh′ŭn	A set of gears through which engine power is transmitted to the drive axle.
49.	tread	trĕd	The distance between the center points of ground contact of wheels on opposite sides.
50.	worm	wûrm	A type of gear that operates on the principle of the screw.

LESSON 84

Aviation Terms

1. **aerodynamics** ā′ēr ŏ dī năm′ĭks — The branch of science that treats of the motion of air and other gaseous fluids and of the forces acting on solids in motion through such fluids.

2. **aeronautics** ā′ēr ŏ nô′tĭks — The science and art of traveling in the air.

3. **aerostat** ā′ēr ŏ stăt′ — A general term for an aircraft whose support is chiefly due to buoyancy derived from containers filled with a gas that is lighter than air.

4. **aileron** ā′lēr ŏn — A hinged or movable portion of an airplane wing, the primary function of which is to control lateral or rolling motion of an airplane.

5. **aircraft** âr′kråft′ — Any weight-carrying device designed to be supported by the air.

6. **airfoil** âr′foil′ — Any surface, such as an airplane wing, aileron, or rudder, designed to obtain reaction from the air through which it moves.

7. **altimeter** ăl tĭm′ĕ tēr — An instrument that measures the elevation of an aircraft above a given plane, usually sea level.

8. **amphibian** ăm fĭb′ĭ ăn — An airplane designed to rise from and alight on either land or water.

9. **autogiro** ô′tŏ jī′rō — A type of motor plane whose support in the air is chiefly derived from airfoils rotated about an approximately vertical axis by aerodynamic forces.

10. **bank** băngk — To incline an airplane laterally; that is, to rotate it about its longitudinal axis.

11. **biplane** bī′plān′ — An airplane with two main supporting surfaces placed one above the other.

158

12. blimp	blĭmp	A colloquial term for a nonrigid airship.
13. catapult	kăt′ȧ pŭlt	A device by which an airplane can be launched at flying speed.
14. ceiling	sēl′ĭng	Height above the ground of the lowest level of a bank of clouds.
15. cockpit	kŏk′pĭt′	An open space in an airplane for the accommodation of pilots or passengers.
16. control column	kŏn trōl′ kŏl′ŭm	A lever for operating the longitudinal and lateral control surfaces of an airplane.
17. control stick	kŏn trōl′ stĭk	The vertical lever by means of which the longitudinal and lateral control surfaces of an airplane are operated.
18. dirigible	dĭr′ĭ jĭ b'l	An airship.
19. elevator	ĕl′ė vā′tēr	A movable auxiliary airfoil, the function of which is to control pitching motions on an aircraft.
20. fairing	fâr′ĭng	An auxiliary member or structure designed to reduce the drag of the part to which it is fitted.
21. float	flōt	A completely enclosed watertight structure attached to an aircraft to give it buoyancy and stability when in contact with water.
22. fuselage	fū′zĕ lĭj	The body to which the wings and tail unit of an airplane are attached.
23. glide	glīd	To descend at a normal angle of attack with little or no power from the propeller.
24. glider	glīd′ēr	An aircraft heavier than air, similar to an airplane but without an engine.
25. ground loop	ground lo͞op	An uncontrollable violent turn of an airplane while taxiing, or during the landing or take-off run.
26. gyroscope	jī′rŏ skōp	A steering apparatus or balancing device dependent on centrifugal force.
27. hangar	hăng′ēr	A shelter for housing airplanes.

28. helicopter	hĕl′ĭ kŏp′tēr	A type of rotor plane whose support in the air is normally derived from airfoils mechanically rotated about an approximately vertical axis.
29. instrument flying	ĭn′strōō mĕnt flī′ĭng	The art of controlling an aircraft solely by the use of instruments; sometimes called "blind flying."
30. landing gear	lănd′ĭng gēr	The understructure that supports the weight of an aircraft.
31. landplane	lănd′plān′	An airplane designed to rise from and alight on the land.
32. longeron	lôN′zhă′rôN′	A principal longitudinal member of the framing of an airplane fuselage or nacelle.
33. loop	lōōp	A maneuver executed in such a manner that the airplane follows a closed curve approximately in a vertical plane.
34. maneuverability	mȧ nōō′vēr ȧ bĭl′ĭ tĭ	That quality in an aircraft that determines the rate at which its altitude and direction of flight can be changed.
35. monoplane	mŏn′ō plān	An airplane with but one main supporting surface.
36. multiplane	mŭl′tĭ plān′	An airplane with two or more main supporting surfaces placed one above the other.
37. nacelle	nȧ sĕl′	An enclosed shelter for personnel or for a power plant. A nacelle is usually shorter than a fuselage, and does not carry the tail unit.
38. parachute	păr′ȧ shōōt	An umbrellalike device used to retard the descent of a falling body by offering resistance to its motion through the air.
39. propeller	prō pĕl′ēr	Any device for driving a craft through water or air.
40. rudder	rŭd′ēr	A hinged or movable auxiliary airfoil on an aircraft for controlling "right" or "left" motions of an aircraft.
41. runway	rŭn′wā′	An artificial landing strip permitting the landing and take-off of airplanes under all weather conditions.

42.	seaplane	sē′plān′	An airplane designed to rise from and alight on the water.
43.	sesquiplane	sĕs′kwĭ plān′	A form of biplane in which the area of one wing is less than half the area of the other.
44.	soar	sōr	To fly without engine power and without loss of altitude, as does a glider in ascending air currents.
45.	stabilizer	stā′bĭ līz′ẽr	Any airfoil intended to increase the stability of an aircraft.
46.	tachometer	tå kŏm′ê tẽr	An instrument that measures in revolutions a minute the rate at which the crankshaft of an engine turns.
47.	taxi	tăk′sĭ	To operate an airplane under its own power.
48.	visibility	vĭz′ĭ bĭl′ĭ tĭ	The greatest distance at which conspicuous objects can be seen and identified.
49.	wind tunnel	wĭnd tŭn′ĕl	An apparatus producing an artificial wind or air stream, in which objects are placed for investigating the air flow about them and the aerodynamic forces exerted on them.
50.	zoom	zōōm	To climb for a short time at an angle greater than the normal climbing angle, the airplane being carried upward by its own momentum.

LESSON 85

Chemical Terms [1]

1.	aldehyde	ăl′dē hīd	Any one of a class of organic products obtained by oxidizing an alcohol.
2.	alkali	ăl′kå lī	Any of a group of compounds that will neutralize acids to form salts; as soda ash, sodium and potassium hydroxides.

[1] See also "Medical and Drug Terms," pages 200–208; "Mining and Metallurgical Terms," pages 208–209.

3. amorphous   á môr′fŭs   That property designating a solid substance that does not crystallize; the opposite of crystalline.

4. atomic   ă tŏm′ĭk   Pertaining to atoms; very minute.

5. benzene   bĕn′zēn   A colorless, volatile, inflammable liquid used as a solvent.

6. calcium   kăl′sĭ ŭm   A white, metallic element that combines readily with other elements to give calcium salts.

7. carbohydrate   kär′bŏ hī′drāt   Any of a group of compounds that are found in plants and that contain carbon combined with hydrogen and oxygen.

8. carbon   kär′bŏn   A nonmetallic element found in all organic substances.

9. cellulose   sĕl′ủ lōs   A carbohydrate that is a constituent of the walls and skeletons of vegetable cells.

10. centigrade (C.)   sĕn′tĭ grād   Graduated into 100 equal parts called "degrees." On the centigrade thermometer, the freezing point of water is 0° and the boiling point is 100°.

11. chlorine   klō′rēn   A greenish-yellow, poisonous, gaseous element.

12. citrate   sĭt′rāt   A salt derived from the lemon or like fruits.

13. colloidal   kŏ loi′dăl   A state of subdivision of matter that consists either of single large molecules or of aggregations of smaller molecules.

14. crucible   kroō′sĭ b'l   A vessel for melting metals or minerals.

15. crystalline   krĭs′tăl ĭn   Of or pertaining to crystals or crystal.

16. dioxide   dī ŏk′sīd   A compound containing two atoms of oxygen in combination with a single atom of another element.

17. effervesce   ĕf′ẽr vĕs′   To give off bubbles of gas.

18. effloresce   ĕf′lŏ rĕs′   To lose moisture and become powdery on exposure to the air.

19. enzyme   ĕn′zīm   A compound of vegetable or animal origin that causes chemical action.

20. ester   ĕs′tẽr   Any organic salt.

21. ethylene   ĕth′ĭ lēn   A colorless gaseous compound contained in illuminating gas.

22. **Fahrenheit (F.)**	făr′ĕn hīt	A thermometer scale on which the freezing point of water is 32° and the boiling point is 212°.
23. **filtrate**	fĭl′trāt	The liquid that has passed through a filter.
24. **halogen**	hăl′ō jĕn	Any one of the elements—chlorine, bromine, iodine, or fluorine—all of which have similar chemical properties.
25. **helium**	hē′lĭ ŭm	A gaseous element found in the atmosphere and in certain minerals.
26. **homologous**	hō mŏl′ō gŭs	Having similar structure; identical in nature.
27. **hydrate**	hī′drāt	Any substance that contains water in chemical combination; for example, hydrate of lime.
28. **iodide**	ī′ō dīd	A compound consisting of iodine and another element.
29. **ionize**	ī′ŏn īz	To dissociate a substance into oppositely charged atoms.
30. **litmus**	lĭt′mŭs	A dyestuff that is turned red by acids and blue by alkalies.
31. **mercury**	mûr′kû rĭ	A silvery-white metallic element remaining liquid at ordinary temperatures.
32. **metallurgy**	mĕt′′l ûr′jĭ	The art or science of extracting metals from their ores.
33. **monoxide**	mŏn ŏk′sīd	A compound containing a single atom of oxygen in combination with a single atom of another element.
34. **mordant**	môr′dănt	Any substance used in combination with a dye to produce a fixed color on a fabric.
35. **nascent**	năs′ĕnt	Uncombined—applied to an element at the instant of being set free from a compound.
36. **nitrate**	nī′trāt	Any salt of nitric acid; for example, silver nitrate.
37. **nitrogen**	nī′trō jĕn	An odorless, colorless gaseous element that makes up about four-fifths of the air we breathe and is found in many chemical compounds.
38. **oxidation**	ŏk′sĭ dā′shŭn	Any chemical action in which oxygen unites with another substance.

39.	phosphate	fŏs'fāt	Any salt of phosphoric acid.
40.	polymerization	pŏl'ĭ mēr ĭ zā'shŭn	A reaction in which two or more molecules of the same substance combine to form a compound of higher molecular weight.
41.	potassium	pŏ tăs'ĭ ŭm	A bluish-white metallic element whose salts are widely distributed in nature.
42.	protein	prō'tē ĭn	A nitrogen-containing organic compound found in animal and vegetable matter.
43.	radioactivity	rā'dĭ ō ăk tĭv'ĭ tĭ	The property possessed by certain substances of spontaneous disintegration accompanied by emission of light rays.
44.	sodium	sō'dĭ ŭm	A bluish-white metallic element that readily forms salts, one of which is common baking soda.
45.	solvent	sŏl'vĕnt	A fluid capable of dissolving substances.
46.	specific gravity	spĕ sĭf'ĭk grăv'ĭ tĭ	The ratio of the weight of a substance to that of an equal volume of some standard substance.
47.	spectroscope	spĕk'trŏ skōp	An optical instrument for analyzing light rays, such as those obtained by burning various substances.
48.	sulphur	sŭl'fĕr	A nonmetallic element entering into many compounds, particularly with metals.
49.	vitriol	vĭt'rĭ ŭl	A sulphate of any of various metals; sulphuric acid.
50.	volatile	vŏl'à tĭl	Evaporating rapidly on exposure to the air.

LESSON 86

Civil Engineering Terms [1]

| 1. | abutment | à bŭt'mĕnt | The end support of an arch or of a bridge span, as distinguished from intermediate supports or piers. |

---

[1] See also "Architectural and Building Terms," pages 152–154; "Mining and Metallurgical Terms," pages 208–209.

2. aggregate	ăg′rĕ gȧt	Stone, gravel, and sand mixed with cement to form concrete.
3. alignment	ȧ. līn′mĕnt	The horizontal plan of a railroad, highway, or canal, showing its curves and straight lines or tangents.
4. altitude	ăl′tĭ tūd	Vertical elevation; height above ground or a specified level.
5. aqueduct	ăk′wĕ dŭkt	A structure carrying a canal across a river or low ground.
6. artesian	är tē′zhăn	A term applied to a bored well in which underground pressure raises the water above the ground level.
7. caisson	kā′sŭn	A box or chamber sunk in water or through soft earth for foundation construction.
8. centrifugal	sĕn trĭf′ů găl	Tending or traveling away from a center; radiating.
9. centripetal	sĕn trĭp′ĕ tăl	Directed or moving toward a center.
10. compression	kŏm prĕsh′ŭn	Pressure exerted tending to reduce the size of a body.
11. concrete	kŏn′krēt	A mixture of cement, sand, stone, or gravel, and water, which hardens into a solid mass of artificial stone.
12. conglomerate	kŏn glŏm′ēr ĭt	Consisting of loosely cemented heterogeneous material.
13. crevasse	krĕ văs′	A deep fissure; breach in a levee or dike.
14. culvert	kŭl′vĕrt	A covered drain for the passage of water through an embankment or under a railway or road.
15. diagonal	dī ăg′ŏ năl	A straight line connecting two nonadjacent angles of a rectangular figure; also an inclined member of a truss or frame.
16. dowel	dou′ĕl	A headless pin or rod fitted into holes in two adjacent pieces to fasten them together.
17. drainage	drān′ĭj	A carrying off of the natural flow of water from a country or district by a natural system of rivers and streams; or the removal of excess water by a system of drains.

18. ductile	dŭk′tĭl	Pliable or capable of being drawn out, as into wire.
19. elasticity	ē lăs′tĭs′ĭ tĭ	The rebounding property of bodies in returning to original shape after being pulled, pressed, or distorted.
20. equilibrium	ē′kwĭ lĭb′rĭ ŭm	A state of balance; equipoise.
21. friction	frĭk′shŭn	Resistance to movement of one body in contact with another.
22. girder	gûr′dēr	A main horizontal member in a framework of steel, wood, or concrete.
23. heterogeneous	hĕt′ēr ŏ jē′nē ŭs	Composed of materials of unlike kinds or quantities.
24. homogeneous	hō′mŏ jē′nē ŭs	Of the same structure or composition throughout.
25. hydraulic	hī drô′lĭk	Pertaining to the movement of, or conveyance by means of, water; also said of materials that harden under water.
26. hydroelectric	hī′drŏ ē lĕk′trĭk	Pertaining to the production of electricity by water power.
27. hydrostatic	hī′drŏ stăt′ĭk	Pertaining to the principles of equilibrium of fluids.
28. impermeable	ĭm pûr′mē á b'l	Not permitting the passage of water or fluid.
29. lamination	lăm′ĭ nā′shŭn	The process of forming into thin plates or sheets.
30. lateral	lăt′ēr ăl	Directed toward or from a side.
31. levee	lĕv′ē	An embankment or dike to prevent overflow of a river or other body of water.
32. pile	pīl	A long, slender timber or column of wood, steel, or concrete driven into the ground as foundation.
33. pneumatic	nû măt′ĭk	Pertaining to the use of air or gas under pressure.
34. profile	prō′fīl	A drawing of a vertical section along a road, railway, or canal showing its relation to the ground surface.
35. reconnaissance	rē kŏn′ĭ săns	Preliminary survey, as for engineering or military purposes.
36. reservoir	rĕz′ēr vwôr	A natural or artificial basin for collecting or storing water.

37.	resilience	rĕ zĭl′ĭ ĕns	The property of changing shape under impact or pressure and returning to original position or shape when released. Not the same as elasticity.
38.	rigidity	rĭ jĭd′ĭ tĭ	The property of being stiff, unyielding, inflexible.
39.	rivet	rĭv′ĕt	A short metal bolt used to join objects, having one head, the projecting end being hammered down to form the other head.
40.	sedimentation	sĕd′ĭ mĕn tā′shŭn	Settlement of solid particles contained in liquids.
41.	segregation	sĕg′rĕ gā′shŭn	Separation of parts in a mixture.
42.	sewage	sū′ĭj	Refuse liquids and solids carried off by sewers.
43.	sewerage	sū′ẽr ĭj	A system of pipes or conduits, called sewers, for carrying away sewage.
44.	siphon	sī′fŏn	A bent pipe, tube, or conduit for withdrawal or passage of liquids by atmospheric pressure.
45.	surveyor	sẽr vā′ẽr	One who sets out land boundaries or property lines by application of geometrical and trigonometrical principles.
46.	tension	tĕn′shŭn	Stress caused by pulling or extension (as distinguished from compression).
47.	torsion	tôr′shŭn	Stress caused by twisting a bar or rod about its longitudinal axis.
48.	trestle	trĕs′'l	A braced framework (as a viaduct) of wood, steel, or concrete, usually having a number of short spans supported by bents or piers.
49.	turbine	tûr′bĭn	A power wheel or rotary engine driven by radial flow of water, steam, or gas between curved blades or guides.
50.	viaduct	vī′å dŭkt	A bridgelike structure to carry a road or railway over a valley, usually having a series of short spans as distinguished from a bridge.

LESSON 87

Educational Terms

1.	academic	ăk′a̍ dĕm′ĭk	Literary or classical, as distinguished from technical or scientific; scholarly.
2.	accredited	ă krĕd′ĭ tĕd	Officially vouched for as conforming to a prescribed standard.
3.	alma mater	ăl′ma̍ mā′tēr	The university, college, or school where one has been educated.
4.	alumnus	a̍ lŭm′nŭs	A male graduate of a college or school.
5.	auditorium	ô′dĭ tō′rĭ ŭm	That part of a public building assigned to the audience.
6.	baccalaureate	băk′a̍ lô′rē ăt	Of or pertaining to the bachelor's degree.
7.	classics	klăs′ĭks	Standard works of literature or art. "The classics," Greek or Latin works or authors.
8.	coeducation	kō′ĕd′û kā′shun	Joint education of both sexes at one institution.
9.	collegiate	kŏ lē′jĭ ĭt	Of or pertaining to a college.
10.	curriculum	kŭ rĭk′û lŭm	The whole body of courses offered in an educational institution or by one of its departments.
11.	disciplinarian	dĭs′ĭ plĭ nâr′ĭ ăn	One who insists upon strict observance of rules of behavior.
12.	emeritus	ē mĕr′ĭ tŭs	Retired from active service but retaining honorary rank and title.
13.	extracurricular	ĕks′tra̍ kŭ rĭk′û lēr	Outside the prescribed course of study.
14.	extramural	ĕks′tra̍ mū′răl	Outside the walls, as of a university or city.
15.	faculty	făk′ŭl tĭ	The teaching staff of a university, college, or school; special mental endowment, natural aptitude.
16.	forum	fō′rŭm	An organization that holds public meetings for the discussion of subjects of current interest; a public meeting place for open discussion.

17.	fraternity	frȧ tûr′nĭ tĭ	A secret society; a body of men banded together by common interests; as, men of the same profession.
18.	graduate	grăd′ū ăt	One who has completed the prescribed course of study in an institution of learning.
19.	honorary	ŏn′ẽr ĕr′ĭ	Designating a title or position held by courtesy, without giving service or receiving pay.
20.	intelligence quotient (I. Q. or IQ)	ĭn tĕl′ĭ jĕns kwō′shĕnt	A number derived from an examination given to measure the intelligence of a person.
21.	journalism	jûr′năl ĭz′m	The occupation of publishing or writing for newspapers; also, the name of a course that prepares for such writing.
22.	literacy	lĭt′ẽr ȧ sĭ	State of being educated; specifically, ability to read and write.
23.	lyceum	lī sē′ŭm	An association for debate and literary improvement.
24.	matriculate	mȧ trĭk′ū lāt	To enroll in a college or society by entering one's name in a register.
25.	oratorical	ŏr′ȧ tŏr′ĭ kăl	Pertaining to eloquent public speaking.
26.	parliamentary	pär′lĭ mĕn′tȧ rĭ	According to or permitted by the rules and usages of deliberative bodies.
27.	parochial	pȧ rō′kĭ ăl	Of or pertaining to a parish, as a *parochial* school; that is, one maintained by a parish or religious body.
28.	pedagogue	pĕd′ȧ gŏg	One who, especially by teaching, has become formal, dogmatic, or pedantic.
29.	philosophy	fĭ lŏs′ŏ fĭ	The science that investigates the facts and principles of reality and of human nature and conduct; practical or moral wisdom; mental serenity.
30.	physics	fĭz′ĭks	The study of mechanics, heat, sound, light, electricity, etc.
31.	physiology	fĭz′ĭ ŏl′ŏ jĭ	That part of biology that treats of functions of the human body alone.
32.	postgraduate	pōst grăd′ū ăt	One pursuing formal studies after graduation.

33.	pragmatism	prăg′må tĭz′m	Dogmatism; practicality; matter-of-factness.
34.	professorial	prō′fĕ sō′rĭ ăl	Of or pertaining to a teacher of the highest rank in a university or college.
35.	psychology	sī kŏl′ō jĭ	The science that treats of the mind.
36.	rhetoric	rĕt′ō rĭk	The art of expressing oneself in writing or speaking.
37.	scholarship	skŏl′ẽr shĭp	An allowance to aid a student to continue his studies; also, erudition or learning.
38.	science	sī′ĕns	Any department of knowledge in which the results of investigation have been systematized and are considered as a distinct field of study.
39.	secondary school	sĕk′ŭn dẽr′Ĭ skōōl	Any school of high school grade.
40.	semester	sĕ mĕs′tẽr	One of the two terms of a school year.
41.	seminary	sĕm′Ĭ nẽr′Ĭ	A special school, as of theology; an academy or private secondary school.
42.	sociology	sō′sĭ ŏl′ō jĭ	The science that deals with human associations—their development, forms, and functions.
43.	sophomore	sŏf′ō mōr	A second-year student in a high school, college, or university.
44.	sorority	sō rŏr′Ĭ tĭ	A secret society or club of girls or women.
45.	syllabus	sĭl′à bŭs	A statement of the main points of a course of study.
46.	technical	tĕk′nĭ kăl	Relating to the useful or mechanical arts of any science, business, profession, sport, etc.
47.	thesis	thē′sĭs	A formal treatise describing original work in research on some subject and presented by the candidate for an academic degree.
48.	tuition	tū ĭsh′ŭn	Charge for instruction.
49.	university	ū′nĭ vûr′sĭ tĭ	An institution organized for teaching and study in the higher branches of learning and empowered to confer degrees, as in arts, law, medicine.

LESSON 88

Electrical and Radio Terms—Electricity [1]

1.	admittance	ăd mĭt′ăns	Measure of degree of ease by which an alternating current is established in a circuit.
2.	alternating	ôl′tẽr nāt′ĭng	Reversing periodically and rapidly in direction of flow.
3.	ammeter	ăm′mē′tẽr	Instrument for measuring the magnitude of an electric current.
4.	ampere	ăm′pēr	A unit of electric current.
5.	amplitude	ăm′plĭ tūd	Peak or maximum instantaneous value of an alternating current or voltage in either direction.
6.	anode	ăn′ōd	The electrode from which or by which electricity enters the electrolyte (*q.v.*) of a cell. The electrode by which it leaves is called the *cathode*.
7.	armature	är′mȧ tụ̈r	In a motor, the part in which the current produces torque and rotation.
8.	capacitance	kȧ păs′ĭ tăns	The ratio of the quantity of electricity stored in a condenser to the voltage across the condenser.
9.	commutator	kŏm′ụ̈ tā′tẽr	Device for changing the direction of flow of an electric current.
10.	condensance	kŏn dĕn′săns	Synonym for "capacitance" and "capacity reactance."
11.	conductance	kŏn dŭk′tăns	A measure of the ease of flow of an electric current in a direct current circuit.
12.	conductivity	kŏn′dŭk tĭv′ĭ tĭ	Property of material determining the ease of flow of electric current through the conductor.
13.	conduit	kŏn′dĭt	Tubing or duct within which electrical conductors are placed.

---

[1] See also "Automobile Terms," pages 155–157.

14.	controller	kŏn trōl′ẽr	Device for reversing or varying the speed of an electric motor.
15.	converter	kŏn vûr′tẽr	Rotating machine for changing alternating currents into direct currents.
16.	coulomb	koō lŏm′	Unit for measuring electrical quantity.
17.	demagnetization	dē măg′nĕ tĭ zā′shŭn	Process of removing the magnetic properties from a magnetized object.
18.	dynamo	dī′nȧ mō	Machine for converting mechanical power into electrical power.
19.	dynamometer	dī′nȧ mŏm′ĕ tẽr	Apparatus for measuring torque, or power input or output of a machine.
20.	electrification	ĕ lĕk′trĭ fĭ kā′shŭn	Process of supplying a charge or service of electricity.
21.	electrode	ĕ lĕk′trōd	Either of the conductors by which the current enters and leaves an electrolyte.
22.	electrodynamics	ĕ lĕk′trō dī năm′ĭks	Branch of physics dealing with electricity in motion.
23.	electrolysis	ĕ lĕk′trŏl′ĭ sĭs	Chemical decomposition into constituents by means of electric currents.
24.	electrolyte	ĕ lĕk′trō līt	A substance that will conduct electricity, or that becomes a conductor when in solution, and undergoes chemical decomposition when an electric current is passed through it.
25.	electromotive	ĕ lĕk′trō mō′tĭv	Applied to the force whose pressure drives an electric current around a circuit.
26.	farad	făr′ăd	A unit of capacitance.
27.	frequency	frē′kwĕn sĭ	Number of complete cycles per second of an alternating current or voltage.
28.	galvanoscope	găl′vȧ nō skōp′	Instrument for detecting presence of small electric currents.
29.	hysteresis	hĭs′tẽr ē′sĭs	Lag in changes of magnetization behind the reversals of the magnetizing force.

30.	impedance	ĭm pēd′ăns	Total opposition to flow of an alternating current.
31.	incandescence	ĭn′kăn dĕs′ĕns	Glow of a body, as a lamp filament, heated to high temperature.
32.	inductance	ĭn dŭk′tăns	The property of a coil that enables it to store energy in an electromagnetic field.
33.	insulation	in′sû lā′shŭn	Nonconducting material used to prevent escape or access of electric current (also heat and sound).
34.	magnetomotive	măg nē′tŏ mō′tĭv	Designating the force whose pressure overcomes reluctance in establishing magnetism.
35.	mho	mō	Unit of electrical conductance; reciprocal of the ohm.
36.	ohm	ōm	The practical unit of electrical resistance.
37.	oscillograph	ŏs′ĭ lŏ grȧf′	Apparatus for observing or recording the wave form of an alternating current or voltage.
38.	permeability	pûr′mē ȧ bĭl′ĭ tĭ	Property of susceptibility to magnetization.
39.	photoelectric	fō′tŏ ĕ lĕk′trĭk	Pertaining to the electrical effects produced by light.
40.	polarization	pō′lēr ĭ zā′shŭn	Accumulation of gas at the electrode in a cell.
41.	reactance	rē ăk′tăns	Portion of impedance attributable to inductance or capacitance.
42.	rectifier	rĕk′tĭ fī′ēr	Apparatus for converting alternating current into direct current.
43.	resistance	rē zĭs′tăns	Opposition offered to the flow of electricity.
44.	shunt	shŭnt	A conductor joining two points of an electric circuit over which part of the current may be diverted.
45.	teletype	tĕl′ē tīp	Electric system by which a typewriter is operated at a distance.
46.	torque	tôrk	A force that tends to produce a rotating or twisting motion.

47.	transformer	trăns fôr′mẽr	Apparatus for transforming electrical energy from high voltage to low voltage, or vice versa.
48.	turbogenerator	tûr′bŏ jĕn′ẽr ā/tẽr	Combination of a generator and the turbine that drives it.
49.	voltage	vōl′tĭj	Electromotive force or potential difference expressed in terms of volts.
50.	watt	wŏt	The practical unit of power. A thousand watts is known as a *kilowatt*.

LESSON 89

Electrical and Radio Terms—Radio

1.	amplifier	ăm′plĭ fī′ẽr	A device to magnify electric impulses; also, a loudspeaker.
2.	antenna	ăn tĕn′å	Wires, supported in the air, for receiving or transmitting electric waves.
3.	attenuation	ă tĕn′ū ā′shŭn	The decrease in amplitude of a wave or current or voltage with increasing distance from the source of transmission.
4.	audition	ô dĭsh′ŭn	A hearing or audience, especially a trial or test hearing before a microphone.
5.	battery	băt′ẽr ĭ	An apparatus for generating electricity.
6.	bias	bī′ăs	A permanent negative voltage applied to the grid of a vacuum tube.
7.	coherer	kŏ hẽr′ẽr	A device employed to detect electric waves.
8.	commentator	kŏm′ĕn tā′tẽr	One who makes observations or interpretations, especially of news events.
9.	condenser	kŏn dĕn′sẽr	An instrument for concentrating electricity.
10.	damping	dămp′ĭng	The progressive diminution of amplitude in alternating current or waves.

11.	decibel	děs′ĭ běl	A unit for measuring sound intensities.
12.	deflection	dĕ flĕk′shŭn	A turning aside from a straight line or given course.
13.	detector	dĕ tĕk′tēr	A device for rectifying high-frequency electric current.
14.	dial	dī′ăl	A plate or face having a pointer for indicating some quantity; in radio, the kilocycles.
15.	dielectric	dī′ĕ lĕk′trĭk	A nonconducting substance; an insulator.
16.	diplex	dī′plĕks	Pertaining to a telegraph circuit arranged for simultaneous transmission of two messages in the same direction.
17.	direction finder	dĭ rĕk′shŭn fīn′dēr	A receiving device determining the direction from which radio waves come to it.
18.	distortion	dĭs tôr′shŭn	Imperfection in the received signal.
19.	duplex	dū′plĕks	Pertaining to a telegraph circuit arranged for simultaneous transmission of two messages in opposite directions.
20.	electron	ĕ lĕk′trŏn	The most elementary charge of negative electricity. Electrons are constituents of all atoms.
21.	electron tube	ĕ lĕk′trŏn tūb	A tube in which the flow of electrons through space forms the essential operation of the device.
22.	filament	fĭl′à mĕnt	In radio tubes, the incandescent wire that provides a source of electrons.
23.	filter	fĭl′tēr	A selective network that permits the discrimination of electrical currents of various frequencies.
24.	grid	grĭd	A perforated or ridged plate of lead for use in a storage battery; the control electrode of an electron tube.
25.	grounded	groun′dĕd	Connected with the earth so as to make the earth a part of an electrical circuit.
26.	heterodyne	hĕt′ēr ŏ dīn′	Pertaining to the production of a difference of frequency between two radio frequencies.

27.	interference	ĭn′tẽr fẽr′ĕns	A confusion of received signals due to undesired signals or other causes.
28.	kilocycle	kĭl′ō sī′k'l	A unit of frequency equal to 1,000 cycles a second.
29.	loud-speaker	loud spēk′ẽr	A form of telephone receiver for producing sounds loud enough to be heard readily without holding it close to the ear.
30.	microfarad	mī′krō făr′ăd	A unit of electrostatic capacity equal to one-millionth of a farad.
31.	microphone	mī′krō fōn	An apparatus for converting sound vibrations into variations of an electrical current.
32.	network	nĕt′wûrk′	A broadcast system having stations at various points connected by wire lines and transmitting signals simultaneously from a central point.
33.	oscillator	ŏs′ĭ lā′tẽr	A radio-frequency generator, especially one of nonrotating type.
34.	quartz crystal	kwôrts krĭs′tăl	In radio transmitters, a small slab of carefully cut and ground quartz whose natural period of vibration determines the frequency of the radiation being generated.
35.	radiogram	rā′dĭ ō grăm′	A message transmitted by radiotelegraphy.
36.	rebroadcast	rē brôd′kȧst′	To broadcast signals, programs, etc., while receiving them from another source.
37.	resonance	rĕz′ō năns	The condition existing in an electrical circuit when that circuit is tuned so that its natural frequency of oscillation is equal to that of the incoming or impressed voltage.
38.	rheostat	rē′ō stăt	A variable or adjustable resistor.
39.	selectivity	sĕ lĕk′tĭv′ĭ tĭ	The degree of ability of a circuit to respond to impulses to the exclusion of others.

40.	sensitivity	sĕn′sĭ tĭv′ĭ tĭ	The degree to which a receiving set responds to incoming waves.
41.	S O S	ĕs′ō′ĕs′	The letters of the international signal of distress for use by ships calling for help.
42.	socket	sŏk′ĕt	A support for a tube.
43.	sponsor	spŏn′sẽr	The concern or organization that pays the broadcaster and performers for a radio program.
44.	static	stăt′ĭk	In radio communication, disturbances due to natural causes of whatever origin.
45.	superheterodyne	sū′pẽr hĕt′ẽr ŏ dīn′	A type of receiver in which the incoming frequency is changed to another frequency (usually lower) before the signals are made audible in the detecting process.
46.	synchronize	sĭng′krŏ nīz	To make agree in time; to regulate and co-ordinate.
47.	telephotograph	tĕl′ē fō′tŏ gråf	A photograph reproduced at some distant point.
48.	television	tĕl′ē vĭzh′ŭn	The instantaneous projection to a distant point, and reproduction on a screen there, of images, views, or objects.
49.	tuning	tūn′ĭng	The process of obtaining the maximum effect by adjusting the time period of one circuit to the same period of another.
50.	wave length	wāv lĕngth	The distance between corresponding points on any two consecutive electric waves.

LESSON 90

Fashion and Textile Terms

1.	accessories	ăk sĕs′ŏ rĭz	Small articles of apparel that add to the effectiveness of a costume, as purse, scarf, gloves, jewelry.
2.	acetate	ăs′ē tāt	Designating a process of making rayon yarn in which acetic acid is used; fabric made from acetate rayon yarn.

3.	appliqué	ăp′lĭ kā′	Material cut in a decorative pattern and applied flat to a garment as ornamentation.
4.	bandanna	băn dăn′á	A large square of fabric, often printed, worn about the neck or around the head.
5.	bandeau	băn dō′	A band worn around the head.
6.	beret	bĕ rā′	A close-fitting, round, flat hat of soft material.
7.	bolero	bŏ lâr′ō	A short jacket usually made to hang loose and stop at the waistline.
8.	bouclé	boo′klā′	A fabric having a knotted and curled appearance, due to the use of a yarn, one thread of which is partly drawn out into a loop.
9.	bouffant	boo′fäN′	Puffed out; full; as a bouffant skirt.
10.	couturier (m.) couturière (f.)	koo′tü′ryā′ koo′tü′ryâr′	A dressmaker (French).
11.	croquis	krŏ′kē′	An artist's rough sketch of a figure or pattern.
12.	culotte	kū lŏt′	Full, calf-length trousers made to give the appearance of a skirt.
13.	décolleté	dā kŏl′tā	Low-necked; said of a dress that exposes the neck and shoulders.
14.	duvetyn	doo′vĕ tēn	A soft fabric with a fine, velvety nap.
15.	ensemble	än sŏm′b'l	The whole costume; often a costume of coat and dress designed to be worn together.
16.	faille	fāl	A fabric of silk or rayon with a ribbed weave.
17.	gabardine	găb′ẽr dēn′	A firmly woven fabric with a narrow diagonal rib.
18.	gilet	zhē′lĕ′	A vest or sleeveless blouse.
19.	grosgrain	grō′grän′	Fabric or ribbon with a heavy corded or ribbed weave.
20.	jabot	zhȧ′bō′	A frill on the front of a dress or blouse.
21.	jacquard	jă kärd′	A type of loom designed to weave patterned fabrics; fabrics woven on a jacquard loom.
22.	lapel	lă pĕl′	Part of a garment that folds back from a center opening and is usually joined to the collar; a revers.
23.	lingerie	lăN′zh′rē′	A woman's underclothing; also a combination of lace and sheer embroidered cotton used as a trimming or for blouses.
24.	mannequin	măn′ĕ kĭn	A living model or a display form.

25.	matelassé	màt′lä′sā′	A fabric with raised pattern in blistered effect usually woven on a jacquard loom.
26.	modiste	mō dēst′	A dressmaker, especially one who makes dresses in the latest mode or fashion.
27.	molded	mōl′dĕd	Shaped; closely fitted.
28.	mousseline de soie	mōōs′lēn′ dē swä′	Sheer, soft silk muslin.
29.	negligee	nĕg′lĭ zhā′	A robe to wear in the boudoir.
30.	notions	nō′shŭns	Small wares used in dressmaking.
31.	organdy	ôr′găn dĭ	A sheer, crisp cotton fabric with a permanently stiff finish.
32.	piqué	pē kā′	A cotton fabric woven with a slightly ribbed pattern.
33.	rayon	rā′ŏn	A textile fiber made from cellulose by one of several chemical processes; also, a fabric made of rayon yarn.
34.	redingote	rĕd′ĭng gōt	A fitted coat that does not lap in front.
35.	revers	rē vēr′	The part of a garment that folds back from a center opening; a lapel.
36.	ruching	rōōsh′ĭng	Pleated or gathered bands of fabric used as trimming.
37.	selvage	sĕl′vĭj	The edge of a fabric so woven as to prevent raveling.
38.	sequin	sē′kwĭn	A small metal or composition disk used for ornamentation; a spangle.
39.	Shantung	shăn tŭng′	A kind of pongee with a rough surface.
40.	shirr	shûr	To gather fullness on rows of thread.
41.	silhouette	sĭl′ōō ĕt′	The outline of a figure; a profile such as is formed by a shadow.
42.	surplice	sûr′plĭs	Having its neckline lapped over to form a diagonal closing.
43.	swatch	swŏch	A small sample of fabric; also, a collection of samples issued by one manufacturer.
44.	taffeta	tăf′ē tà	A smooth silk or rayon fabric with a crisp finish.
45.	tailleur	tä′yûr′	A tailored suit.
46.	texture	tĕks′tụr	The surface appearance and character of a fabric determined by the weave and yarns.
47.	tiers	tẹrs	Ruffles placed one above the other.
48.	tulle	tōōl	A very fine open-meshed fabric.
49.	voile	voil	A sheer, soft cotton fabric.
50.	worsted	wŏŏs′tĕd	A hard-twisted woolen yarn; also, a fabric woven of worsted yarns.

LESSON 91

Fuel and Oil Terms [1]

1. **acetone** ăs′ê tōn — An inflammable liquid, with a biting taste, used in making chloroform and as a solvent for fats, camphor, and resins.
2. **acetylene** ă sĕt′ĭ lēn — The most brilliant of the illuminating gases.
3. **Allegheny** ăl′ê gā′nĭ — A range of mountains in Pennsylvania, Maryland, Virginia, and West Virginia.
4. **anthracite** ăn′thrȧ sīt — A hard, lustrous coal.
5. **anticline** ăn′tĭ klīn — A fold or arch of rock in which the layers dip in a rooflike form.
6. **Appalachian** ăp′ȧ lăch′ĭ ăn — A great mountain system in the eastern part of North America, extending from the Gulf of St. Lawrence to Alabama.
7. **bakelite** bā′kĕ līt — A trade-marked synthetic resin used for the same purpose as hard rubber and celluloid.
8. **bituminous coal** bĭ tū′mĭ nŭs kōl — Soft coal.
9. **calorie** kăl′ȯ rĭ — The unit of heat quantity—the heat required to raise 1 kilogram of water 1 degree C.
10. **cannel coal** kăn′ĕl kōl — A coal of fine texture, containing much volatile matter and burning with a bright flame.
11. **carbon monoxide** kär′bŏn mŏn ŏk′sīd — A colorless, poisonous gas resulting from the incomplete combustion of carbon when burned with an insufficient supply of air or oxygen.
12. **carbonaceous** kär′bō nā′shŭs — Pertaining to, containing, or composed of carbon.
13. **charcoal** chär′kōl′ — Impure solid carbon formed by highly heating (charring) wood in the absence of air.
14. **chimney** chĭm′nĭ — An upright flue of brick or stone usually extending above the roof.

---

[1] See also "Mining and Metallurgical Terms," pages 208–209.

15.	coke	kōk	A substance left after coal has been subjected to distillation; used as a fuel.
16.	colliery	kŏl′yẽr ĭ	A coal mine.
17.	combustion	kŏm bŭs′chŭn	The process of burning; the chemical process of combining oxygen with a fuel to obtain heat and sometimes light.
18.	creosote	krē′ŏ sōt	An oily antiseptic fluid obtained by the distillation of coal tar or wood tar; used as an antiseptic in medicine and as a wood preservative.
19.	croppings	krŏp′ĭngz	Portions of a vein or bed as seen exposed at the surface.
20.	dehydrator	dē hī′drā tẽr	An apparatus in which water is removed from oil.
21.	Diesel engine	dē′zĕl ĕn′jĭn	An internal-combustion oil engine of high efficiency in which atomized fuel is ignited by high temperature due to high-compression pressure.
22.	distillation	dĭs′tĭ lā′shŭn	The process of separating a volatile fluid or fluids from a heavier fluid by evaporation and condensation.
23.	flash point	flăsh point	The temperature to which an oil must be raised to produce enough vapor for a momentary flash when the vapor is ignited under certain standard conditions.
24.	gasoline	găs′ŏ lēn	A light distillate of petroleum.
25.	graphite	grăf′īt	A form of carbon. It is intensely black, has a metallic luster, a greasy feeling, and leaves a black mark on paper; used in the manufacture of paints, pencils, and as a lubricant.
26.	gusher	gŭsh′ẽr	A flowing oil well, especially if the discharge is with force.
27.	hydrocarbon	hī′drŏ kär′bŏn	A compound containing only carbon and hydrogen.
28.	kerosene	kĕr′ŏ sēn′	A thin mineral oil produced by distillation, chiefly from petroleum.

29.	lampblack	lămp′blăk′	A product obtained by burning natural gas with insufficient oxygen.
30.	lignite	lĭg′nīt	A brownish-black coal in which the alteration of vegetal material has proceeded further than in peat, but not so far as in bituminous coal.
31.	lubricant	lū′brĭ kănt	A fluid, semifluid, or solid substance used to reduce friction and wear between rubbing surfaces.
32.	naphtha	năf′thȧ	Any of several volatile inflammable liquids obtained by distilling petroleum; used in dry cleaning, varnish making, and as a fuel.
33.	ozocerite	ŏ zō′kĕ rīt	A mineral wax.
34.	paraffin	păr′ă fĭn	A tasteless, odorless, colorless waxy substance obtained by the distillation of wood, coal, peat, etc., and from crude petroleum.
35.	peat	pēt	A carbonaceous deposit, occurring principally in swamps and marshy places, composed of partly decayed vegetable matter.
36.	petrolatum	pĕt′rṑ lā′tŭm	Soft petroleum ointment.
37.	petroleum	ρĕ trō′lĕ ŭm	In general, an oily, dark-colored, inflammable liquid mixture of highly complex hydrocarbons, occurring naturally and obtained by drilling into earth or rock.
38.	receptacle	rĕ sĕp′tȧ k'l	That which is used to hold things; a vessel.
39.	refinery	rĕ fīn′ẽr ĭ	A building and apparatus for separating many products from crude petroleum.
40.	residuum	rĕ sĭd′ṹ ŭm	A by-product obtained on the distillation of crude petroleum after the constituents boiling below 620° F. have been removed.
41.	saturation	săt′ṹ rā′shŭn	The state of being fully soaked or impregnated.

42.	screenings	skrēn′ĭngs	Small particles of coal remaining after the coal has been passed through a sifter or coarse sieve.
43.	sedimentary rock	sĕd ĭ′mĕn′tå rĭ rŏk	Rock formed by the compacting of sediment containing petroleum oils.
44.	shale	shāl	A rock of clayey origin, easily split into thin layers.
45.	stratified rock	străt′ĭ fīd rŏk	Rocks deposited in distinct, generally parallel, layers.
46.	syncline	sĭng′klīn	A fold in rocks in which the layers dip inward from both sides—the opposite of an anticline.
47.	thermal	thûr′măl	Relating to heat or heating.
48.	thermodynamics	thûr′mō dī năm′ĭks	The science of heat energy and its conversion into mechanical energy.
49.	Vaseline	văs′ĕ lēn	A trade name for petrolatum.
50.	viscosity	vĭs kŏs′ĭ tĭ	The property of an oil that determines its rate of flow.

LESSON 92

Furniture and Interior-Decoration Terms

1.	bird's-eye maple	bûrdz′ī′ mā′p'l	Maple wood marked with spots resembling birds' eyes.
2.	boudoir	bōō′dwär	A small, elegantly furnished retiring room for ladies.
3.	bureau	bū′rō	A chest of drawers for clothing, often equipped with a mirror.
4.	burnish	bûr′nĭsh	To cause to shine; polish.
5.	cabriole	kăb′rĭ ōl	A curved leg ending in an ornamental foot, common in Queen Anne and Chippendale furniture.
6.	chaise longue	shāz′ lông′	An elongated couch having a back rest at one end only.
7.	chiffonier	shĭf′ŏ nẽr′	A high and narrow chest of drawers.
8.	chintz	chĭnts	Printed cotton cloth, often glazed.
9.	Chippendale	chĭp′ĕn dāl	A graceful, sometimes ornate, style of furniture designed by Thomas Chippendale in England in the eighteenth century.

10.	colonial	kŏ lō′nĭ ăl	The style of furniture in vogue in this country while it was a British colony.
11.	console	kŏn′sōl	An ornamental table to be set against a wall.
12.	cretonne	krē tŏn′	A strong, unglazed cotton cloth, printed on one or both sides.
13.	dado	dā′dō	The lower part of any wall when differently decorated from the upper part.
14.	damask	dăm′ȧsk	Fabrics so woven that a pattern is made, without contrast of color.
15.	decorative	dĕk′ȯ rā′tĭv	Suitable for decorating or embellishing; adorning.
16.	drapery	drā′pẽr ĭ	A fabric used for decorative purposes.
17.	ebony	ĕb′ŭn ĭ	A hard, heavy, durable Asian or African wood used in cabinetwork, etc.
18.	Empire	ĕm′pīr	A dignified style of furniture developed in France under Napoleon I.
19.	escritoire	ĕs′krĭ twär′	A writing desk.
20.	frieze	frēz	A twisted weave used in broadloom rugs and drapery fabrics; also, any sculptured or richly ornamented band in a building.
21.	fumed oak	fūmd ōk	Oak given a weathered appearance by exposure to fumes of ammonia.
22.	Georgian	jôr′jĭ ăn	A term descriptive of the furniture and decoration used in the reigns of the four Georges, kings of Great Britain.
23.	girandole	jĭr′ăn dōl	An ornamental, branched candleholder.
24.	hassock	hăs′ŭk	A thick mat or cushion used as a footstool.
25.	Hepplewhite	hĕp′′l hwīt	A light and elegant style of furniture developed in England under George III.
26.	highboy	hī′boi′	A tall, commodious chest of drawers mounted on legs.
27.	Jacobean	jăk′ȯ bē′ăn	Pertaining to a style of decoration in England in the early seventeenth century.
28.	jardiniere	jär′dĭ nẽr′	An ornamental jar for flowers or plants.
29.	mahogany	mȧ hŏg′ȧ nĭ	The hard wood of a tropical American tree having a characteristic grain and much used in fine furniture.
30.	mattress	măt′rĕs	A tufted sack of ticking or other cloth, stuffed with hair, felt, or the like, and used as a soft pad for a bed.
31.	modern	mŏd′ẽrn	A style of furniture and decoration characterized by severely plain lines.

32.	mohair	mō′hâr′	A fine fabric woven from the long, silky hair of the Angora goat.
33.	moquette	mŏ kĕt′	A kind of upholstery fabric having a velvety pile.
34.	ottoman	ŏt′ŏ măn	A stuffed seat without a back, originally used in Turkey.
35.	parquetry	pär′kĕt rĭ	Cabinetwork or flooring consisting of an inlay of geometric or other patterns.
36.	penthouse	pĕnt′hous′	Any small structure, with sloping roof, joined to a building; also, a recessed apartment or dwelling house built on a roof and having a terrace.
37.	petit point	pĕt′ĭ point	A very small sloping stitch used in embroidery; tent stitch.
38.	pilaster	pĭ lăs′tĕr	An upright architectural member, treated as a column, with a usual projection from the wall of one-third of its width.
39.	porcelain	pōr′sĕ lĭn	A fine, translucent chinaware or earthenware.
40.	portiere	pōr tyâr′	A curtain hanging in a doorway.
41.	rattan	ră tăn′	Very tough, long stems from a certain palm, used for wickerwork, etc.
42.	Renaissance	rĕn′ĕ säns′	The revival of art in Europe in the fourteenth century.
43.	rococo	rŏ kō′kō	A style of decorating distinguished by elaborately executed ornament, prevalent during the seventeenth and eighteenth centuries.
44.	Sheraton	shĕr′ȧ tŏn	A light, elegant style of furniture, designed about 1800, in England, by Thomas Sheraton, characterized by straight lines and graceful proportions.
45.	tapestry	tăp′ĕs trĭ	An ornamental fabric used for hangings and upholstery.
46.	tassel	tăs′′l	A hanging ornament, ending in a tuft of loose threads.
47.	Tudor style	tū′dĕr stīl	The latest variety of English Gothic, characterized by shallow moldings and profuse panels.
48.	upholstery	ŭp hōl′stĕr ĭ	The materials used to stuff or cover furniture, as fabric, webbing, nails.
49.	Venetian blind	vĕ nē′shăn blīnd	An inside shutter, having horizontal wooden slats, capable of being adjusted to admit varying amounts of light.
50.	wainscot	wān′skŭt	A lining for the lower portion of inner walls, usually paneled.

LESSON 93

Government Terms

1.	alien	āl′yĕn	A person of another family, race, or nation; a foreigner.
2.	allies	ă līz′	Sovereigns or states united by treaty.
3.	ambassador	ăm băs′à dẽr	A government agent of the highest rank representing his country's interests at a foreign capital.
4.	amendment	à mĕnd′mĕnt	A change in, or an addition to, the constitution of a country, state, or society.
5.	assessor	ă sĕs′ẽr	One appointed to estimate the value of property for taxation.
6.	attaché	ăt′à shā′	A member of the diplomatic staff of an ambassador or minister.
7.	autocracy	ô tŏk′rà sĭ	Independent or self-derived power; absolute supremacy.
8.	bureaucracy	bû rŏk′rà sĭ	A system of carrying on government by means of departments; often used to imply undue emphasis on "red tape."
9.	campaign	kăm pān′	A connected series of operations to bring about some desired result.
10.	censorship	sĕn′sẽr shĭp	The action of an official empowered to examine written or printed matter in order to forbid anything objectionable.
11.	civilian	sĭ vĭl′yăn	One engaged in occupations other than those of a soldier or sailor.
12.	constitutional	kŏn′stĭ tū′shŭn ăl	Relating to a constitution or established form of government.
13.	consulate	kŏn′sû lăt	The office or jurisdiction of an official appointed to reside in some foreign country; also, the premises occupied officially.

14.	contraband	kŏn′trȧ bănd	Illegal or prohibited traffic; also, the goods or merchandise prohibited.
15.	court-martial	kōrt′ mär′shăl	A court consisting of military or naval officers.
16.	demagogue	dĕm′ȧ gŏg	An insincere political leader who appeals to the masses for his leadership.
17.	democracy	dḙ mŏk′rȧ sĭ	A government by the people; practical or social equality as opposed to an aristocracy.
18.	diplomacy	dĭ plō′mȧ sĭ	Art and practice of conducting negotiations between nations.
19.	disfranchise	dĭs frăn′chīz	To deprive of a political right, as the right to vote.
20.	embassy	ĕm′bă sĭ	The function, business, or official residence of an ambassador.
21.	envoy	ĕn′voi	One dispatched upon an errand or mission.
22.	expatriate	ĕks pā′trĭ ăt	One banished or in exile.
23.	federal	fĕd′ēr ăl	Pertaining to a state formed by the consolidation of several states.
24.	fusion	fū′zhŭn	A union of political parties.
25.	imperialism	ĭm pēr′ĭ ăl ĭz′m	The power or government of an emperor.
26.	inauguration	ĭn ô′gu̇ rā′shŭn	Formal induction into an office; investiture.
27.	legation	lḙ gā′shŭn	The place of business or official residence of a diplomatic minister at a foreign court or seat of government; an embassy.
28.	legislature	lĕj′ĭs lā′tu̇r	The lawmaking body of a state.
29.	lobbying	lŏb′Ĭ ĭng	Trying to get a bill passed by personal influence exerted on the legislators.
30.	logrolling	lŏg′rōl′ĭng	A combining to assist in furthering the schemes of others in expectation of receiving assistance in return.
31.	monarchy	mŏn′ēr kĭ	Government by a single ruler.
32.	naturalization	năt′u̇ răl ĭ zā′shŭn	Admission to the rights and privileges of citizenship.

33.	neutrality	nū trăl′ĭ tĭ	State of refraining from taking part in a controversy.
34.	opponent	ŏ pō′nĕnt	An adversary.
35.	Pan-American	păn à mĕr′ĭ kăn	Pertaining to North and South America, or all Americans.
36.	parliament	pär′lĭ mĕnt	The supreme legislative body of Great Britain; also, a similar body in any of the self-governing British colonies.
37.	partisan	pär′tĭ zăn	A strongly devoted adherent to a party, faction, or cause.
38.	plenipotentiary	plĕn′ĭ pō tĕn′shĭ ĕr ĭ	A diplomatic agent invested with full power to transact business for his government.
39.	precinct	prē′sĭngkt	A district within certain boundaries set up for governmental purposes.
40.	proletariat	prō′lĕ târ′ĭ ăt	The wage-earning class.
41.	propaganda	prŏp′à găn′dà	A scheme or plan for spreading a doctrine or system of principles.
42.	protectorate	prŏ tĕk′tēr ĭt	A relation of authority assumed by one state over a dependent one.
43.	protocol	prō′tŏ kŏl	A preliminary memorandum as a basis for a final convention or treaty.
44.	quorum	kwō′rŭm	The proportion of members of an organization that must be present at a meeting in order to transact business legally.
45.	reactionary	rē ăk′shŭn ĕr′ĭ	Tending toward a former condition, policy, or form of government.
46.	reciprocity	rĕs′ĭ prŏs′ĭ tĭ	A relationship between two nations in which each grants the other special advantages in trade.
47.	referendum	rĕf′ēr ĕn′dŭm	The principle of referring measures to the voters for approval or rejection.
48.	republic	rē pŭb′lĭk	A state in which the power resides in the people.
49.	revenue	rĕv′ĕ nū	The general income of a government from taxes, customs, and other sources.
50.	suffrage	sŭf′rĭj	The right or act of voting; franchise.

LESSON 94

Grocery Terms [1]

1.	artichoke	är′tĭ chōk	A plant with a flower head, which is cooked as a vegetable.
2.	asparagus	ăs păr′ȧ gŭs	A plant that, when young, has tender stalks much prized as a vegetable.
3.	avocado	ăv′ȯ kä′dō	Pulpy fruit similar in size and shape to a large pear; also called "alligator pear."
4.	banana	bȧ năn′ȧ	The fruit of a tropical tree.
5.	biscuit	bĭs′kĭt	A kind of unraised bread—plain, sweet, or fancy—formed into flat cakes and baked.
6.	bluing	blōō′ĭng	A preparation of indigo or the like used in laundering to bring out the whiteness of fabrics.
7.	Bologna	bȯ lō′nyä	A large sausage of mixed beef, veal, and pork, chopped fine, seasoned, and enclosed in a skin.
8.	Brie cheese	brē chēz	A soft cream cheese made in Brie, France.
9.	broccoli	brŏk′ȯ lĭ	A hardy variety of cauliflower.
10.	canape	kȧ′nȧ′pā′	A small piece of bread or biscuit on which anchovies, cheese, and relishes are served.
11.	caviar	kăv′ĭ är′	The prepared and salted roe (eggs) of sturgeon and other fish, served as a delicacy.
12.	cayenne pepper	kī ĕn′ pĕp′ẽr	A very hot and pungent powder made by grinding the fruits or seeds of several peppers; also called "red pepper."
13.	chile con carne	chē′lȧ kŏn kär′nȧ	A Mexican dish consisting of minced red peppers and meat.
14.	chop suey	chŏp′sōō′ĭ	A Chinese dish of celery, bean or bamboo sprouts, onions, sliced meat, etc.
15.	chow chow	chou′ chou′	Chopped mixed pickles in mustard sauce.
16.	cocoa	kō′kō	A powder made from the ground seeds of the cacao tree.
17.	coconut	kō′kȯ nŭt′	The fruit of the coco palm, a tropical product.

---

[1] See also "Agricultural Terms," pages 150–151.

18.	consommé	kŏn′sŏ mā′	A strong, clear soup made from meat.
19.	deviled	dĕv′′ld	Chopped and highly seasoned.
20.	endive	ĕn′dīv	An herb, whose curled, blanched leaves are used for salads.
21.	farina	fȧ rē′nȧ	A fine flour or meal; starch.
22.	hominy	hŏm′ĭ nĭ	Coarsely ground Indian corn (maize), used as a cereal.
23.	kohlrabi	kōl′rä′bĭ	A variety of cabbage, with an enlarged, turniplike stem.
24.	kumquat	kŭm′kwŏt	A Chinese citrous fruit used chiefly for preserves and confectionery.
25.	lentils	lĕn′tĭls	The seeds of a plant of the pea family.
26.	macaroni	măk′ȧ rō′nĭ	An article of food made of paste, chiefly of wheat flour, and dried in the form of long, slender tubes.
27.	maraschino	măr′ȧ skē′nō	A liqueur distilled from the marasca cherry and flavored with the bruised cherry kernels.
28.	marjoram	mär′jŏ răm	A very fragrant mint used in cookery for flavoring.
29.	marron	măr′ŏn	The large sweet European chestnut.
30.	marshmallow	märsh′măl′ō	A confection in the form of a sweetened paste.
31.	matzoth	måt′sōth	Unleavened bread eaten at the Passover.
32.	mayonnaise	mā′ŏ nāz′	A thick sauce used in dressing salads, fish, etc.
33.	Mocha	mō′kȧ	A variety of coffee.
34.	mulligatawny	mŭl′ĭ gȧ tô′nĭ	An East Indian curry soup.
35.	oleomargarine	ō′lĕ ŏ mär′jä rēn	A butter substitute made from fats and oils derived from certain animals and plants.
36.	pâté de foie gras	pä′tā′ dē fwȧ′ grä′	Patty of fattened liver, usually goose liver.
37.	piccalilli	pĭk′ȧ lĭl′ĭ	A pickle of chopped vegetables and pungent spices.
38.	pistachio	pĭs tä′shĭ ō	The flavor of the pistachio nut.
39.	pomegranate	pŏm′grăn′ĭt	The fruit, resembling an orange in size and color, of a tropical African and Asiatic tree.
40.	potpourri	pō′poō′rē′	A mixture of various meats and vegetables.
41.	raisin	rā′z′n	A special type of grape dried in the sun or by artificial heat.

42.	rhubarb	rōō′bärb	Tall, coarse herbs with thick, succulent stalks.
43.	Roquefort	rōk′fẽrt	A highly flavored cheese made at Roquefort, France.
44.	sauerkraut	sour′krout′	Cabbage cut fine and allowed to ferment.
45.	sirup	sĭr′ŭp	A thick, sweet liquid made from the sap of trees, juice of fruits, etc.
46.	sorghum	sôr′gŭm	A cereal grass cultivated as a fodder or grain plant or for making molasses or sirup; also, the molasses or sirup.
47.	spaghetti	spå gĕt′ĭ	A variety of macaroni made in cords of small diameter.
48.	thyme	tīm	A pungent aromatic herb used in seasoning.
49.	vermicelli	vûr′mĭ sĕl′ĭ	A wheat paste forced through cylinders till it takes a slender, wormlike form.
50.	Zwieback	tsvē′bäk′	A kind of biscuit or rusk baked in a loaf and then cut and toasted.

LESSON 95

Hardware and Cutlery Terms [1]

1.	andirons	ănd′ī′ẽrns	A pair of supports on which wood is laid in a fireplace.
2.	asbestos	ăs bĕs′tŏs	A fibrous incombustible material used for fireproofing.
3.	auger	ô′gẽr	A carpenter's tool for boring, used with a brace; also, a T-handled tool for hand boring.
4.	carborundum	kär′bŏ rŭn′dŭm	An artificial compound of carbon and silicon made in an electric furnace and used for abrasive purposes.
5.	caster	kȧs′tẽr	A small roller on a pivot fastened under a piece of furniture to enable it to be moved easily.
6.	chisel	chĭz′'l	A metal tool with a cutting edge at the end of a blade.

---

[1] See also "Architectural and Building Terms," pages 152–154; "Machinery Terms," pages 197–199.

7.	cleaver	klēv′ēr	A tool for splitting, as a meat cleaver.
8.	corrugated	kŏr′ů gāt′ĕd	Bent into a series of ridges to give stiffness.
9.	currycomb	kûr′ĭ kōm′	A comb having rows of metallic teeth, used in dressing the coat of a horse.
10.	door check	dōr chĕk	A device to prevent a door from slamming when being shut.
11.	emery	ĕm′ēr ĭ	A very hard black mineral substance; when powdered, used for grinding.
12.	faucet	fô′sĕt	A fixture for drawing a liquid, as water, etc.
13.	forceps	fôr′sĕps	A pair of pincers or tongs for grasping or holding objects.
14.	galvanized iron	găl′vȧ nīzd ī′ērn	Iron sheets coated with zinc.
15.	gauge	gāj	A standard measure.
16.	gimlet	gĭm′lĕt	A small tool with a screw point for boring into wood or other material.
17.	grindstone	grīnd′stōn′	A flat, circular stone for grinding or sharpening edge tools.
18.	handle	hăn′d'l	That part of a tool that is intended to be grasped by the hand.
19.	hinge	hĭnj	A joint on which a door turns or swings.
20.	hoe	hō	An implement for weeding or loosening the earth.
21.	holster	hōl′stēr	A leather case for a pistol carried at the belt.
22.	hose	hōz	A flexible tube for conveying water or other liquid.
23.	knob	nŏb	A handle or ornament used to open a door or drawer.
24.	knocker	nŏk′ēr	A loose hammer hinged to a door, to be used for rapping.
25.	ladle	lā′d'l	A spoon or dipper, with a long handle, for conveying liquids.
26.	latch	lăch	A fastening device or catch for a door or gate.
27.	mattock	măt′ŭk	A tool having two blades set in different planes, used in digging or loosening the soil.
28.	maul	môl	A heavy hammer used for driving wedges.

29.	nozzle	nŏz″l	A rigid tube tapering at the end to form a vent, as of a hose or pipe.
30.	pail	pāl	A bucket.
31.	pincers	pĭn′sẽrz	An instrument for gripping and holding, having two handles and two hinged jaws.
32.	pliers	plī′ẽrs	Small pincers used for bending or cutting wire, etc., or for holding small objects.
33.	plumb	plŭm	A weight, as of lead, attached to a line used to indicate vertical direction.
34.	putty	pŭt′ĭ	A paste used for filling holes or cracks and for securing window panes.
35.	razor	rā′zẽr	A cutting implement for shaving hair from the skin.
36.	reamer	rēm′ẽr	A rotating tool with a sharp edge for enlarging holes.
37.	scissors	sĭz′ẽrz	A cutting instrument consisting of a pair of pivoted blades with handles.
38.	screen	skrēn	A portable covered framework for shelter or protection.
39.	screw driver	skrōō′ drīv′ẽr	A tool for turning screws so as to drive them into place.
40.	sheathing paper	shēth′ĭng pā′pẽr	A material used for lining or covering walls, roofs, floors, packing cases, etc.
41.	sickle	sĭk″l	An implement with a curved blade mounted on a short handle used for cutting grain or grass.
42.	sieve	sĭv	A utensil with meshes, used to separate the finer particles of a pulverized or granulated substance from the coarser particles.
43.	sledge	slĕj	A large hammer.
44.	solder	sŏd′ẽr	A metal alloy used, when melted, to join metallic surfaces.
45.	tongs	tŏngz	An instrument consisting of pivoted levers for grasping objects, as ice or coal.
46.	trowel	trou′ĕl	A tool used to spread or shape plastic material; also, an implement used in setting plants.
47.	twine	twīn	Strong cord.

48.	wedge	wĕj	A piece of wood, metal, etc., tapering to a thin edge, used in splitting wood, rocks, etc.
49.	wrench	rĕnch	A tool for turning or twisting bolts, nuts, pipe, etc.
50.	wringer	rĭng′ēr	A machine or device for pressing water out of anything, as from clothes after they have been washed.

LESSON 96

Jewelry and Silverware Terms

1.	alloy	ă loi′	A substance composed of two or more metals intimately mixed and united; as brass, which is an alloy of copper and zinc. Also, a base metal mixed with a more valuable metal to give durability or some other quality.
2.	amethyst	ăm′ĕ thĭst	A clear variety of quartz, pale violet to deep purple in color.
3.	baguette	bă gĕt′	A long, narrow rectangular form of cut stones.
4.	bezel	bĕz′ĕl	Oblique side or face of cut gems; the flange in which a watch crystal is set.
5.	cameo	kăm′ĕ ō	A carved gem of two layers of different colors, the lower layer forming the background for a raised figure.
6.	carat	kăr′ăt	The unit of weight for precious stones, especially diamonds; also, a twenty-fourth part, used to express the fineness of a gold alloy.
7.	carnelian	kär nēl′yăn	A bright-red variety of chalcedony, much used in making seals.
8.	cloisonné	kloi′zŏ nā′	A method of enameling in which thin metal is soldered to metallic background and the spaces filled with enamel.
9.	crystal	krĭs′tăl	Quartz that is transparent or nearly so; also applied to glass of superior brilliancy, made into articles for the table and other decorative objects.
10.	culet	kū′lĕt	The small, flat facet at the bottom of a brilliant-cut diamond.
11.	facet	făs′ĕt	One of the small planes that form the sides of a natural crystal, or of a cut gem.

12.	filigree	fĭl′ĭ grē	Ornamental work of fine wire.
13.	hallmark	hôl′märk′	The official mark stamped on gold and silver articles at Goldsmiths' Hall, London, to attest their purity; hence, any mark similarly used.
14.	lorgnette	lôr′nyĕt′	A pair of eyeglasses fixed to a handle.
15.	loupe	lōōp	A magnifier used by jewelers; used in the hand or mounted in a cup to be held in the eye socket.
16.	marcasite	mär′kȧ sīt	Metallic crystals, pale bronze or grayish-yellow, used in moderately priced jewelry.
17.	marquise	mär kēz′	A gem cut, or a ring having gems set, in an oval with pointed ends.
18.	opaque	ȯ pāk′	Not reflecting or giving out light; not transparent.
19.	pewter	pū′tẽr	Any of various alloys having tin as their principal constituent.
20.	platinum	plăt′ĭ nŭm	A heavy, almost silver-white metal widely used in jewelry.
21.	rhinestone	rīn′stōn′	A colorless stone of high luster, made of paste, widely used in inexpensive jewelry.
22.	sapphire	săf′īr	A precious stone of transparent rich-blue corundum.
23.	solitaire	sŏl′ĭ târ′	A single diamond or (sometimes) other gem set alone.
24.	sterling	stûr′lĭng	An alloy in the proportion of 925 parts of silver to 75 parts of copper.
25.	turquoise	tûr′koiz	An opaque, green-to-blue stone, widely used in moderately priced jewelry.

LESSON 97

Leather Goods Terms

1.	alligator	ăl′ĭ gā′tẽr	A crocodilian reptile having a tough hide with pleasing markings, the skin of which is serviceable and popular for luggage, purses, shoes, etc.
2.	brief case	brēf kās	A leather or fabricoid case or envelope for carrying business papers or other articles.
3.	buckskin	bŭk′skĭn′	The name applied to those leathers used for shoes and gloves that are made from elk and deer skins.

4.	chamois	shăm′ĭ	The name of an Alpine antelope, now virtually extinct. The term is applied to oil-dressed, suede-finished leather made from the undersplit or fleshers of sheepskins; chamois leather is used for making gloves and for cleaning and polishing purposes.
5.	doeskin	dō′skĭn′	A trade term designating lambskins and sheepskins that have been tanned by the formaldehyde and alum process.
6.	gauntlet	gônt′lĕt	A glove with a long, wide wrist extension.
7.	grain	grān	The hair side or outer layer of a hide or skin that has been split into two or more layers.
8.	kangaroo	kăng′gȧ roō′	Leather from the hide of an Australian mammal of the same name.
9.	leash	lēsh	A line or thong for holding a dog.
10.	leatherette	lĕth′ẽr ĕt′	A paper or composition product, embossed in imitation of the grain of leather.
11.	moccasin	mŏk′ȧ sĭn	A type of footwear developed from styles worn by the American Indian, and generally made entirely in one piece and of buckskin.
12.	mocha	mō′kȧ	A soft, pliable leather for gloves, especially leather from the skin of an Arabian goat.
13.	morocco	mŏ rŏk′ō	Originally leather from Morocco; later applied to all goatskin leather.
14.	patent leather	păt′ĕnt lĕth′ẽr	A leather with a hard, glossy surface finish.
15.	pelt	pĕlt	The skin, in its raw state, of a small fur-bearing animal.
16.	pigskin	pĭg′skĭn′	An exceedingly durable leather widely used in the manufacture of gloves, handbags, and brief cases, and the binding of books.
17.	portmanteau	pōrt măn′tō	A case, usually of leather, for carrying apparel—now made with hinges in the back so that it opens like a book.
18.	rein	rān	A leather strap attached to the bit, by which one controls a horse or other animal.
19.	saddle	săd′′l	A padded cushion to support a rider on a horse or bicycle.

20. suede	swād	A finish in which the fibers are separated in order to produce a nap on the leather, usually accomplished by running the surface of the leather on a carborundum or emery wheel.
21. tannery	tăn'ēr ĭ	A factory where hides and skins are turned into leather by a process known as "tanning."
22. tool	tōōl	To shape, form, or finish with a tool; especially, in bookbinding and other fancy leathers, as cardcases, picture frames, etc., to impress or carve a design with a hand instrument.
23. valise	và lēs'	A case for toilet articles, clothes, etc., designed to be carried in the hand.
24. vellum	vĕl'ŭm	A fine-grained lambskin, kidskin, or calfskin made clear and white, for writing upon, binding books, etc.
25. wallet	wŏl'ĕt	A flat pocketbook for carrying paper money unfolded.

LESSON 98

Machinery Terms [1]

1. annealing	ă nēl'ĭng	The process of treating metals or glass by heating and cooling, so as to remove hardness and brittleness.
2. anvil	ăn'vĭl	A block, usually of iron, on which metal is shaped by hammering.
3. axis	ăk'sĭs	A straight line about which a body rotates or is considered as rotating.
4. Bessemer	bĕs'ĕ mēr	A kind of steel; named for the inventor of the process by which it is made.
5. blowtorch	blō'tôrch'	A lamp with a flame directed by an air blast.
6. brake	brāk	A device for checking the motion of a wheel, vehicle, etc.
7. burr	bûr	Roughness left by a tool in cutting or shaping metal.
8. cable	kā'b'l	A strong rope of wire or a chain for securing great weight.

[1] See also "Hardware and Cutlery Terms," pages 191–194.

9. caliper	kăl′Ĭ pēr	An instrument with two legs, used for determining the diameter of objects or the distance between surfaces.
10. chain	chān	A series of links joined together; in surveying, a measure of 100 links, or 66 feet.
11. chamfer	chăm′fēr	A beveled surface.
12. chuck	chŭk	A contrivance for holding securely a tool or piece of work in a lathe or drill press.
13. conveyer	kŏn vā′ēr	Any of various mechanical devices for carrying things from place to place.
14. crane	krān	A machine for raising and lowering heavy weights and transporting them through a limited lateral distance.
15. cylindrical	sĭ lĭn′drĭ kăl	Having the form or properties of a cylinder.
16. disk	dĭsk	A flat, round plate, or a structure likened to it.
17. dovetail	dŭv′tāl′	An interlocking joint between two pieces that resists pulling apart in all directions except one.
18. eccentric	ĕk sĕn′trĭk	A device for converting a circular motion to a backward and forward motion.
19. foundry	foun′drĭ	A place where metals are cast.
20. fusion	fū′zhŭn	Union or blending of metals, by actual melting.
21. gear	gēr	Cog wheels, serving to transmit motion or change its rate or direction.
22. guy	gī	A rope or chain attached to an object to steady it.
23. hoist	hoist	To raise or lift a heavy weight by means of tackle.
24. jack	jăk	A portable contrivance or device for lifting a heavy body a short distance.
25. lever	lē′vēr	A mechanical device, often consisting of a straight bar, turning freely on a fixed point, and serving to impart pressure or motion from a source of power to a resistance.
26. machinist	ma̍ shēn′ĭst	A skilled operator of machine-shop tools.
27. malleable	măl′ê a̍ b'l	Capable of being extended or shaped by beating with hammers.
28. mandrel	măn′drĕl	A piece of steel, like a short shaft, used for holding work or tools.
29. mangle	măng′g'l	A machine for smoothing cloth by roller pressure.

30.	mechanic	mė kăn′ĭk	A workman skilled in constructing, repairing, or using machinery.
31.	mold	mōld	To form into a particular shape; also, a form for shaping any fluid or plastic material.
32.	pendulum	pĕn′dụ lŭm	A body suspended from a fixed point so as to swing freely.
33.	periphery	pė rĭf′ẽr ĭ	The line bounding a circle.
34.	pinion	pĭn′yŭn	The smaller of two gears that engage with one another.
35.	pivot	pĭv′ŭt	The end of a shaft that rests and turns in a support.
36.	pulley	poŏl′ĭ	A small wheel with a grooved rim through which a flexible rope or chain passes.
37.	pumice	pŭm′ĭs	Hardened volcanic glass froth, widely used in powder form for smoothing and polishing.
38.	ratchet	răch′ĕt	A bar or tooth working with a toothed wheel.
39.	resiliency	rė zĭl′ĭ ĕn sĭ	Act of rebounding or recoiling; elasticity; power of recovery.
40.	rotor	rō′tẽr	A part that revolves in a stationary part; the rotating member of an electrical machine.
41.	smelting	smĕlt′ĭng	Act of melting or fusing, as ore, to separate and refine the metal.
42.	sprocket	sprŏk′ĕt	A projection shaped so as to engage with a chain.
43.	swivel	swĭv′′l	A part that turns on a headed bolt or pin.
44.	template	tĕm′plĭt	A guide or pattern used in mechanical work.
45.	tenon	tĕn′ŭn	A projection on the end of a timber for inserting it in a hollowed-out space (a mortise) in another timber.
46.	tensile	tĕn′sĭl	Capable of being drawn out or extended in length or breadth.
47.	trunnion	trŭn′yŭn	Either of two opposite projections that provide a means of turning an engine cylinder or other piece of machinery.
48.	vise	vīs	A device for holding objects firmly, as in filing metal surfaces.
49.	welded	wĕl′dĕd	Pressed or beaten into union, as the ends of two iron bars, usually while softened by heat.
50.	wrought iron	rôt ī′ẽrn	The purest form of iron, containing only about one-half of 1 per cent of carbon; purified ore.

LESSON 99

Medical and Drug Terms—Medicine [1]

1.	abdomen	ăb dō′měn	The main body cavity, containing the organs of digestion.
2.	abscess	ăb′sĕs	A collection of pus, usually causing a swelling.
3.	acidosis	ăs′ĭ dō′sĭs	A condition in which body fluids are more acid than normally.
4.	adolescence	ăd′ŏ lĕs′ĕns	State or process of growing up from childhood to maturity.
5.	alimentary	ăl′ĭ mĕn′tà rĭ	Pertaining to food or nutrition or to the entire canal or tube through which food passes from the mouth to the anus.
6.	allergic	ă lûr′jĭk	Special sensitivity to foods, drugs, or other substances normally harmless.
7.	amputation	ăm pû tā′shŭn	Act or process of cutting off a limb or other member of the body.
8.	anatomy	à năt′ŏ mĭ	The science of the structure of living things.
9.	anemia	à nē′mĭ à	A deficiency in the quantity of the blood or in its red cells.
10.	anesthetic	ăn′ĕs thĕt′ĭk	An agent that produces insensibility to pain, as chloroform, ether, etc.
11.	antiseptic	ăn′tĭ sĕp′tĭk	A substance used to destroy bacteria or counteract putrefaction.
12.	antitoxin	ăn′tĭ tŏk′sĭn	A substance found in body fluids to counteract poisons.
13.	aorta	à ôr′tà	The main artery leading directly from the heart.
14.	appendicitis	à pĕn′dĭ sī′tĭs	Inflammation of the appendix.
15.	artery	är′tẽr ĭ	A blood vessel leading away from the heart.
16.	asthma	ăz′mà	A disease accompanied by coughing and difficulty of breathing.

[1] See also "Chemical Terms," pages 161–164.

17.	astigmatism	á stĭg′má tĭz′m	A defect of the eye, generally due to irregularity in the formation of the cornea, causing imperfect vision.
18.	atrophy	ăt′rō fĭ	A wasting away of a part or of the entire body to the point where it fails to function.
19.	autointoxication	ô′tō ĭn tŏk′sĭ kā′shŭn	Poisoning as a result of the failure of the body to eliminate its own toxins.
20.	autopsy	ô′tŏp sĭ	Dissection of a dead body for the purpose of ascertaining the cause of the death; a post-mortem examination.
21.	bacteria	băk tēr′ĭ á	A group of microorganisms, some of which cause disease, while others are harmless or even beneficial.
22.	bronchitis	brŏn kī′tĭs	Inflammation of the lining of the tubes between the windpipe and the lungs.
23.	carbuncle	kär′bŭng k'l	An acute and painful local inflammation of the skin and deeper tissues, more serious than a boil.
24.	cardiac	kär′dĭ ăk	Pertaining to the heart.
25.	cartilage	kär′tĭ lĭj	A tough, elastic tissue; gristle.
26.	cerebral	sĕr′ĕ brăl	Of or pertaining to the brain.
27.	chiropodist	kĭ rŏp′ō dĭst	One who treats corns, calluses, and minor foot ailments.
28.	chiropractor	kī′rō prăk′tēr	A practitioner of a system of adjusting the joints, especially of the spine, for the curing of bodily disorders.
29.	chronic	krŏn′ĭk	Continuing for a long time.
30.	clinical	klĭn′ĭ kăl	Relating to the bedside of a patient or to the course of his disease.
31.	congenital	kŏn jĕn′ĭ tăl	Existing from birth.
32.	contagious	kŏn tā′jŭs	Communicable by contact.
33.	convalescence	kŏn′vá lĕs′ĕns	The period of gradual recovery of health.
34.	corpuscle	kôr′pŭs′l	A small mass or body, such as a blood cell.
35.	debility	dĕ bĭl′ĭ tĭ	Weakness, especially in body functioning; languor.

36.	delirious	dē lĭr′ĭ ŭs	Wandering in mind.
37.	diabetes	dī′à bē′tēz	A disease characterized by excess sugar in body fluids.
38.	diagnosis	dī′ăg nō′sĭs	The art or act of recognizing the presence of disease from its symptoms.
39.	diaphragm	dī′à frăm	The muscular partition separating the cavity of the chest from that of the abdomen.
40.	diphtheria	dĭf thēr′ĭ à	An infectious and contagious disease of the air passages, especially of the throat.
41.	dispensary	dĭs pĕn′sà rĭ	A place where medicines are distributed, especially where one can obtain them free or at a nominal price.
42.	dissect	dĭ sĕkt′	To cut apart the tissues of the body.
43.	epidemic	ĕp′ĭ dĕm′ĭk	Affecting many in a community at the same time; also, a widely spread disease in a certain region.
44.	epileptic	ĕp′ĭ lĕp′tĭk	Suffering from a nervous disorder characterized by convulsive attacks.
45.	esophagus	ē sŏf′à gŭs	The tube that leads from the throat to the stomach.
46.	fluoroscope	floō′ŏ rō skōp	An instrument for observing the shadows cast in the path of the X rays.
47.	germicide	jûr′mĭ sīd	Any agent that destroys germs.
48.	glandular	glăn′dụ lēr	Relating to glands.
49.	hemoglobin	hē′mō glō′bĭn	The normal coloring matter of red blood corpuscles.
50.	hemorrhage	hĕm′ŏ rĭj	An excessive bleeding.

LESSON 100

Medical and Drug Terms—Medicine (*Continued*)

1.	hiccup	hĭk′ŭp	A short, spasmodic cough.
2.	homeopathic	hō′mē ō păth′ĭk	Pertaining to a special type of medical treatment, in which very small doses of medicine are prescribed.

3.	hydrophobia	hī′drŏ fō′bĭ á	An infectious disease, usually transmitted to a human being from the bite of a diseased animal.
4.	hygiene	hī′jēn	The science that treats of the preservation of health.
5.	immunity	ĭ mū′nĭ tĭ	Freedom or exemption from; state of resisting the development of a disease.
6.	inflammation	ĭn′flă mā′shŭn	State of being swollen, congested, or irritated.
7.	insomnia	ĭn sŏm′nĭ á	Prolonged inability to sleep; abnormal wakefulness.
8.	larynx	lăr′ĭngks	The organ of voice production.
9.	malignant	má lĭg′nănt	So severe as to endanger life.
10.	mastoiditis	măs′toid ī′tĭs	Inflammation in the region of the mastoid bone, behind the ear.
11.	melancholia	měl′ăn kō′lĭ á	A type of mental unsoundness characterized by extreme depression of spirits, delusions, and brooding.
12.	metabolism	mě tăb′ŏ lĭz′m	The chemical changes proceeding continually in living cells, by which the energy is provided for the vital processes (commonly studied now by means of the basal metabolism test).
13.	microbe	mī′krōb	Organism or germ, invisible to the naked eye; popularly applied to bacteria.
14.	microscope	mī′krŏ skōp	An optical instrument for making enlarged images of minute objects.
15.	migraine	mī′grān	A sick, nervous headache of great severity, usually affecting one side of the head only.
16.	morbidity	môr bĭd′ĭ tĭ	Unsound or gloomy state; also, in medical terminology only, the amount of disease or the sick rate.
17.	nasal	nā′zăl	Pertaining to the nose.
18.	nausea	nô′shē á	A sickness of the stomach, accompanied by an inclination to vomit.
19.	neuralgia	nū răl′já	A severe throbbing or stabbing nerve pain.
20.	neurotic	nū rŏt′ĭk	Pertaining to or affecting the nerves; nervous.
21.	obese	ŏ bēs′	Extremely fat.
22.	orthodontia	ôr′thŏ dŏn′shĭ á	Straightening of irregular teeth.
23.	orthopedic	ôr′thŏ pē′dĭk	Pertaining to a branch of surgery dealing with the joints or spine.

24.	osteopathy	ŏs'tĕ ŏp'å thĭ	A system of treatment based on the theory that diseases are due to deranged mechanism of the bones, with a resultant pressure on nerves and blood vessels.
25.	pallor	păl'ẽr	Lack of color; paleness.
26.	pancreas	păn'krē ăs	One of the most vital glands in the body, necessary for digestion.
27.	paralysis	på răl'ĭ sĭs	Loss of power of voluntary movement.
28.	paroxysm	păr'ŏk sĭz'm	Any sudden, violent, and uncontrollable action; a convulsion or fit.
29.	pediatrician	pē'dĭ å trĭsh'ăn	A doctor specializing in children's diseases.
30.	pharynx	făr'ĭngks	The part of the alimentary canal between the mouth and the esophagus.
31.	phlegmatic	flĕg măt'ĭk	Sluggish, apathetic; like phlegm or mucus.
32.	podiatrist	pŏ dī'å trĭst	One who cares for the feet in health and disease.
33.	poultice	pōl'tĭs	A soft composition to be applied, on a cloth, to inflamed parts of the body.
34.	psychiatry	sī kī'å trĭ	The treatment or study of mental diseases.
35.	ptomaine	tō'mān	A type of poisoning, often resulting from eating spoiled foods.
36.	pulmonary	pŭl'mŏ nẽr'ĭ	Pertaining to the lungs.
37.	quarantine	kwŏr'ăn tēn	To compel to remain in a given place when having, or suspected of having, a contagious disease.
38.	respiratory	rĕ spīr'å tō'rĭ	Pertaining to the act or process of breathing.
39.	rheumatism	rōō'må tĭz'm	A painful condition of joints and muscles.
40.	sanitarium	săn'ĭ târ'ĭ ŭm	A hospital for convalescents or those taking rest cures.
41.	serum	sẽr'ŭm	The watery portion of the body; also an antitoxin solution.
42.	stethoscope	stĕth'ŏ skōp	An instrument used to convey to the ear sounds produced in the body, particularly the beats of the heart.
43.	surgeon	sûr'jŭn	One whose profession is curing diseases and body injuries by operation.

44.	symptom	sĭmp′tŭm	Any perceptible change in the body that indicates disease, or the kind or phase of a disease.
45.	thyroid	thī′roid	A ductless gland on either side of the windpipe in the neck.
46.	tonsillitis	tŏn′sĭ lī′tĭs	Inflammation of the tonsils.
47.	trachea	trā′kĕ à	The windpipe in the body of an animal or human.
48.	typhoid	tī′foid	An acute, infectious disease generally acquired from infected water or milk.
49.	vaccine	văk′sēn	A virus used to immunize the body against a disease.
50.	vertebra	vûr′tĕ brà	One of the bony segments composing the spinal column or backbone.

LESSON 101

Medical and Drug Terms—Drugs

1.	alcohol	ăl′kŏ hŏl	A colorless, volatile, inflammable liquid that is the intoxicating principle in fermented and distilled liquors.
2.	ampoule	ăm pool′	A small, sealed glass tube containing a solution for use with a hypodermic needle.
3.	analgesic	ăn′ăl jē′sĭk	Capable of dulling pain; sedative.
4.	anodyne	ăn′ŏ dīn	A drug that relieves pain.
5.	antacid	ănt ăs′ĭd	A drug designed to counteract stomach acidity.
6.	aperient	à pēr′ĭ ĕnt	Gently laxative.
7.	aromatic	ăr′ŏ măt′ĭk	Fragrant; spicy; also, a plant, drug, or medicine having such characteristics.
8.	belladonna	bĕl à dŏn′à	A drug used as a narcotic and anodyne and to dilate the pupils of the eyes.
9.	benzoin	bĕn′zŏ ĭn	A white crystalline substance obtained from oil of bitter almonds and some other sources.
10.	bicarbonate	bī kär′bŏn āt	A type of chemical compound, such as bicarbonate of soda.

11.	bismuth	bĭz′mŭth	A chemical element used in drugs for stomach conditions and venereal diseases.
12.	caffeine	kăf′ê ĭn	A substance contained in coffee and tea, used in medicine as a stimulant.
13.	camphor	kăm′fẽr	A fragrant gumlike compound obtained from an Asiatic evergreen tree; also manufactured artificially.
14.	capsule	kăp′sūl	A small container of soluble or digestible matter in which disagreeable-tasting doses are enclosed to be swallowed.
15.	chloroform	klō′rô fôrm	A colorless anesthetic.
16.	cocaine	kō kān′	A bitter drug of the opium family.
17.	codeine	kō′dê ēn	A drug similar to morphine, but feebler in its action.
18.	collodion	kŏ lō′dĭ ŭn	A solution used as a coating for wounds.
19.	dentifrice	dĕn′tĭ frĭs	A powder, paste, or liquid used in cleaning the teeth.
20.	digitalis	dĭj′ĭ tā′lĭs	A drug compounded from the leaves of the purple foxglove, used as a heart stimulant.
21.	elixir	ê lĭk′sẽr	A solution of a drug in sugar, water, and alcohol.
22.	emulsify	ê mŭl′sĭ fī	To make a true mixture of oil and water.
23.	essence	ĕs′ĕns	An alcoholic solution of the volatile constituents of a substance in concentrated form.
24.	ether	ē′thẽr	A light, inflammable liquid, used as an anesthetic.
25.	formaldehyde	fôr măl′dĕ hīd	A colorless gas, with a sharp odor, used as a preservative and disinfectant.
26.	gauze	gôz	A very thin, transparent material used in surgical dressings.
27.	glycerin	glĭs′ẽr ĭn	A sweet, sirupy liquid used as a solvent and preservative and as an ingredient in toilet preparations and ointments.
28.	hormone	hôr′mōn	A substance, internally secreted, that has a specific effect on body cells.

29. insulin	ĭn'sû lĭn	A preparation that regulates the amount of sugar in the blood, used in treating diabetes.
30. iodoform	ī ō'dŏ fôrm	A disinfectant, used largely in hospitals.
31. lanolin	lăn'ŏ lĭn	A fatty substance obtained from sheep's wool; used as a basis for many ointments.
32. lozenge	lŏz'ĕnj	A medicated cough drop, originally diamond-shaped.
33. magnesia	măg nē'shȧ	A mild antacid laxative.
34. menthol	mĕn'thōl	A white crystalline substance having the odor and cooling taste of peppermint.
35. mercurochrome	mûr kū'rŏ krōm'	An antiseptic containing mercury.
36. narcotic	när kŏt'ĭk	A drug that in moderate doses relieves pain and produces profound sleep. Usually applied to habit-forming drugs.
37. nicotine	nĭk'ŏ tēn	A poisonous substance found in tobacco.
38. novocain	nō'vŏ kān'	A local anesthetic much less toxic than cocaine.
39. oxygen	ŏk'sĭ jĕn	A colorless, tasteless, gaseous element in the atmosphere, indispensable to breathing.
40. paregoric	păr'ĕ gŏr'ĭk	A medicine containing opium extract; used in cough preparations.
41. pharmaceutical	fär'má sū'tĭ kăl	Pertaining to pharmacy.
42. poisonous	poi'z'n ŭs	Having the properties or effects of poison; destructive; noxious.
43. prescription	prē skrĭp'shŭn	Written directions for the preparation and use of a medicine.
44. prophylactic	prō'fĭ lăk'tĭk	A medicine that defends against disease; a preventive.
45. quinine	kwī'nīn	A bitter drug extracted from the bark of the cinchona tree, used in the treatment of malaria.
46. saccharin	săk'ȧ rĭn	An extremely sweet substance, with no food value; used as a sugar substitute, as in cases of diabetes.
47. salve	säv	An ointment.
48. strychnine	strĭk'nĭn	A poisonous alkaloid employed in medicine as a powerful nerve stimulant.
49. tincture	tĭngk'tůr	A solution of a drug in alcohol.

50.	vitamin	vī′tȧ mĭn	A constituent found in most foods in extremely small quantities, but essential to life and health.

LESSON 102

Mining and Metallurgical Terms [1]

1.	bonanza	bŏ năn′zȧ	A rich mine, vein, or find of ore; also, a profitable speculation.
2.	cleavage	klēv′ĭj	A cleft or division; a tendency in a rock or crystal to divide in certain directions.
3.	corrosion	kŏ rō′zhŭn	Gradual disintegration; an eating or wearing away by a chemical process, usually by oxidation.
4.	derrick	dĕr′ĭk	An apparatus for hoisting and swinging heavy objects into place.
5.	dredge	drĕj	An appliance for bringing up sand, silt, etc., from under water.
6.	dynamite	dī′nȧ mīt	An explosive, safer than nitroglycerin.
7.	erosion	ē rō′zhŭn	The natural wearing away of rocks or soil.
8.	explosion	ĕks plō′zhŭn	A violent bursting or expansion, with noise.
9.	fissure	fĭsh′ĕr	A narrow opening made by the parting of any substance.
10.	flux	flŭks	A substance that promotes the fusing of minerals or metals
11.	fossil	fŏs′ĭl	Any remains, impression, or trace of an animal or plant of past geological ages, preserved in a stratified deposit.
12.	geological	jē′ō lŏj′ĭ kăl	Pertaining to the science that treats of the history of the earth and its life, especially as recorded in the rocks.
13.	glacial	glā′shăl	Pertaining to, or caused by, ice masses.
14.	hydrometer	hī drŏm′ē tẽr	A floating instrument for determining specific gravities.
15.	infiltration	ĭn′fĭl trā′shŭn	Act or process of penetration, as of water into a porous substance.
16.	ingot	ĭng′gŏt	A mass of cast metal from a furnace or a crucible, as a bar of gold or a mass of cast steel.

---
[1] See also "Chemical Terms," pages 161–164; "Civil Engineering Terms," pages 164–167; "Fuel and Oil Terms," pages 180–183.

17.	limestone	līm′stōn′	A rock composed wholly or in part of calcium carbonate.
18.	lode	lōd	A somewhat continuous, unstratified, metal-bearing vein.
19.	mineralogy	mĭn′ẽr ăl′ō jĭ	The science of minerals, dealing with their physical and chemical properties in general.
20.	nitroglycerin	nī′trō glĭs′ẽr ĭn	A colorless, heavy, oily liquid used as an explosive.
21.	nugget	nŭg′ĕt	A lump or mass, especially a native lump of a precious metal.
22.	slag	slăg	Metallic dross; the fused refuse from refined ore.
23.	sluice	slo͞os	A trough for separating gold from dirt.
24.	stratum	strā′tŭm	A body of sedimentary rock or earth formed by natural causes and usually lying in layers.
25.	tunneling	tŭn′ĕl′ĭng	The digging of an underground passage.

LESSON 103

Motion Picture and Photographic Terms

1.	achromatic	ăk′rō măt′ĭk	Said of lenses that are "color corrected," so made as to avoid distortion of color values in photography or the projection of pictures.
2.	aperture	ăp′ẽr tụr	The opening in cameras through which the picture is made, or in projection machines, through which it is thrown on the screen.
3.	binoculars	bĭn ŏk′ụ lērs	Field glasses.
4.	cinema	sĭn′ē má	A motion picture; also, motion pictures collectively.
5.	comedienne	kŏ mē′dĭ ĕn′	An actress who plays comedy.
6.	contrasty	kŏn′trăs tĭ	Having very dark shadows and very white high lights.
7.	emulsion	ē mŭl′shŭn	A solution used for coating photographic plates.
8.	exposure	ĕks pō′zhẽr	The subjecting of a film or plate to light; also the length of time a negative is exposed to light during the taking of a picture.

9.	focusing	fō′kŭs ĭng	The process of adjusting the position of the lens to bring the photographic image to the desired degree of sharpness or definition.
10.	ingénue	ăN′zhă′nü′	An actress who portrays the part of a naïve young woman.
11.	klieg light	klēg līt	A trade name for a type of very bright light used in motion pictures.
12.	Kodak	kō′dăk	A trade name for a hand camera.
13.	lens	lĕnz	A piece of glass so ground that rays of light may be made to converge or diverge.
14.	orthochromatic	ôr′thō krō măt′ĭk	Producing tone values of light and shade in a photograph corresponding to the tone of nature.
15.	playwright	plā′rīt′	A maker or writer of plays; a dramatist.
16.	portraiture	pōr′trȧ tụr	Act or art of making portraits, or a pictorial likeness of a person.
17.	prismatic	prĭz măt′ĭk	Showing the colors formed by passing a ray of light through a prism.
18.	projection	prŏ jĕk′shŭn	The display of motion pictures by throwing an image from them upon a screen.
19.	reel	rēl	A spool on which a photographic film is wound; also, a strip of motion-picture film.
20.	reflector	rē flĕk′tẽr	A polished surface or body for reflecting light or heat, as a mirror.
21.	scenario	sĕ nä′rĭ ō	An outline or synopsis of a play or book, giving the scenes and rôles of the actors.
22.	silhouette	sĭl′o͞o ĕt′	A photograph of only two tones, showing the subject against a light background.
23.	stereoscope	stĕr′ē ō skōp′	An optical instrument with two eyeglasses enabling the observer mentally to combine the images of two pictures, thus getting the effect of solidity, or relief.
24.	Technicolor	tĕk′nĭ kŭl′ẽr	The trade name of one of a number of processes used for making colored motion pictures.

25. telephoto — tĕl′ė fō′tō — A combination of lenses for photographing objects at extreme distances.

LESSON 104

Musical Terms

1. adagio — à dä′jō — Slowly; in an easy, graceful manner.
2. allegro — ä lā′grō — Brisk; lively.
3. arpeggio — är pĕj′ō — The notes of a chord executed in rapid succession.
4. baritone — băr′ĭ tōn — A male voice between tenor and bass.
5. chord — kôrd — A combination of tones sounded simultaneously, in agreement with the rules of harmony.
6. coloratura — kŭl′ēr à tū′rà — Florid ornaments in vocal music, as trills and runs. A high soprano voice of clearness and great flexibility.
7. concerto — kŏn chĕr′tō — A composition for a solo instrument with orchestra, written especially to display the powers of the solo instrument.
8. crescendo — krĕ shĕn′dō — Swelling; gradually increasing in loudness.
9. encore — äng′kōr — A musical number repeated, or added to a program, in response to applause by the audience.
10. forte — fôr′tā — Loud.
11. fortissimo — fôr tĭs′ĭ mō — Very loud.
12. fugue — fūg — A composition in which an original theme is repeated and imitated throughout.
13. hymn — hĭm — A song of praise, adoration, or supplication, addressed to the Deity.
14. libretto — lĭ brĕt′ō — The literary text of an opera or dramatic composition.
15. obbligato — ŏb′lĭ gä′tō — An accompanying part, usually by a single instrument, necessary to the completion of the musical thought.
16. oratorio — ŏr′à tō′rĭ ō — An elaborate composition, usually on a sacred theme, for chorus, full orchestra, and solo voices.

17.	orchestral	ôr kĕs′trăl	Pertaining to, or performed by, an orchestra.
18.	rhapsody	răp′sŏ dĭ	An instrumental or vocal composition irregular in form and of a strongly romantic nature.
19.	rhythm	rĭth'm	The regular appearance of stress or accent.
20.	scherzo	skĕr′tsō	A sprightly, humorous composition commonly in quick triple time; a musical joke or humorous tale.
21.	soprano	sŏ prä′nō	The highest female or boy's singing voice.
22.	staccato	stȧ kä′tō	Notes executed in a short, crisp, and detached manner.
23.	symphony	sĭm′fŏ nĭ	An elaborate instrumental composition in sonata form for full orchestra.
24.	syncopation	sĭng′kŏ pā′shŭn	A temporary displacing or shifting of the regular metrical accent.
25.	virtuoso	vûr′tṳ ō′sō	One skilled in the technique of some musical instrument.

INDEX

Abbreviations,
  commercial, 148
  states, 87–88
Able, suffix, 36–37
Accounting terms, 110–113
Advertising terms, 114–117
Agricultural terms, 150–151
Ance, suffix, 34–35
Ant, suffix, 32–33
Antonyms, 74–76
Apostrophe, use of, 20–21
Architectural terms, 152–154
Automobile terms, 155–157
Aviation terms, 158–161

Banking terms, 118–125
Building terms, 152–154
Business terms, 95–148
  general, 96–109
  of Latin origin, 86
Businesses, special, terms used in, 149–212

Capitals, of North and South American countries, 89
Chemical terms, 161–164
Cities,
  North and South American, 89
  of the world, 91
  United States, 87–88, 90
Civil engineering terms, 164–167
Commercial abbreviations, 148
Compound words, 22–23
Cutlery terms, 191–194

Dictionary, use of, vii–ix
Division of words, back fly leaf
Drug terms, 200–208

E, final, silent
  omitted, 2–3
  retained, 4–5

Educational terms, 168–170
Ei words, 12–13
Electrical terms, 171–177
Ence, suffix, 34–35
Ent, suffix, 32–33
Er, suffix, 40–41

F, nouns ending in, plurals, 16–17
Fashion terms, 177–179
Fe, nouns ending in, plurals, 16–17
Ff, nouns ending in, plurals, 16–17
Final consonant,
  doubled, 6–7
  not doubled, 8–9
Foreign words and phrases, 83–85, 94
  legal and business terms, 86
Fuel terms, 180–183
Furniture terms, 183–185

General business terms, 96–109
Geographic names, 87–91, 94
Government terms, 186–188
Grocery terms, 189–191

Hardware terms, 191–194
Homonyms, 46–53
Hyphenated words, 22–23

I, when final *y* is changed to, 10–11
Ible, suffix, 36–37
Ie words, 12–13
Industries, terms used in special, 149–212
Insurance terms, 126–129
Interior decoration terms, 183–185
Investment terms, 118–125
Ise, suffix, 38–39
Ize, suffix, 38–39

Jewelry terms, 194–195

Latin origin, legal and business terms, 86

Leather goods terms, 195–197
Legal terms, 130–137
  of Latin origin, 86

Machinery terms, 197–199
Medical terms, 200–208
Metallurgical terms, 208–209
Mining terms, 208–209
Mispronounced words, frequent, 25, 43, 79, 93
Misspelled words, frequent, 24, 42, 78, 92
Motion picture terms, 209–211
Musical terms, 211–212

New words, 82
North American countries and their capitals, 89

O, nouns ending in, plural, 16–17
Office supplies and equipment terms, 138–141
Oil terms, 180–183
Old words with new meanings, 82
Or, suffix, 40–41

Photographic terms, 209–211
Plurals,
  irregular, 18–19
  nouns ending in,
    f, fe, ff, 16–17
    o, 16–17
    y, 14–15
  regular, 14–15
Possessives, 20–21
Prefixes, 27–41, 44
  common, 28–29
Prepositions, 77
Printing terms, 114–117
Pronunciation, words frequently mispronounced, 25, 43, 79, 93
Publishing terms, 114–117

Radio terms, 171–177
Real estate terms, 142–143
Rules, spelling, 1–23, 26

Shipping terms, 144–147
Silverware terms, 194–195

Sion, suffix, 38–39
South American countries and their capitals, 89
Spelling rules, 1–23, 26
States and territories of United States, 87–88
Suffixes, 27–41, 44
  able and *ible*, 36–37
  ance and *ence*, 34–35
  ant and *ent*, 32–33
  common, 30–31
  er and *or*, 40–41
  ise and *ize*, 38–39
  tion and *sion*, 38–39
Synonyms, 66–73

Territories and states of United States, 87–88
Tests,
  on Part I, 26
  on Part II, 44
  on Part III, 80
  on Part IV, 94
Textile terms, 177–179
Tion, suffix, 38–39
Transportation terms, 144–147

United States, states and territories, 87–88

Word usage, 45–77, 80
Words,
  commonly mispronounced, 25, 43, 79, 93
  commonly misspelled, 24, 42, 78, 92
  foreign, 83–85, 94
  new, 82
  that mean the opposite thing, 74–76
  that mean the same thing, 66–73
  that sound and look somewhat alike, 54–65
  that sound exactly alike, 46–53
  used in business, 95–148
    special, 149–212

Y, when final, is changed to *i*, 10–11
  plural, 14–15

THE DIVISION OF WORDS

Note: The following summary has been placed in the back of this book to supply a convenient and quick reference for the student who has difficulty in dividing words correctly when typing.

The point at which a word may be divided at the end of a line is governed by its syllabication and by the appearance on the printed or typewritten page.

Words may be divided only between syllables; therefore, one-syllable words should not be divided.

bruise   search   sound   through   would   Charles

In the past tense, many short verbs are still one-syllable words.

trimmed   scrapped   stripped   hauled   helped

The following rules represent accepted typewriting and printing practice for the division of words of more than one syllable. If one is in doubt as to the syllabication of any word, the dictionary should be consulted.

1. A one-letter syllable—whether at the beginning or at the end of a word—should not be separated from the rest of the word.

One-Letter Beginning Syllables   *One-Letter Ending Syllables*

adulterate	obedience	rainy	hysteria
agreeable	idolize	camera	bindery
enumerate	unification	radio	heavy

2. Two-letter final syllables should not be carried over to a second line.

idiomatic   beautify   exceptional   commissioner   interested

3. Four- and five-letter words, even though of more than one syllable, should not be divided.

only   Asia   exit   idea   rabid   carry   ideal

Note: In the examples that follow, hyphens represent points of division. Do not confuse these with hyphenated compound words.   *(Over)*

4. When a word begins with a prefix of two or more letters, division should be after the prefix.

dis-similar	with-drawing	super-ficial	con-centrate
sub-ordinate	pre-conceived	mis-addressed	per-pendicular
over-influence	under-value	inter-relate	sub-sidize

5. When a word ends with a suffix of three or more letters, division should be before the suffix.

sudden-ness	tempera-ment	lubrica-tion	comfort-able
treacher-ous	justify-ing	statisti-cal	temper-ance
primi-tive	motor-ist	digest-ible	appar-ent

Exception to Rules 4 and 5. Sometimes, however, division after a prefix or before a suffix would misrepresent the pronunciation—that is, would not coincide with the syllabication.

Prefixes

antic-ipate	signifi-cance
pref-erence	abun-dant
prel-ude	compe-tence

Suffixes

crea-tive	trium-phant
vigi-lance	combus-tible
impenetra-ble	spar-kling

6. When the final letter of a word is doubled because of the addition of *ing, er, est, en,* etc., the division is between the doubled letters.

refer-ring   rob-ber   allot-ted   red-dest   glad-den

Such words should not be confused with words ending in a double consonant, in which the original form is retained.

full   full-est   pass   pass-ing   fulfill   fulfill-ing

7. A single-vowel syllable should not be carried over to a new line

medi-cine   facili-tate   deli-cate   approxi-mate   simi-lar

except with a two-letter syllable in order to make a division possible.

simplic-ity   propri-ety   durabil-ity

8. Compound words, whether solid or hyphenated, should be divided only between the elements of the word.

Solid Compounds		*Hyphenated Compounds*	
inasmuch	inas-much	heart-rending	heart-rending
southwestern	south-western	above-mentioned	above-mentioned
newsstand	news-stand	machine-made	machine-made